BALLANTINE BOOKS + NEW YORK

TINKER
DABBLE
DOODLE
TRY

BY SRINI PILLAY, M.D.

Life Unlocked:
7 Revolutionary Lessons to Overcome Fear

Your Brain and Business:
The Neuroscience of Great Leaders

Tinker Dabble Doodle Try:
Unlock the Power of the Unfocused Mind

Advance Praise for *Tinker Dabble Doodle Try*

"I highly recommend this book to anyone looking to accomplish more by doing less. It shows why relentless focus and a cultish adherence to overwork are counterproductive. And it explains how innovation and insight—true markers of success in our new working reality—are more in our control than we might think. Read *Tinker Dabble Doodle Try* to strengthen both your ability and your resolve to slack off, strategically."

—CHRISTINE CARTER, PH.D., author of *The Sweet Spot*

"Dr. Srini Pillay's new book, *Tinker Dabble Doodle Try*, will help you create a new, fun, more playful destiny and unlock your brain's inner potential."

—DANIEL G. AMEN, M.D., founder of Amen Clinics
and co-author of *The Brain Warrior's Way*

"This book is that rare combination of fascinating narrative and practical prescription. It not only gives you license to step off the hamster wheel of focus, focus, focus, but it will show you how to strategically and productively do so."

—JJ VIRGIN, author of *The Virgin Diet* and
JJ Virgin's Sugar Impact Diet

"The story of how the brain takes the 'ingredients' of our lives—smells, sounds, experiences, memories—and spins them into new ideas, innovations, and creative inspirations is one of the most fascinating narratives I have read in some time. *Tinker Dabble Doodle Try* leaves me in awe of all that quietly goes on between our ears."

—JOHN ASSARAF, author of *Having It All*
and chairman and CEO of NeuroGym

"Cognitive rest is the new exercise! *Tinker Dabble Doodle Try* is great medicine for those who have long suspected that multitasking and always being on the go aren't all they are cracked up to be."

—SARA GOTTFRIED, M.D., author of *The Hormone Cure; The Hormone Reset Diet;* and *Younger: A Breakthrough Program to Reset Your Genes, Reverse Aging, and Turn Back the Clock 10 Years*

"This brilliant book shows how to harness a hidden neurological process that taps into your creativity, reducing stress while simultaneously boosting your productivity at work. When you learn how to manipulate your brain to alternate between intense concentration and deliberate mind-wandering you'll solve problems more quickly and experience more satisfaction in life."

—MARK ROBERT WALDMAN, co-author of
How God Changes Your Brain

"In this insightful new book, Srini Pillay describes important strategies for purposeful focusing and, conversely, 'unfocusing' of our minds to improve resourcefulness, creativity, optimism, and mental well-being. As a lifelong business and social entrepreneur and survivor of a recent brain injury, I can attest to the great value of these practices."

—DAVID SHAW, biotech entrepreneur and founder of Idexx

"*Tinker Dabble Doodle Try* masterfully guides us to become the conductors of our own neural symphonies. By developing routines that deliberately oscillate between focus and strategic distraction, we become more fully present in the moments that matter most to us, decreasing our perceptions of stress and aligning the brain and body in healthy harmony. I'm excited to schedule even more tinker-time in my day, and to have scientific validation to post on the door when I'm in my self-induced time-out."

—HEIDI HANNA, author of
The SHARP Solution and *Stressaholic*

"Celebrating the usually untapped power of the *entire* mind, as opposed to the mere focused mind, Dr. Srini Pillay offers a brilliant, deeply researched, and even more deeply imagined blueprint for using one's full mental armamentarium, conscious, unconscious, and all the undiscovered rest! A fantastic book!"

—EDWARD M. HALLOWELL, M.D.,
co-author of *Delivered from Distraction*

TINKER
DABBLE
DOODLE
TRY

UNLOCK THE POWER OF THE UNFOCUSED MIND

SRINI PILLAY, M.D.

Published in the United States by Ballantine Books, an imprint of
Random House, a division of Penguin Random House LLC, New York.

BALLANTINE and the HOUSE colophon are registered trademarks of
Penguin Random House LLC.

Library of Congress Cataloging-in-Publication Data
Names: Pillay, Srinivasan S., author.
Title: Tinker dabble doodle try : unlock the power of the unfocused mind /
Srini Pillay, M.D.
Description: New York : Ballantine Books, 2017. | Includes bibliographical
references and index.
Identifiers: LCCN 2016043974| ISBN 9781101883655 (hardback) | ISBN
9781101883662 (ebook)
Subjects: LCSH: Creative ability. | Self-actualization (Psychology) | BISAC:
PSYCHOLOGY / Personality. | PSYCHOLOGY / Creative Ability. | SELF-HELP /
Personal Growth / Success.
Classification: LCC BF408 .P485 2017 | DDC 153.4—dc23
LC record available at https://lccn.loc.gov/2016043974

Printed in the United States of America on acid-free paper

randomhousebooks.com

2 4 6 8 9 7 5 3 1

First Edition

Book design by Liz Cosgrove

This book is dedicated to all of those people in the world who dare to tap into their ingenuity and brilliance— and to those who defy the naysayers to explore their greatest and most heartfelt possibilities

CONTENTS

LEAVING THE CULT OF FOCUS

For oft, when on my couch I lie
In vacant or in pensive mood,
They flash upon that inward eye
Which is the bliss of solitude;
And then my heart with pleasure fills,
And dances with the daffodils.

—William Wordsworth,
"I Wandered Lonely as a Cloud"

One Friday night in 1983, a man and his girlfriend were driving down California Highway 128 from Berkeley to Mendocino, where he was building a cabin in the woods. It was late, it was a long drive, and he was feeling a little tired and spacey. As his girlfriend dozed in the passenger seat, the man's mind wandered back to his work—in his case, research on DNA.

As he put it, "My little silver Honda's front tires pulled us through the mountains. My hands felt the road and the turns. My mind drifted back into the laboratory. DNA chains coiled and floated. Lurid blue and pink images of electric molecules injected themselves somewhere between the mountain road and my eyes."

Like an enthusiastic puppy just unleashed, his thoughts darted to and fro, mulling, comparing, and connecting fragments of information. Suddenly something new fell into place for him. He pulled off to the side of the road—mile marker 46.58, to be exact, he found himself noticing—and began to connect the dots of his thoughts. Science would never be the same.

That man was Dr. Kary Banks Mullis—a biochemist who, ten years later, would win the Nobel Prize in chemistry for his invention of the polymerase chain reaction, also known as PCR. A way of making synthetic DNA, it has proven crucial in a wide range of disciplines, from obstetrics to forensics. It was on that restless, late-night journey that his mind collected ideas and put them together in new and strange ways. Later he would sort and hone what his wandering mind had pooled before him. The magic of that process—both the collecting and the sorting—is the stuff of this book.

As a physician, psychiatrist, and executive coach, I am privy to people's hope for change and their yearning for change strategies. In every consultation—whether in a boardroom or on the therapeutic couch, whether about work flow and workplace efficiency, leadership, learning, parenting, marriage, or weight loss—everyone wants to figure out how to overcome a hurdle, reach their goal, and get ahead. Most people I talk to are convinced that more focus—maybe in the form of better organization, more detailed plans, or even an advanced degree—will be the solution to their issues. They use focusing tools—timetables, to-do lists, calendar reminders, and noise-blocking headphones—though they often come to see that these technologies don't actually move the needle on the quality of their lives or productivity in quite the way they were hyped.

Some have read about meditation and mindfulness and how very healthy and productivity-inducing the development of these kinds of here-and-now "mental muscles" can be. They try to fit them into their daily lives, although not always successfully. Others come to me with the vague sense that they have distractibility, procrastination, attention deficit hyperactivity disorder (ADHD), or follow-through issues. Many even hope I'll make a formal diagnosis and prescribe medication to keep them on task. These people believe their inability to focus and stay focused is what is getting in the way.

Oftentimes focus appears to be exactly what they need (though medication is much overused). Indeed, focus can be a *tremendous* change agent. It keeps you on target until a job is finished, allowing you to coordinate your thinking, emotions, and movements to execute and finish it. Kids need focus in quantity to sit through a traditional school day's worth of instruction. Leaders need it to unify people around a mission or objective. Businesses need it to build and grow their market share. Try to thread a needle or follow a recipe or build "some assembly required" furniture without it!

In the long run, focus can selectively—and often profitably—hone your interests. Unless you're a polymath genius like Michelangelo (I have to pause to ask: would someone like him be medicated today?), having a wide range of interests may make you a jack-of-all-trades but master of none. Focused specialization gives you greater depth of understanding, insight, practice, and experience. Over time it gives you confidence in your abilities and gives others confidence in you. If you had to have a heart bypass, wouldn't you choose the surgeon who has performed a thousand bypasses rather than one who has performed three hundred bypasses, three hundred gut resections, and four hundred brain surgeries? In the business realm, the company that focuses on one specific market need is often the company that meets the need best.

Neurologically, focusing plays an essential role in keeping information online in your brain, a process that has far-ranging—

almost unquantifiable—value. While you're completing a task, your brain is busy relaying and conveying information to your short-term memory, which is housed in a region called the *dorsolateral prefrontal cortex*. I like to call this region the *memory cup* because it collects information that we need to access as we're completing a task. Focus is one of the key determinants (along with emotion and intuition) of what gets deemed relevant, which in turn can make us better/faster/smoother/smarter at that task in the future.

For all the "clear" benefits of focus, however, I believe that too many of us have (unwittingly) bought into the *cult of focus:* the belief that focus is the capability above all capabilities, the core competency to strive for. In truth, focus in isolation will actually work against you and disempower you.

Think of it this way: focus is your brain's flashlight. But while a bright and narrow beam of light cast straight out in front of you is terrifically helpful if that's where you need to be looking, what about your peripheral vision and the light you might need to see into the murky middle distance? In the extreme, this kind of "blinker vision" becomes a phenomenon known to psychologists as *inattentional blindness,* wherein you are blind to some things because you simply cannot pay attention to everything; your brain makes a choice about what to focus on, sometimes to your detriment.

For instance, in 1995, a police officer in Boston ran right past someone who was being viciously beaten while he was chasing a suspect in another crime. The officer claimed not to have seen the assault, but jurors didn't believe he could possibly have been so blinkered. They convicted him of perjury and obstruction of justice, and he was sentenced to more than two years in jail, plus a fine. Interested in the possibility that the officer might have been experiencing inattentional blindness—a focus overload due, in this case, to his zeal to catch a suspect—researchers simulated the scene and found that many test subjects too would have missed the violence in their peripheral vision. At night only 35 percent of experimental subjects noticed the fight; during the day 56 percent noticed it.

A more fun example of how focus can compromise our ability to take in relevant information and cause *selective attention* was brought to life through the invisible gorilla experiment. Search for "invisible gorilla" online, and you can experience it yourself. The study participants were watching a basketball game onscreen, between teams wearing white and black shirts. The researchers asked them to count how many times the white-shirted team members passed the ball to one another. A person in a gorilla suit walked right through the basketball game. But most of the participants, focusing on the white shirts and preoccupied with counting the passes, missed seeing the person in the gorilla suit.

If focus makes you miss seeing a gorilla, what else are you missing in life?

Perhaps you're concentrating so hard on developing your company that you neglect to see the competition gathering momentum in the proverbial wings. Or you're so in love with someone that you don't notice changes in their behavior until they break up with you—"I just didn't see the signals," you explain sadly. Or if you're a psychiatrist, you may be so consumed with uncovering the emotional root of your patient's anxiety that you neglect to investigate whether adrenal problems are causing it. As the saying goes, to the guy with a hammer (or medical specialty), everything looks like a nail (or biased diagnosis).

Related to blinker vision and selective attention is the issue of too much focus or hyperfocus. Hyperfocus can make you miss out on what truly matters to you. In college, you may become so absorbed in your academic pursuits that you "forget" to socialize or date, then afterward find it difficult to meet potential life partners. I see this a lot as a therapist. There's a scientific name for this too—it's called *long-term discounting*. It's your brain's tendency to minimize the importance of things in the future because they're too far off. Many studies show that long-term discounting is the brain's default. In my opinion, it's one of the biggest reasons we come to regret things—our inability to shift into and out of the long view as much as we need to.

Another consequence of hyperfocus is what psychologists refer to as *loss of caring*. In one study of this phenomenon, subjects were asked to focus intently on a video of a woman talking. They were asked to ignore the bottom corner of the screen, where words appeared every ten seconds. If they got distracted, they were to quickly start watching the woman again. Other subjects watched the video normally and more casually, without being instructed not to look at the words. Later, after the viewing, all the subjects were asked to volunteer to help victims of a recent tragedy. Researchers found that those in the hyperfocused group were less likely to volunteer, less generous with their help, and more prone to loss of caring. Why? Hyperfocus depletes the brain's *prefrontal cortex* (PFC), which helps us make moral decisions. In other words, hyperfocus can drain your brain of the resources needed to balance your own weariness with helping others.

Focus may also stymie innovation. In an article in *Harvard Business Review,* business professor Rosabeth Moss Kanter points to some of the problems associated with limiting the scope of innovation or staying too focused. For example, the Gillette Company had a toothbrush unit (Oral B), an appliance unit (Braun), and a battery unit (Duracell) but failed to make a battery-powered toothbrush. Each division stayed too focused on its own products and practices. And yet our brains are wired to make these connections if we allow them to map similarities across apparently unrelated domains.

So how, exactly, do we do this? What's the sweet spot between focus that galvanizes you and focus that calcifies or exhausts your thinking? How do you achieve a workable balance between a zoomed-in perspective and a more panoramic view of the world? The answer lies in developing the capacity for what I call *unfocus*.

When I raise the idea of unfocus to clients and patients, I often automatically get a little pushback: they think it means they should relax their standards or flit around aimlessly. They don't want to become (or continue to be) dilettantes; they want to be producers and problem solvers. The mention of tinkering, dabbling, doodling, and trying elicits a similar reaction. Tinkerers tend not to finish what they start. Dabblers dip a toe in an endeavor but don't get really wet. Doodling is mere child's play. Trying is important—as we tell our children—but succeeding is more often rewarded, unfortunately all the more so once we're adults.

I get it: unfocus *sounds* like a negative. But disregard semantics for a moment, and come back to the metaphor of a flashlight. Focus and unfocus are *two different settings*. Focus is the close and narrow beam that illuminates the path directly ahead. Unfocus is the beam that reaches far and wide, enabling peripheral vision. Either beam in isolation is helpful only up to a point. Combining them will keep your battery charged the longest, and you will be better able to find your way in the dark too.

Many important discoveries have come from what appear to be unfocused career trajectories. If, for example, you tried to emulate Dr. Mullis's path through life to his discovery, you might, logically, do well in school, obtain a Ph.D. in biochemistry, then systematically approach the question of DNA duplication. But little in Dr. Mullis's history suggests that this was how he arrived at his eureka moment. If anything, the journey to his goal was marked by deviations from the straight-and-narrow path.

After obtaining his Ph.D., he left science to write fiction. Then he quit writing to become a biochemist. Following this, he quit bioscience and managed a bakery for two years. When he returned to science, he was anything but focused. Earlier in his life, he had tried to make rockets before he made DNA. Much of his life has been an emotional roller coaster. He is currently on his fourth marriage. These are the parts of the story that we leave out, yet they are probably as important to his insights and intellectual development as his actual work in biochemistry. You couldn't mimic them. But within you is an unfocused story waiting to be told, if it has not been told already.

Every experience contributes to brain development. Deviations from the straight-and-narrow path can offer unanticipated insights, raise new perspectives on the same issue, and build the character you need to gain the fortitude to pursue your passions. There's no saying what would have happened if Dr. Mullis had become a biochemist sooner, stuck with his first marriage, and never worked in a bakery. But few, if any, successful people have such linear paths to their goals, even if it seems that way in retrospect.

Nor may such a focused career path even be desirable. As London Business School professor Lynda Gratton points out in *The 100-Year Life,* in this age of longevity, we have to rethink how we build our lives. Focus may be a quick and dirty way to make sense of how people get to their goals. But in many cases, it is powerful and persuasive fiction.

Learning to unfocus *and* focus will make you more effective, productive, and nimble as a thinker and problem solver. Getting into a new and conscious rhythm with them both is the key to the productivity, creativity, ingenuity, or general happiness you seek. Indeed, one of the ironic by-products of learning to unfocus is that doing so will sharpen your focus when you need it. And that's because they are two sides of the same mental coin. (By the way, if you've come to this book seeking validation for *already being quite unfocused*—if people criticize you for having that quality—it'll likely be music to your ears to hear that unfocus is a valuable skill.

The key for you will be to learn to hone and harness it instead of letting it run rampant in your life.)

Consider an orchestra. Each member has to practice (focus) to master his or her own individual part. But at concert time, orchestra members must be able to blend their expertise and sound into the greater whole (unfocus). They have to focus just enough to perform their music and keep track of the score, while also being unfocused enough to interact with and hear one another (not to mention keep an intermittent eye on the conductor). Letting go of tight focus and melding their sound with others around them is indeed a skill.

So it is in sports. To be a great tennis player, for example (and assuming a good level of fitness), you need to practice a number of specific, focused skills: how to grip the racket for each kind of shot and where to follow through; the position of your feet in relation to your body; how high to toss the ball up when serving; how much power to put behind your strokes in order to place the ball where you want it to go. And you have to play the game repeatedly to develop a sense for ball placement. It takes hours and hours of focused practice to program this, but all those hours will create a blueprint in your brain, and if you trust it, at match time you simply need to watch the ball and let your body do what it has learned to do. You allow unfocus to take over. And in that state of mind your body will carry out the many tiny adjustments that are needed to get the ball where it should go without your having to actively think them all through.

In the basest and broadest sense, unfocusing is the process of relaxing your brain so that it can be ready, recharged, coordinated, and innovative when you need it to be. This isn't wishful thinking—it's proven neurology. Unfocusing reduces amygdala activation and creates calmness. It activates the *frontopolar cortex* and enhances innovation. It increases *anterior insula* activity and strengthens a sense of self. It limits the grip of the part of the brain called the precuneus, the "observing ego" that makes us self-conscious. (This, essentially, is the getting-out-of-your-own-way ability I'm talking about for the violinist or tennis player.) It restores *prefrontal cortex* activity so that we can become reenergized in our thinking and have less burnout. It improves long-term memory and retrieval of relevant experience. And perhaps its most consistent and profound effect is that it increases activity in the *default mode network* (DMN)—a collection of brain regions that are active during rest and that usually deactivate during focused tasks. We will also call the DMN the *unfocus network,* yet it is vitally important for focus too. If, for example, this network did not deactivate during focused tasks, it would interrupt your ability to focus.

This, tragically, is what happens in diseases like Alzheimer's. Patients with this disease have a DMN that is not synchronized—its various components metaphorically shoot randomly in the dark. Reduced connectivity in the unfocus network has also been linked to problems in thinking in several other neurologic and psychiatric disorders, including autism, frontotemporal dementia, multiple sclerosis, and vegetative states when people have severe brain damage and can be partially aroused but not aware. Studies indicate that if you build cognitive reserve by training your brain with both focused and unfocused activities, you have a backup should something go wrong. Simply put, unfocus can protect your thinking brain over the course of your life. And if you change your lifestyle and train your brain so that unfocus serves you, you're likely to see the changes sooner than you think.

In my opinion, there is nothing—absolutely nothing—more beautiful than the tinkering brain in action.

Brain scanners can photographically capture the flow of blood to and between the engaged circuits and brain regions—the sure sign that the billions of neurons in a brain are working extra-hard.

Think of neurons as modern dancers, moving around and coming together in unexpected ways, pushing off one another, and changing directions suddenly. Instead of just two arms and two legs, however, these lithe and shapely dancers have millions of limbs, exponentially multiplying the ways in which they can connect and interact. Each new thought or action discharges a burst of electricity more dazzling than the most extravagant fireworks display. And this discharge mobilizes and transports information across the brain's circuits. The shifts in blood flow light up the images like a sparkly, starry night. The picture is utterly mesmerizing.

Arranged largely by function, some brain circuits *perceive* information, others *retrieve* it, and still others *conceive* of what might be. Yet separate though these functions may be, they come together when we're thinking—being creative, learning, doing many things at once, or problem solving. These functions make the neuronal "arms" and "legs" reach out and intertwine with one another in acts of agile grace. Sometimes the dancers in your brain take turns carrying out their functions, conserving energy, and relying on one another. Each new moment of sensing, responding, and acting changes neuronal communications and connection—the choreography. Whether you're focused (studying for a test) or unfocused (daydreaming or imagining how you would like to be graded!), the rhythm of focus and unfocus determines how, where, and when the dancers in our brain will rise or fall, rest or run, connect or pull away. And it determines which set of neurons will take center stage.

In this mystical and magical brain dance, logic finds a home. Here you learn how to bake bread, deal with a lover's rejection, pursue an interest that has captured your imagination, believe in God, or build the business of your dreams. Mysteriously, the conductor of this magic is as yet unknown or absent. But here you have some control over the shunting of blood to and from different regions; here you are the choreographer.

When you learn to switch back and forth from focus to unfocus, something profound will change in how you manage stress and risk and in how you understand life. You will find formidable parts of yourself that you never knew you had. You will even stop hating your unfocused mind. Learning it will require you to be *purposeful and skilled* in how you unfocus and include it in your daily activities. You may already be doing it accidentally—stumbling upon a creative idea, perhaps when you don't mean to—but this book will teach you how to actively control or at least steer the process.

When people try out even a few of these methods in workshops, or in my private therapy and coaching practice, they often suddenly feel relieved or they have the kind of aha moment I mentioned above. Nearly everyone once in a while finds his or her mind floating out through a window in the middle of a day. If you knew how to harness that tendency for something positive, wouldn't it be amazing? Aha indeed!

TINKER
DABBLE
DOODLE
TRY

THE BEAT OF
YOUR BRAIN

Thought is the labor of the intellect, reverie is its pleasure. To
replace thought by reverie is to confound poison with nour-
ishment.

—Victor Hugo

I was a straight-A student prior to my second year at medical
school, but during that year, in the context of an escalating workload, my grades suddenly slumped.

Even though I burned the midnight oil, I wasn't able to make
headway. I sat for hours studying human anatomy, trying to mem-
orize where muscles attached, and where in the body nerves and
blood vessels traveled. On more than one occasion, I ran myself
ragged, only to wake up with my head buried in a pile of bones.

Nobody could have spent more time than I did studying and
working, yet the harder I focused, the worse I seemed to do. Little
did I know that I was operating my brain like a teenager driving a
car for the first time, taking off at breakneck speed, then jerkily
screeching to an abrupt halt. The result: too much wear and tear
on the brake pads and gears!

I struggled to wrap my head around what was happening. And

I didn't even register that I was physically exhausted until the penny eventually dropped during the vacation between my second and third years. That's when I decided to make a few changes.

Desperate, I determined to start working smarter instead of just harder. I saw my failings as a code I had to crack, so I tinkered with habit and lifestyle changes. Even though it went against my work ethic, I took short breaks every forty-five minutes while studying. I made an effort to spend more time away from work and with my friends. I committed to sleeping well before undertaking any big stretches of studying. And because I had always heard such great things about its restorative power, I began meditating for twenty minutes twice a day.

My grades improved. My energy level rose. Eventually, I was at the top of my class again. I had no idea exactly how my lifestyle hacks had worked, but I was certainly happy with the results, so I strove to include these strategies throughout the rest of medical school—with great results.

But I didn't really learn the lesson I should have from that episode. My subsequent residency in psychiatry started off with a bang as I burned the proverbial midnight oil anew. Eager to immerse myself in my cases, I spent hours with patients in the hospital. And when I got home, I threw off my work clothes, ate dinner, and read books and psychiatric journals voraciously. After my first clinical rotation, I looked forward to my feedback session with my supervisor.

But the meeting went very differently than I thought it would. "You are a really dedicated doctor," he said. "It must be a little frustrating that your knowledge base is far more developed than your peers'. You probably can't have the conversations that you want to, right?"

I didn't really feel that way, but I *thought* I heard positive feedback and took it gladly. Then came a comment that I will never forget for the rest of my life.

"We're a little concerned that you spend as much time as you do on the inpatient units. If you keep this up, I'm afraid you'll have a ton of information in your head, but you won't receive a superior education. I presume that's why you wanted to come to Harvard in the first place?"

The question was ironic and chilling, to say the least. I realized I had reverted to my old bad habits. I was trapped by the wrong assumptions about ambition, exhausting myself both physically and mentally all over again.

My supervisor explained that taking breaks to allow thoughts to congeal is one of the most important aspects of a true education. He prescribed walking through the woods in the middle of the day, spending more time on park benches with my colleagues, and even going into therapy to see if I could develop insights that could help me unpack my days.

Now, having studied how our brains manage focus and unfocus, I understand what my supervisor already knew: there was no nuance to my *cognitive rhythm.*

When you think of great rhythm, you likely think first of music—say, Michael Jackson's or Elvis Presley's dancing—or you conjure the amazing riffs of a guitarist like Jimi Hendrix, Kurt Cobain, or Keith Richards. In all those instances, a run of notes or movement repeats with regularity—a defining beat with on and off moments. Play "Voodoo Child," "Come as You Are," or "Jumpin' Jack Flash," and you'll connect instantly with an extraordinary rhythm.

But rhythm is not only a musical concept. It's essential in your body as well. Your heart has to expand and contract on time. You have to breathe in and out with great regularity. And you can't escape the circadian rhythm of sleep-wake cycles. Cognitive rhythm is the ability to intermingle focus and unfocus (the on and off moments) in the most effective way.

On any given day, you have to be prepared for and respond accordingly to the tumult of life: the constant starting, stopping, negotiating of "bumps," and changing direction. As I discovered in medical school, if the only tool that you have in your thinking toolkit is focus, you will quickly become fatigued. Your brain will shut down prematurely. That's far from optimal. It's far better if you proactively learn to prevent it before it crashes. Furthermore, even though you aren't aware of it, studies show that you spend close to half of your day in mini–mental journeys away from the task at hand. This kind of spontaneous fluctuation is no more an effective use of brainpower than the switching off that happens when you're completely exhausted.

Like the difference between a light bulb blowing a fuse and dimming the lights to save energy, there's a huge difference between running out of steam and putting your brain on one of its dimmer modes. In the latter case, you can metaphorically turn the light back on to bright again when you need or want it. In the former, you're finished for the time being!

SURFING YOUR BRAINWAVES

Although a brain cell's resting voltage is less than that of an AA battery, electricity passing across the cell membrane generates a massive force—about fourteen million volts per meter, more than four times the force required to produce lightning during a thunderstorm. Multiply that by 100 billion brain cells, and that's the magnitude of your brainpower! It's impressive, to say the least.

From the moment of birth, your brain is generating these electrical impulses across its complex landscape. The impulses occur as waves, and every thought, feeling, and behavior corresponds with a different combination of such waves. Attention is no exception. It's useful to think of waves of attention as musical notes— the low-pitched notes of a trombone, the high-pitched notes of a flute, and everything in between. Even at baseline, your brain's attention fluctuates, aiming for a harmony among these different notes with astounding speed, power, and accuracy. Doctors can detect these "notes" with an EEG (electroencephalogram) much as they can capture your heart's rhythm with an EKG (electrocardiogram). When we look at all the waves that people can generate, they appear on a continuum from more to less frequent and, therefore, from faster to slower.

Beta waves are the "focus" waves. They would appear on your EEG when your eyes are glued to whatever task you're doing. Following beta down the "musical scale" are alpha, theta, and delta waves, each respectively slower, reflecting states of unfocus ranging from pure relaxation to meditation and deep sleep. Gamma waves are the odd ones out. Faster than beta waves, they nonetheless come on when you're either focused or unfocused, suggesting that focus and unfocus are not as separate as we might think.

Each of these brainwave "settings" correlates with a different brain function. Being a peak performer at anything—a homemaker, a teacher, a CEO, a chess player, a researcher—requires knowing when and how to switch between the different settings. And, most important, it requires understanding that these waves work together to create the best brain states to perform the task at hand.

YOUR CIRCUITS IN SYNC

Some people have astounding lucidity. They impress us with their seemingly tireless productivity and razor-sharp clarity. Georg Philipp Telemann, for example, composed two hundred overtures in a two-year period, and Benjamin Franklin invented the lightning rod, a flexible catheter, bifocal eyeglasses, and umpteen other things. They were masters of the frontoparietal cortex, or what I call the *focus circuit*. Always on task, they have focus on demand.

Part of a larger *central executive network* (CEN), the focus circuit keeps you on task even when you're not as extreme as Telemann or Franklin. Whether you're following a recipe or performing a complex procedure, filling out your tax forms or listening carefully to your GPS as you make your way through unknown territory, your focus networks are like a flashlight, lighting up the path just ahead.

Yet this faculty by itself is woefully insufficient, and on its own, razor-sharp clarity can feel shallow. It's like a piano player playing all the right notes but without heart. To be sure, if you have ever played or heard the music of Telemann, you know that he relied on much more than focus to create his music. That said, this shallowness manifests in those who, unlike him, in so many other areas of life, stick *only* to focus: the bureaucratic boss, the one-dimensional bottom-liner, the workhorse colleague whose reports are precise yet lack depth. Their pronouncements are clear, yet they leave us wanting more nuance. To extend the GPS metaphor: You want to know what awaits you farther along your trip. You want to at least know the midterm future, or be able to anticipate the next hour, rather than see only the road immediately ahead.

Nuance and depth require diffusing the beam of the focus flashlight so that you can see important objects and details in your periphery as well. The brain circuit that allows for this broadening of vision is the *default mode network,* or what I refer to as the *unfocus circuit.* Before science understood its true function, the DMN was thought of as the "Do Mostly Nothing" circuit. But over time, we have come to see that it is one of the greatest consumers of energy in the brain. Moreover, it is extensively connected with the focus circuits, in a kind of brainwave overflow and integration. Focus and unfocus are like a good red sauce: it's hard to tell if the meat is flavoring the sauce or the sauce is flavoring the meat. They simply work together.

In the brain, a mix of brainwaves enters and leaves each circuit with a preponderance of one type of wave for any particular function. For instance, at the peak of unfocus, alpha waves may appear in the DMN, but delta waves may also appear in certain unfocus regions, and they may be mixed with beta waves, because focus and unfocus circuits are constantly "talking" to each other. Similarly, more beta than delta waves may appear in the focus circuit, to orient your focused attention. But it's rarely just one type of wave alone. Which is why talking about focused and unfocused circuits is a false dichotomy. They are acting at the same time and are designed to work together. It's we who stop this natural connection in our brains when we overfocus.

The musician who is connected to a past tragedy while singing a sad song pulls on our heartstrings more effectively. It's not just the technical execution of the voice that produces an amazing performance but also the convergence of technicality and precision with the diffuse past and future, with self and other. Unfocus circuits bring on this rich complexity and authenticity. And they can be trained too.

Fritz Reiner, a twentieth-century Hungarian-born conductor, is one of the greatest conductors of all time. Many attribute the world-class ascent of the Chicago Symphony Orchestra (CSO) to his leadership. And it must have been entertaining to watch him at work: using his entire body, he would usher in the strings with his hands, then puff out his cheeks when it was the brass section's turn, and when a section to his right had to stop while he was looking left, he would kick out a foot. As a testament to how great the CSO was under his direction, after hearing a performance in Boston, Arthur Fiedler, the conductor of the Boston Pops Orchestra, said to the CSO, "You're not men. You're gods."

As amazing a conductor as Reiner was, by most reports he was also tyrannical. He did not tolerate imperfections, and when he was rehearsing with the orchestra, he allowed nobody to be a slacker. When you were playing for him, you had to play perfectly. You had to attend to all of him. One slip, and you were in trouble. And when you were silent, you had to listen without distraction.

A musician playing for Reiner or any exacting conductor, as you can imagine, faces the cognitive challenge of being internally connected just enough to play deeply from the heart, but simultaneously of being exquisitely sensitive to what the others are playing and what the conductor is asking of him or her. A musician who becomes lost in the playing risks missing cues and really hearing what others are playing. A musician who focuses too intently on what others are doing or on what the conductor is prompting is likely to play with less heart and emotion. Somehow the brain has to manage the delicate balance between focus and unfocus.

But in our day-to-day lives, we sometimes forget this and behave like a musician who is paying attention only to Fritz Reiner and not to the other musicians. We may be so absorbed in a task that we notice nothing else. Leaders, parents, and sports team players face the same challenge: to be "in the zone," yet also to be aware of their surroundings—to remember to focus and unfocus as well.

THE MANY NOTES OF YOUR DMN

When you understand the quality and extent of the DMN's connections in the brain, the "working together" of focus and unfocus becomes more apparent.

It acts as a distraction filter: Paradoxically, unfocus circuits play an active and crucial role in keeping you focused; they act almost like sponges, absorbing distractions to keep you on a short-term task.

It builds mental flexibility: Unfocus circuits act as a pivot, helping you switch your attention from one task to the next. Engage your unfocus circuits enough, and your thinking becomes very flexible indeed.

It connects you more deeply with yourself and others: Unfocus circuits connect you with elements of your own story, stored in different parts of your brain. They are the chief writers of your autobiography. Your personal traits and self-reflections can all become part of the moment because your unfocus circuits can activate them at the same time. Unfocus circuits reach far back into your stored memories, letting your history inform every moment of focus. In this sense, they transport you toward yourself.

Deep unfocus activates "social connection" circuits too. That's why leadership development coaches will tell you that the quintessential quality of being a leader is becoming yourself. It's why vocal coaches will tell you to find your own voice. And why any great educator will encourage you to discover your originality. Deep self-connection connects your brain to things far and wide beyond the moment and yourself.

It integrates the past, present, and future: Past, present, and future are all "happening" now in your brain. The past is stored as memories. The present is experienced through your five senses. And the future is represented by planning and imagination. Your DMN can bring them all together and help you comprehend the story that is unfolding. It connects the dots on the timeline of your life.

It helps you express your creativity: Because unfocus circuits bridge such vast areas of your brain, they can help you develop unique associations and originality. With this, you can also be more spontaneous.

It helps you dredge up intangible memories: The DMN can also help you integrate memories that lie outside the line of focus. Consider the experienced cook whose meals are inexplicably delicious because they embody more than just following a recipe to the letter. Having watched her grandmother as a child, the adult chef has taken in something that no book could ever teach. It may have to do with the rhythm of stirring the red sauce or the precise finger movements when sprinkling the cheese on the casserole or quesadilla. These are the kinds of emotions that the DMN can dredge up.

A case in point is my favorite Italian meatball recipe. Enter "Anthony's meatballs" into an online search, and you'll see for yourself that it calls on a number of intangibles in the creation process. In addition to the ingredients list and the actual step-by-step instruction to measure, mix, and cook, it includes the direction to put on some "Italian background music" to set the right mood! The result is a magically and exponentially more delicious dinner than a more literal recipe will yield.

YOUR RHYTHM BUSTERS

As helpful as unfocusing—or tapping into your DMN—will be to your brain and your life, some systems and defaults that are already built into your life may challenge your cognitive rhythm. Beware of these rhythm busters, and use them as signals to press your brain's reset button—a skill you will learn to hone throughout this book:

Habits: Your brain likes to maintain the status quo. It's most comfortable cruising along in habitual, familiar behavior. Trying to make a meaningful habit or attitudinal change causes a kind of stress in the mind, or *cognitive dissonance,* which is visible on brain scans. Your brain is trying to reconcile two things here: you want to change, but you can't change without psychological discomfort.

Take, for instance, the habit of focus itself. Even though all the brain biology research points to the value of unfocus, if you're used to focusing for productivity, your brain will reject or avoid making a change; unfocusing just doesn't compute to your rational, focus-habit brain.

Even after you do a few unfocus practices, your brain's default response will be to go back to what it was doing before, to continue your habitual behavior. That's what will settle it down. You must pay a price for change, and you have to be willing to pay it. It's called *switch cost*.

Switch cost comes in the form of fear, uncertainty, and unfamiliarity. Your brain doesn't like these things; they are "expensive." You have to be certain that reenergizing your brain is worth it to you, and convince your brain that your current structure in life is not working (as I did when I changed my study habits).

One alternative is to stay stuck where you are (alternative A)—in a shop-till-you-drop kind of mentality at Christmas, for example. The other is to change (alternative B)—to take a lunch or coffee break, or to spread your shopping out over several days. The more obvious the advantages of B over A, the more your brain is likely to comply. Also called *spreading of alternatives* (SOA), this obvious difference between A and B needs to be spelled out. When it is, SOA resolves cognitive dissonance. You can even see this resolution on brain scans. Blood flows away from the conflict center and back to regions that will help you complete your daily tasks.

Uncertainty: Uncertainty is generally a negative to your brain, not just because of itself but also because it also biases you to believe that the sky is falling.

When you're uncertain, all goals look like moving targets. Panicked, you may revert to focus, in the hope that you can detect the dangers coming your way and hit the targets as you need to. But there's more to uncertainty than meets the eye.

In 2010, radiology professor Issidoros Sarinopoulos and colleagues examined how uncertainty affects the brain. They showed people emotional expressions—some neutral and some frightening. Just before the neutral pictures, they were shown an *O*, and just before the negative pictures, they were shown an *X*. And in some trials they did not know what to expect and were shown a *?*

When people saw the *?*, it freaked them out more than when they saw the *X*.

Then they were asked, "What do you think the next face is going to be?" The people in the *?* group were completely off target. Seventy-five percent of them said it was going to be threatening when it was not. Their uncertain brains simply kept expecting the worst. In these people, the conflict (anterior cingulate cortex) and disgust (insula) centers were in overdrive.

Bottom line—being uncertain shakes up your brain and skews the way you see the world. But once you recognize this fact, you will see that uncertainty's bark is worse than its bite. Unfocusing to correct this bias should be the first step in the order of things.

Focus addiction: Sometimes focus casts a magic spell because you can get so much done when you're in that focused zone. Plus, to come full circle to the idea of habits and avoiding cognitive dissonance, it's sometimes just a whole lot more psychologically comfortable to get through your day the way you always have and the only way you know how: through focus. But while it's desirable to have things go smoothly, you need to make sure you don't flatline your way through life.

Instead, recognize that focus can impact your brain much as any addiction would. You'll get exhausted, have a one-track mind, feel depleted, and not be able to think clearly either. When you unfocus, on the other hand, your brain has time to recover, and you can go back to focusing, rejuvenated and refreshed.

Focus relapses: Imagine you've just come back from a restful, rejuvenating, and mentally unfocused vacation. But now you face a huge pile of work and the associated stress about getting it all done. So you relapse into hyperfocus, relying on your pre-vacation habit of getting up early, working late, and not taking lunch breaks. This kind of U-turn into focus is common, and it's often very helpful—you'll certainly catch up on the work that's piled up. But after the necessary focused binge, you're depleted all over again. What good was the vacation?

Instead, even when you get back into the saddle, remember to unfocus as well as focus. That will take you to the finish line and not exhaust you in the process.

EARLY SIGNS OF A JAMMED-UP BRAIN

Nobody stays in a healthy cognitive rhythm all the time. Like the rude awakening I had in medical school, when my grades and energy dropped precipitously, and again at the beginning of my residency, when my adviser pointed out my narrow-mindedness, you eventually know when you have been operating out of rhythm. But if you know the early signs of a jammed-up brain, you can self-correct *before* you get off track.

Not having as much energy as you used to: If you're feeling more drained than usual, you may be starting to lose your cognitive rhythm, and if you've felt this way for a few days in a month, then it might be time to see how you're utilizing your days. That's a good time to choose one of the roads to unfocus.

Not closing the deal: A lot of people work hard to get what they want, but they either choke or just can't close the deal. From the tennis player who surrenders several match points, to the negotiator who makes it to the final round but then can't bring about a settlement, or the politician whose campaign loses steam (and followers), closing the deal requires maintaining energy right to the end. You can't do this on your last breath. When you start to feel like you're repeatedly one number short of winning the lottery, it may be time to do a rhythm check.

Not reaching your goals: Similarly, you don't reach your goals because your mind, fatigued by focus, will not only *not* reach a goal, it won't be anywhere near the actual goal that needs to be reached. Here you're barking up the wrong tree of life. It's time to reset your rhythm and revisit your goals.

Repeated mistakes: Everybody makes mistakes, and many mistakes are helpful if we can learn from them. But making the same mistake over and over isn't efficient. When your life has one too many deletes, rewrites, spills, or schedule snafus, it may be time to reset your brain's rhythm.

Feeling easily overwhelmed: In our fast-paced technologically stimulating world, occasional overwhelm of the "I've had a very taxing day and need to shut the world out tonight" variety is understandable. But if you find that you're easily or quickly or repeatedly overwhelmed, it's time to take stock of your life. Your brain is a beautiful organ that you can use to advance your life and the lives of those you care about. Don't feed it trash or expect it to run on the nutritional equivalent of junk food! If you're feeling overwhelmed, it might be time to reestablish your brain's focus-unfocus rhythm.

Settling: When we're young, we are filled with dreams, hopes, and ambitions. But when we get older, those dreams seem to fade away. This is so common that some say settling is a sign of mature behavior! At times it may be, but most of the time, settling is a sign of emotional fatigue. You're unable to take on another challenge because you don't have the brain rhythm that you need to do so. But unfocus can help your brain get back in rhythm.

Finding yourself far from your hopes, dreams, and goals: Think about your life for a moment. How congruent is it with your earlier dreams and expectations? Are you working toward goals that still matter to you? If you find yourself disenchanted with where you are today, or if you suddenly realize that you're speeding toward a destination that no longer holds much appeal, you may need to uncouple yourself from your present focus. It's time to unfocus to begin a whole new search.

THE MANY ROADS TO UNFOCUS

Think of how you feel when you lie in a hammock on a hot summer day. With your eyes half closed and your mind adrift, your brain has the time and ability to bring back long-forgotten memories. In that state it can become a "memory fetcher," giving you a valuable glimpse of the past so you don't make the same mistake twice.

Or recall how you sometimes have epiphanies while standing in the shower. Here you're not necessarily in some dreamy state—just in a different place. Your mind is off the tasks that previously occupied your attention. All of a sudden, eureka! You've got it. Something you've been trying to figure out all week unexpectedly becomes crystal clear.

In other unfocused states, you may be doing something less demanding, like knitting or gardening. Here you're neither half asleep nor in the shower frame of mind. You're cruising along on autopilot, getting stuff done. When you do, your brain gets a much-deserved rest, but it also brings the puzzle pieces of memory together to increase the accuracy of future predictions.

Lying in a hammock, showering, knitting, and gardening are all things you can do to unfocus and relax. But there are more formal, useful, and possibly surprising ways you can unfocus too. These are the methods you will learn to use in context throughout this book.

Reverie: When you speak to another person about your own uncensored thoughts as they arise, thoughts about something fanciful, imaginary, or hypothetical, you're engaging in reverie. Reverie is a form of unfocus used extensively in psychoanalysis, but you can use it in your everyday life too. More seriously and practically, engineers and entrepreneurs use it when they invite others (colleagues, investors, followers) into their strategic thinking at an early and low-impact stage of invention. As a group, you're just thinking out loud, but incorporating some of the generated ideas at an early stage can lead to more support and buy-in from those same people when it's time to act.

The same principle applies when you're trying to make a change in your relationship or even move furniture around your house. The more you invite someone else into your thinking at an early stage, the more ideas you'll generate and the more likely the others will agree with the final outcome, especially if you incorporate some of their suggestions into your plan. Rearranging furniture a gazillion times is a drag, so why not invite new perspectives and ideas early on, before you do the actual moving? In a relationship, where there is usually a whole lot more at stake, you can use reverie to imagine a better or different future together without getting entrenched in your respective agendas and going off in two different directions: that's when people grow apart. In either scenario, you're using a collective unfocus to find solutions you might not have landed on if you focused on your own.

Mind-wandering: A more obvious form of unfocusing, letting your mind wander, is a great way to unearth tangible and intangible memories that enrich your actions. You can do this from a beach chair or in front of a fireplace. You can do it in brainstorming sessions at work. Somewhere in your life, in increments short and long, you can train your unfocus circuits by allowing your mind to wander. Unlike mindfulness, which involves focusing on your breath but taking your attention off your mental chatter, mind-wandering requires letting go of a task with no particular focus.

Imagination: When you imagine something, you're effectively suspending disbelief about the reality of its possibility. This is unfocus writ large! Trading increasingly zany "what if's" about the future or about ways to deal with a scenario is a playful form of using imagination that is also called *prospection*. Regardless of what you call it, projecting into the future (imagining) has been shown to activate the DMN and will spill over into your ability to imagine new outcomes for old problems or situations. In my practice, people who are stuck—either in a relationship or in their businesses—use "reality" to escape their traps, when imagination is often a far better way to discover solutions.

Daydreaming: Then there's the all-important tool of daydreaming. Of course, one person's daydreaming is another person's nightmare. You may have an analyzing, task-focused brain that can more or less switch into autopilot and go daydreaming while you're tinkering on machines. For me, this would be a nightmare—I need every ounce of focus I can muster in order to fix something.

But you can choose your activity for daydreaming. What are you likely to be able to do with little effort—painting by numbers or reorganizing your closet? The key is that it must not be stressful or effortful. Throughout this book you will learn about the differences between positive constructive daydreaming and wasting time.

Self-talk: In many strategies, I will be recommending that you talk to your brain. At first glance, this may seem slightly deranged since when most of us see people talking to themselves, we think they've lost their marbles! But recent research increasingly points to the usefulness of self-talk, especially as a stress-reducing strategy. Speaking in the second person (addressing yourself as "you" or by your name) is more effective than simply talking to yourself. You've probably seen professional athletes engage in this: Serena Williams sometimes shouts "C'mon, Serena!" instead of just

"C'mon!" Basketball great LeBron James is famous for speaking to himself like this. It may sound implausible at first, but if you can tell your brain to lift up your right hand, why shouldn't you be able to tell it to approach a situation differently? In fact, you can. And it works!

A huge body of scientific study points to the value of reframing your thoughts to yourself, even silently. These reframes can range from the overt (e.g., reframing "I'm useless" to "I need to acquire certain skills") to more subtly shifting our self-narratives. For example, asking yourself, "Why does this always happen to me?" will probably send your brain on a wild goose chase to find the answer to this question—not a good use of your unconscious time. But shifting the query to "How do people with my disadvantages overcome them to get to their goal?" is a much more useful question to pose to your conscious and unconscious brain.

As long as you frame things in the positive, you're in the black. But try to prevent yourself from doing something by telling yourself not to do it, and you will lose ground. Psychologist Daniel Wegner studied this phenomenon and found that when people are under stress, and they give themselves a "do not" instruction, their brains will do the exact opposite of what they want. So ditch the self-admonitions!

You can also use self-talk to stop and reevaluate what you're doing—to course-correct when necessary. Sometimes you do this naturally, but making it a habit will give you an automatic reminder to break away from your focused task from time to time to check in with yourself.

Using your body: You can use your body to activate cognitive rhythm. Like daydreaming, doing certain activities will activate focus or unfocus for different people. One person may want to go for a hike on an unknown path to activate unfocus. Another may want to go on a very familiar hike (like a daily walk around a park in the same direction, along the same paths), since only in the familiar can they really get "lost." And you can use your body in specific ways to get creative too!

Meditation: There are many forms of meditation: Transcendental (using a mantra or word as a point of focus and return); mindfulness (using your breath as a point of focus and return); walking (using walking as a focus while venturing on a path); open monitoring (having no point of focus—just closing the eyes); loving kindness (generating loving and kind feelings with eyes closed); devotion (e.g., to a god or field of interest); and simple self-inquiry (e.g., asking, "Who am I?" regularly). Regardless of the technique you use, when you meditate, you can get unstuck, learn better, become more creative, multitask like a juggler, and access a part of your greatness that is unavailable to a focused mind alone.

So now the big question is *where to start?*

RHYTHM-BUILDING TRAINING WHEELS

When you first learn musical rhythm, you tap single beats, then two beats with an emphasis on the first, then three beats with an emphasis on the first, and so on. Gradually, you learn to break beats up into two or three, and when you become more advanced, the rhythmic complexity is much greater. Then you learn how to improvise and ornament, almost imperceptibly robbing a beat and making up for it by prolonging another beat without losing step with the basic rhythm.

And so it goes with the rhythm of your thinking. You start with the basics, and eventually you will march to the beat of your own drummer. Initially, though, you need to hold yourself to your promises, and you may need some help along the way.

Use an alarm: Let's face it, it's unlikely that you're going to build unfocus time into your day automatically. An alarm can act like your coach, reminding you to do what you really should do. Start small, and set an alarm for one period of unfocused activity a day. Prepare to obey it when you hear it, no matter what. Whether you decide to push back from your desk and let your mind wander on an undemanding task for ten minutes (which will feel like a long time at first) or go for a walk or even take a catnap, using an alarm takes deciding to take a break out of the equation. You hear the alarm, and you just do it.

Create a tinkertable: You already spend close to half your day in mini–mental journeys away from the task at hand. Why not take control of what your mind is intent on doing anyway? Why not harness your mental power? A tinkertable will help you regulate and make better use of those mental flights of attention.

Almost by definition, timetables encourage you to book up every moment, every hour of your day, with focused work. How often have you said, "I'm booked back to back"? Paradoxically, a tinkertable is *not* as open and flexible. Whereas in a timetable you fill in time slots as needed and move appointments around, a tinkertable blocks off periods of time that are off-limits to your day-to-day work and chores.

That said, I know that life's challenges change on a day-to-day basis. Don't obsess about the rules of tinkertable creation. (That's a focus trap if ever there was one!)

Since everyone's day is different, there is no set time of day that you should focus and unfocus, and the number of periods of unfocused time you schedule per day depends on you. There is no hard data on this point, but I find it's most effective to take fifteen minutes off for every forty-five minutes you spend focusing. Your first focused period can be longer than the rest—you can go more like seventy-five minutes before breaking for some unfocus—but thereafter strive for fifteen minutes of unfocus for every forty-five minutes of focus. When you make up your tinkertable, write in these fifteen-minute segments, or if you manage your time with an online calendar, set a calendar reminder every fifteen minutes every day. You can stay at your desk, and maybe in your unfocused time you will listen to music, do a crossword puzzle, or play a video game. The critical thing is that it be undemanding for *you*. Getting up and moving around while unfocusing—going for a walk around the block or in nearby greenery *without your phone*—is even better since you can't cheat and get back to work before you're back at your desk!

In addition to these short daily breaks, build in a time slot for an event that will break up the monotony of your week—perhaps a night out with friends or by yourself at the movies. This longer unfocused period is a little more flexible—you may not be able to get away or organize a get-together rigidly the same day of every week. But make sure you *plan* to do something other than work and your daily routine once a week. It may require leaving work a little early on the given day, but the hours you *are* at work in the days ahead will be more productive because your brain has had some time off.

Your tinkertable will also contain bigger time slots—for a vacation, a retreat, or a protracted "staycation" (no travel, but no work either) that you take three or four times a year for a week at a time. If you don't have that much vacation time at work, be sure to tinkertable out the days or weeks that you *do* get from work. Don't leave vacation time up in the air! Plan it so that it becomes a priority and not something that you keep postponing. Also, plan to be refreshed and excited when you start the vacation, not ragged and exhausted from trying to get ahead before leaving work. How? Commit to the short hourly breaks!

I would also recommend creating a placeholder called *flexitime* in your weekly calendar. This is time when you can decide on the spot what you want to do. You can work, or you can take a break. But you're in charge. For these two hours, you will have no appointments or commitments to others. It's your time to do what you want with it. You've blocked it out!

Putting It All Together for a Rhythmic Life

Understanding that there is *such a thing* as cognitive rhythm is the first step to improving your own. Likewise, becoming aware of the moments in your life when you surely lack it—when you're exhausted, short-tempered, or failing to "close the deal"—will help you tune in to your increased need for unfocus. And setting alarms or keeping a tinkertable will be tangible reminders to *keep at* your practice. But after you've internalized these concepts and strategies, you'll fundamentally need to get out of your own way! Rhythm is never achieved through *rules*.

To keep yourself on track and in rhythm, it's useful to approach challenges through the lenses of four identities as you course through this book: the Jazz Musician, the Dancer, the Futurist, and the Inventor. You have at least one of each of these identities in you!

THE JAZZ MUSICIAN

To stay true to your best cognitive rhythm, you have to be able to trust yourself and be willing to step outside of, and back into, your rhythm. For different days, this may be different. And you may wonder if there are rules to be followed. But to develop impeccable cognitive rhythm, it's preferable to develop the capability to respond rather than simply to follow rules.

Jazz musicians are masters of responding. The same brain regions that allow us to have a synchronized conversation with someone also allow jazz musicians to anticipate what they will each next play. In 2014, brain researcher Ana Luisa Pinho and her colleagues demonstrated that the brain's focus circuits are turned off when this happens, and the unfocus circuits are turned on so that the brain can make quick associations to help predict the next note.

We can take a page out of the jazz musician's book to implement cognitive rhythm. It all starts with self-trust and a conscious willingness to improvise.

If you think you're not an improviser, think again. As a toddler, you had to learn to crawl, then walk, then run. And now not only can you walk without being consciously in charge of your movements, you can walk on a busy sidewalk and effortlessly avoid bumping into the oncoming walkers. If they look like they're coming toward you, you automatically move away, or you stagger your steps to avoid their path. That's improvisation at its most basic. Similarly, as you build up the capability (and through your tinkertable, the habit) for unfocused time, you can throw off the conscious triggers for it, the training wheels. You'll have internalized the need for unfocus and will tap into it more naturally.

THE DANCER

In 2015, when clinical psychologist Anika Maraz and her colleagues questioned 447 salsa and/or ballroom dancers, they found that there are many motivations for their dancing: improving fitness, enhancing mood, finding intimacy, socializing, entering a trance, achieving mastery, building self-confidence, and escaping. When you learn to include unfocus in your daily life, you will invite exactly these experiences into your life. Your DMN, when active and honed, will improve your cognitive fitness, enhance your happiness, increase your sensitivity to yourself and others, give rise to useful daydreaming, and improve your learning and productivity while changing your consciousness state so that you're in the zone. You become a mental dancer!

That's why you should stop overthinking and practice letting go—all the while thinking of yourself as dancing through life. Dancing is a highly demanding activity, not only in the physical sense. It requires a balance of focus and unfocus and the ability to access emotions, detect rhythm, and express rhythm too. Dance integrates movement and thought, all the while impelling you to control your posture, learn sequences, and use your imagination. While dancing and learning these skills require focus, they also require unfocus. Can you imagine someone dancing while focusing only on the "right" moves? Good dancing, like good cognitive rhythm, occurs when you stop overthinking, let go, find the beat, and join it by anticipating the next beat.

THE FUTURIST

In 1900, Smithsonian Institution curator John Elfreth Watkins accurately predicted that we would one day have wireless phone networks, television, MRI machines, aerial warfare, and food trucks in cities throughout America. He also predicted some things that have yet to pass—like the letters *C, X,* and *Q* being removed from the English alphabet! When people like Watkins predict things correctly, they are using a form of thinking known as *intelligent guessing.* They may not always be correct, but when they dare to guess from time to time, they use the DMN and unfocus to look into the future.

If you were on vacation in Miami for the first time and saw only the radiant sun in the sky, then heard the TV weather report that there would be intermittent thundershowers, you might balk at this idea. Yet if you turned your beach-weary head and saw a pall of gray clouds slowly making its way toward you, you would likely put two and two together, pack up your stuff, and head for the hills (or back to your hotel!). In this instance, you're an intelligent futurist—and your hazy, unfocused, sun-drenched mind may be just the thing you need to see the connection between the weather report and those clouds. You don't even need explicit clues to be a good guesser.

In 2012, neuroscientist Julia Mossbridge and her colleagues reported on the findings of a meta-analysis of twenty-six studies on "guessing" from seven independent laboratories. They found that the human body can detect stimuli presented one to ten seconds in the future. For example, if I show you a photograph of a violent scene or a neutral landscape, your actual physiology will accurately change—to anxiety when the image you're about to see is violent, or to calmness when it is serene. In that sense, you're capable of guessing correctly, more often than not, what you're about to see before you do.

Called *predictive anticipatory activity,* this phenomenon may reflect the brain's unconscious ability to know the future. Part of the DMN, the frontopolar cortex, is thought to play an active role in this prediction ability, but the precise reasoning behind this surprising reality is not known. Some kind of unconscious mirroring may be at play—our brains may be able to sense what's about to come because brain circuits can act like mirrors without us even knowing. And there are other theories based on quantum physics. The point is, you don't always have to wait for perceptible knowledge. You know more than you may be willing to admit.

The paradox is that the more you unfocus and give yourself over to this anticipation, the more likely you are to get it right. Furthermore, there's a snowball effect of taking that leap. Study after study has shown a direct correlation between musical training and thinking abilities. Children who learn to play music have better verbal memory, second language pronunciation accuracy, reading ability, and executive functions, not to mention fluency of speech.

Why does this happen in our brains? Well, focus alone brings the brain's attentional system to life and activates the frontoparietal cortex (the brain's flashlight). But it also turns off the DMN. It is unfocus together with focus that connects us to rhythm, dance, and music—and, more loosely, to walking, pausing before jumping into someone's arms, and having sex. Can you imagine if you thought your way all through an orgasm?

THE INVENTOR

As useful as I believe the strategies in this book will be to you, I have to admit that I am always skeptical when authors or advice-givers compartmentalize things so neatly. It's important to remember—and to know that I appreciate—that no two people are alike, and that effective generalizations are hard to make. I don't offer policy! Let my recommendations be a map to help you navigate your own unique complexity. There is no right way or time to do anything except what feels right to you. You will get the maximum value of the ideas I share only if you apply the science and adjust the findings to yourself. Take the ideas, strategies, and information I offer, and adapt them to your own brain: tinker! As much as I have learned about the brain and human psychology, I can provide the information, but only you can be the expert on your own life.

Unfocus is an intelligent form of letting go. It allows our thinking to be flexible, enables us to surrender at crucial moments, provides a friction-free zone within which we can move to the next stage of thinking, and supports a greater connection with the essence of who you are.

It may feel counterintuitive to rest, stop, daydream, turn your intensity down, or temporarily abandon a project just as things are heating up. You may feel like you're giving up or wasting time. But when you shift from *focus-focus-focus-fatigue* to *focus-tinker-focus-*

rest-focus-dabble-focus-try, for example, you leave fatigue out of the equation and use unfocusing moments (tinkering, dabbling, trying) instead to reenergize your brain. Furthermore, *focus-knit-focus-rest-focus-hammock* is different from *focus-meditate-focus-shower-focus-sleep*. Throughout the book, you will learn how to use these different forms of unfocus in context.

Whether you want to become more creative, get unstuck, learn more effectively, master multitasking, or discover your own greatness, employing cognitive rhythm will help you develop competencies that are relevant in a world where constant brain change is necessary if you want to thrive.

When you feel off your game, in a rut, in a haze, overwhelmed, or down on life, the rhythm of life is calling you to join it. Learn how to specifically unfocus for different challenges, and you will be fascinated by the jewels of your very own intellect. That journey begins now!

CONJURING CREATIVITY

I began by tinkering around with some old tunes I knew. Then, just to try something different, I set to putting some music to the rhythm that I used in jerking ice-cream sodas at the Poodle Dog. I fooled around with the tune more and more until at last, lo and behold, I had completed my first piece of finished music.

—Duke Ellington

If I placed dirt, sugar, string, and chocolate syrup in one big bag and gave it to you, what would you do with it all?

In all likelihood, this bag of odd-lot things would not inspire you to take photographs, let alone apply them in original and evocative ways to a photographic canvas. More likely you would toss it into the garbage. Yet this is the kind of thing that the renowned Brazilian artist Vik Muniz thinks to do time and again. He once daubed peanut butter and jelly in a painterly way on top of two close-up shots of the *Mona Lisa*. In everyday life, peanut butter, jelly, and Da Vinci rarely go together. But Muniz suspends traditional thinking about how to pair things and in so doing brings to life potential conflicts between mind and matter (you wouldn't expect the *Mona Lisa* to be made of peanut butter and jelly!), showcases the unexpected, and bridges mental gaps between concepts that would otherwise never be associated. His unexpected combinations capture our attention and stimulate our imagination to run a little wilder. That's why a lot of people take to his work. But whether his art is to your taste or not (some people joke that it inspires them to make artwork of their children's spilled food, or from the dirt that someone tracked onto their brand-new carpet), most people would agree that it is dramatic, provocative, and stunningly creative.

Even if you don't consider yourself creative at the Vik Muniz level, it's important to acknowledge that creativity takes many forms. It requires creativity to manage conflicts diplomatically, to cook a delicious meal from scratch, to convince your stubborn teenager to see things your way, and to put together an outfit in an unusual but eye-catching way.

Still, you may think of creative types as a breed apart, and of creativity as something that you either have or you don't (and you don't). If you *do* think of yourself as creative, you may not truly understand the ways your mind doodles its way to inspiration. And regardless of how creative you feel *you* are, most people would agree that creativity is elusive, not a capability that can be conjured or rushed.

A popular myth has it that creativity is a right-brain phenomenon, so some people declare that they are not right-brained. But recent studies indicate that creativity actually activates a widespread network in the brain, favoring neither hemisphere over the other.

For instance, when brain researcher Melissa Ellamil and her colleagues examined the brains of people who were designing book cover illustrations, they found that both sides of the brain pitched in to stimulate creativity. When the designers were generating ideas, the medial temporal lobe on both sides of the brain, known for storing facts and memories, played a major role. And when the designers were evaluating ideas, it was as if the brain called a town hall meeting—a widespread network had a say. While this network did have two sides, they were not left and right. Rather, they were the focused and unfocused networks on both sides of the brain, bringing analytical versus emotional or gut-level perspectives respectively.

In other words, when you're creative, you don't need to throw your logical brain away. Analysis, association, and inference work hand in hand to ensure that the creative process flows smoothly. This chapter will show you how to activate unfocus to join focus so as to become creative—and how to ignore your brain's assertions that you're not genetically endowed with creativity, a right brain, or the capacity to figure out the mysterious path to your most creative self. It's far less mysterious than you think.

It feels good to have creative insights, and we are often praised for having them. In 2014, Adobe Systems hired Edelman Berland, an insight and analytics company, to ask more than one thousand college-educated professionals whether creative thinking was critical for problem solving. Somewhat predictably, 85 percent of them said yes. In fact, nine out of ten people ranked creativity among the top factors that they believed drove salary increases. Yet even as we laud creativity as a vital attribute, many of us are unconsciously uncomfortable with it.

The Implicit Association Test (IAT) is used to measure and test this unconscious discomfort. In a recent study, management professor Jennifer Mueller and her colleagues used the IAT to uncover hidden biases about creativity in situations of uncertainty. Participants were told to match a positive word like *sunshine* or a negative word like *vomit* with a creativity-related word like *novel* or a practicality-related word like *useful,* by pressing a computer key. The speed of their response was factored into the calculation. Mueller found that when participants were uncertain, they automatically associated creativity with negative words. Our unconscious aversion to novelty and uncertainty under these conditions seems instinctual, in part because the unknown is a formidable obstacle to a mind set in its ways. That's why you may resist creativity, and why your creative abilities may seem to max out.

FROM CONCRETE TO FLUID THINKING

Our society lauds the person who lives as an open book, as a straight shooter, behaving predictably. The slogan "What you see is what you get" is often applied as a badge of honor. And these concrete traits are indeed all good, especially when negotiating the price of a new car, or doing a complicated business deal. There's nothing wrong with concrete thinking when you need to impose order in your life.

But too much order can actually lead to disorder. In a sense, *order* implies stiffening up rather than allowing the fluid flow of thoughts. It suggests prematurely packing thoughts away rather than giving your brain the time to form new associations between them.

Concrete thinking is a kind of poison to creativity. It engages the brain's focus circuits, but when you focus exclusively—having only one "beat" in your cognitive rhythm—you necessarily switch off your DMN, the home of abstract thought. The result? Instead of finding a creative solution to a problem, you see only option A and option B. Instead of seeing the grays, you see only black and white. If you're a black-and-white thinker, learning to see gray will require challenging some of your habits of thought.

Embrace Chaos

Creative people recognize that disorder and chaos are precursors to a new order, a new burst of creative thought, a new solution to an old problem. Creativity requires the fast and unconscious reorganization of information in the brain. New associations have to be made to find novel solutions to the problem at hand. That can happen if your DMN is turned on—but to achieve it, you have to unfocus from the chaos and give your brain time to work things out. In effect, you have to surrender to the chaos. You don't bother with it—you let go. Instead of resisting the momentum, you join it.

Of course, you can't live in the la-la land of floating ideas forever, but when you develop the temperament to live on the edge of chaos for a longer and longer time, you allow a more creative brain to develop. Indeed, the ability to surrender to chaos yet not be overwhelmed by it is a hallmark of the creative mind. The study of the brain biology of creativity has shown that the creative brain is often in a state of tension between chaos and control. You are less inhibited but not so disinhibited that you fall off the deep end; you make extensive connections, but not so many that you lose your train of thought; you dismiss linear solutions but stay true to the problem that needs to be solved; and in general, you tend toward controlled chaos more than toward order.

The scientific process itself is more chaotic than orderly. As Richard Feynman, winner of the 1965 Nobel Prize in physics, somewhat wryly pointed out, "Philosophy of science is about as useful to scientists as ornithology is to birds." There's no one way to do things. In fact, there are usually too many—a chaos of facts that you have to navigate.

In support of this view, Kevin Dunbar's research on how scientists work is revealing. In the early 1990s, he observed four Stanford labs and found that although scientists followed established techniques, more than 75 percent of their findings were unexpected, and their findings kept contradicting their elaborate theories. Scientific models pave the way for exploration (as I hope the models in this book do), but they often do not lead to the answer on their own.

Suppose you are a scientist conducting an experiment. Your experiment fails, and you're at a loss. Things feel up in the air. *What went wrong?* you ask. Was it the method? The middle stage? The way you analyzed things? So many things could have gone wrong, it would drive you up a wall trying to figure out what happened. At this point of chaos, you need not prepared knowledge but an insight—your focus and unfocus circuits need to chime in to generate ideas and evaluate them. You need to surrender to this process without tipping over into chaos. Learning to do this is an art, a delicate balancing act, but we are wired for it. Vik Muniz does it, and so do free-form tattoo artists. You do it too whenever you find an original combination of clothes, make up a joke, or learn calligraphy.

Charles Limb is a doctor and a musician who researches how creativity works in the brain. In 2008, he and another doctor-colleague, Allen Braun, studied six full-time musicians using functional magnetic resonance imaging (fMRI) while they performed piano pieces they had memorized and others that they improvised. They found that spontaneous improvisation was associated with widespread deactivation of the lateral prefrontal cortex (PFC, the conscious "thinking brain"). To be spontaneous, the PFC has to be out of the way. Also, improvisation activated the more intuitive brain integrator, the medial PFC (mPFC). In other words, they found that unfocus was key to improvisation.

At first, the idea of trying to embrace chaos may sound frustratingly glib and counterintuitive, akin to taking your foot off the brake when your car is careening out of control. However, if you think of being out of control as analogous to driving on black ice, releasing the brake may make more sense. When you do, you avoid skidding into chaos.

On a day-to-day basis, this would imply practicing what I call *delay and deliver* thinking. Imagine that on a given day you have set yourself a to-do list in a particular order. If someone or something unexpectedly puts a demand on your time that day, a kind of chaos ensues: your to-do list is shot to hell or at least interrupted. In delay and deliver thinking, you examine whether you can actually delay one or two of your to-do list items in order to accommodate the unexpected demand. If you find you *can* make this adjustment, you will still feel productive and in control of the day. Of course, you won't always be able to do this, but if you practice this kind of thinking, you will get used to not resisting the chaos that comes your way.

One advantage of inserting small chaotic time periods into your day—times when you take in or allow chaos—is that it can lead to mini-epiphanies. For example, in 2008 health behavior expert Kenneth Resnicow, in conjunction with complexity expert Scott Page, looked at why people suddenly change their behavior: stop using drugs, start exercising, or eat more healthily. He found that sudden changes are not the result of step-by-step escalations in the desire to change but rather of a creative process or sudden realization in which motivation "arrives." The changes are not planned: rather, "resident chunks of knowledge or attitude may unexpectedly coalesce to form a perfect motivational storm." That's creative motivation—not "intention" as we know it. When you want to go to the gym, but just can't do it, you need creative motivation, in the form of a "motivational storm." When you need to cut back on sugar, but can't resist the apple pie, you need creative motivation. A few blessed people are able to resist temptation, but for the rest of us, creative motivation is often our only hope.

Whether you see chaos as a thunderstorm or as an invigorating fountain is up to you. Self-talk can help you shift from one to the other. (*I'm going to treat this deluge of requests like a waterfall under which I'm standing on a hot summer's day.*) Observing chaos—pondering it even—is often far superior to escaping it.

Case in point: in 1964 two astronomers in New Jersey, Arno Penzias and Robert Wilson, set out to study vast tracts of the universe devoid of bright stars, in order to map them. They decided to make a detailed survey of radiation in the Milky Way but needed a receiver that was exquisitely sensitive, able to pick up the slightest sounds in the vast emptiness. They retrofitted an old radio telescope, then installed amplifiers and a calibration system so that the signals coming from space would be a bit louder.

To their dismay, whenever they pointed their telescope at the sky, they heard a persistent background noise that disturbed their observations—a kind of static sound. You can imagine how frustrating this was—like watching your favorite game on television, but having the commentary turn to static from time to time. What was the source of the static? Was it Manhattan noise, or even pigeon droppings on the antenna? No matter how much they conjectured about the source, they couldn't find it. Unable to remove the noise, they decided to accept all this chaos and just try to get the data they wanted. But they couldn't distinguish the faint radio echoes from the static. They scrapped the experiment, even as they continued to mull the possible source of the sound.

In 1965, Penzias called Robert Dicke, a Princeton nuclear physicist, to ask what he thought about this sound. Dicke, who had been looking for evidence of the Big Bang, even building his own telescope, knew immediately what it was: radiation left over from the beginning of the universe! His interpretation gave rise to investigations that allowed astronomers to confirm the Big Bang theory. Fast-forward to 1978: Penzias and Wilson won the Nobel Prize in physics for their astounding "accidental" discovery. In chaos, tinkering can often unveil unanticipated meaning.

Many businesses recognize that controlled chaos is necessary for innovation. They pay close attention to the changing needs of people who use their products, initially avoiding detailed plans and remaining flexible. They don't mind entertaining many new ideas, especially when they can quickly and inexpensively test them. A certain chaos of new ideas comes in, and most of the ideas quickly fail, but the promising ideas go on to the next stage of development. This high turnover and controlled chaos gives a company the momentum it needs to stay relevant and competitive.

To really grasp this concept, think of how airplane pilots can take advantage of a tailwind to move faster, or how a masterful sailor maneuvers a sailboat in a strong wind. Similarly, you can take advantage of brain chaos. Rather than defaulting to hunkering down and lowering your sails, you can surrender to the winds of change and use them to give yourself the push you need.

Surrender to Inspiration

A big part of developing creativity and creative surrender is practicing the art of letting go. You detach from the external world as a guide for a time and turn to your internal stream of attention.

When artists speak about their creations or the creative process, they often point out that they are not guided exclusively by clarity and single-mindedness. Instead, periods of clarity are usually intermixed with significant ambiguity and even doubt. This ambiguity may even be defining. Indeed, for creative people, *expression* of conflict, ambiguity, or vagueness often trumps the *resolution* of it.

In our relentless quest for meaning and understanding, we may inadvertently shut ourselves off from experiences by too quickly trying to make sense of them or analyzing them. Worse, we sometimes deny ourselves experiences because we don't understand them or see them as relevant to our lives. In so doing, the creative process is compromised, to say the least.

Inspiration usually manifests like a mind pop—a spontaneous burst of creativity to which you can't quite attribute a starting point. Yet inspiration actually has an architecture, a three-part structure that we can discern, implement, and allow.

Inspiration starts with an aesthetic appreciation of something through one of the five senses. For some people, a sunrise is inspiring. For others, it's a walk on the beach, as much for the feeling of sand between the toes as for the smell of salt and seaweed in the air. For still others, inspiration may be far more detailed and specific, like watching the movie *Secretariat* to see the great horse win the Triple Crown. You would be doing yourself a favor to "collect" or note these experiences and have them readily available in a metaphorical (or literal) box of ideas. That way you don't have to rack your brain every time you need inspiration to create.

After that appreciative, inspired feeling has been triggered, you need to allow your mind to wander in its presence, in the phase known as *passive evocation*. When you give yourself both the time and the permission to bathe in your aesthetic appreciation, a swell of inspiration will grow inside you like the King Kong of all soap bubbles. It mesmerizes and entrances you, and it is just the power you need to float into your creativity.

The third part of being inspired is having the desire to act on it—being motivated. When unfocus blows soap bubbles of inspiration into your mind, you have to have the breath to keep those bubbles coming. This part of inspiration is simply the desire for something new to happen. Desire can also be difficult to generate spontaneously, but there are things you can do to foster it.

Find an online community of people who share and breathe life into your passion. Look for a neighborhood group that shares your interests. Think of how your creative desire connects to your well-being and how it relates to your meaning and purpose in life. These groups and thoughts will help keep you motivated.

Two other pathways to desire are novelty and originality. Look for unusual things that pique your interest. They could be unusual and beautiful objects that you place in your office. Or you may try to draw something. (A friend once decided to paint original patterns over the tiles in her front hall.) Don't be self-conscious about getting it right. Picasso was famous for saying that he painted objects as he thought them and not as he saw them. Paint your thoughts. See what comes out.

Practice Abstraction

A natural way to prompt your brain to live in the gray and be more fluid is through *symbolization*. Symbols convert concrete problems into forms of themselves that are easier to work with. They are representations of things.

Symbols are also more prevalent in your life than you may initially think. We use mathematical symbols all the time: + and =. Every word is a symbol—a shorthand way of denoting something. Children often use symbolic thinking, playing in dirt as if they were making food, wearing a towel as a superhero cape, or using a stick as a sword.

As an adult, symbolic thinking can be helpful when you're struggling to let go of a relationship. For example, one creative solution might be to place a picture of your former lover in a bottle, then release the bottle into the ocean, symbolically letting go of the person, and using your emotional reaction as the start to resolving your grief.

You could use a symbol of something you know to model something that you don't know. For instance, you may not know how to foster cross-sector collaborations within an organization, but if you're at an impasse, you may turn to symbols of cross-sector collaborations. Even in the brain itself, the right brain works with the left, focus works with unfocus, and the thinking and feeling brains talk to each other. If they can work together, why can't your designers and programmers? Using such symbols may help you recognize that your brain stops its "cross-sector collaboration" when fear is the dominant emotion, or when there is no cognitive rhythm and it is stuck in focus rather than moving between focus and unfocus. This, in turn, may help you address the fears associated with interdepartmental collaboration and how the teams communicate so that both teams can brainstorm more (unfocus) prior to executing a plan (focus).

Symbols are also helpful when something unknown must be dealt with. Say you want to decide where a desk should go in a room. If you draw the desk fully into an architectural sketch, you may have trouble even thinking about moving it. But if you depict it as an *X* instead, you will suddenly be able to associate it with a wall or fireplace and then infer where it should go. You will stop being caught up in the details, and your creative thought flow will increase. Symbols, also called *simplified semantic structures,* can help you accelerate your creativity.

Metaphors are implicit comparisons that bring ideas to life: they are symbolization in words. Using them can help you tame chaos in your mind. For example, "a roller coaster experience" is much easier to understand than "the edge of chaos." Thinking of life as a box of assorted chocolates—unpredictable but not terrifying—may be the best metaphor of all.

Alternatively, you might think of a challenge as a wall you have encountered. When thinking about your options for dealing with this challenge, extend the wall metaphor: drill right through it, scale it, go around it, or dig under it. The creative process is necessarily abstract, but practicing such metaphors will help your brain work in a different way. It will activate your DMN—and you will be more likely to discover creative solutions.

The higher the quality of a metaphor, the more it will activate the brain regions responsible for openness to experience. Higher-quality metaphors are those that are more remote, novel, and clever. It's subjective, but you can use these criteria to see if your metaphor works. Keep reworking your metaphors as a creative exercise. Instead of comparing obstacles to your creativity to "a wall," you could compare them to "going uphill." If neither metaphor quite communicates the chaos of creativity, you might try comparing your challenge to "controlling a bumper car," or to "skiing down a black diamond slope." These metaphors, however, may feel too frivolous or dangerous respectively. To strike the right balance, you may finally think of the challenge of creativity as "trying to concoct the perfect cocktail"—a few tastes, a few tests and mixers, and you're there. Spread out the testing times so that you don't get too drunk, and be experimental enough with the mixers that your creations are unique. Different people will prefer different metaphors, but playing with metaphors this way will stimulate your creative brain.

Switch Lenses

When you analyze a situation, you engage in "split thinking" or in "lumping." Creative thinking involves both. Split thinking focuses tightly on the specifics, while lumping steps back to consider the big picture, grouping things by similarity in order to understand them. Say that you're an anthropologist studying the population of a remote island. In lumping, you look at the people as a whole, getting a bird's-eye view of the inhabitants. In split thinking, you focus on the differences between things and sort individuals by age, gender, or village.

Consider the usefulness of this exercise, for example, with the concepts of "mind" and "body." For many years, doctors and scientists saw these things as separate parts of the human makeup. The common "split thinking" was that there was no discernible connection between the two. The gut and its bacteria, for example, were separate entirely from the brain and from psychological health or moods. Seeing the gut and brain as separate is helpful when you specialize, but viewing them as connected within the body—as we have come to do—has allowed fascinating new insights to develop. Now we can detect signals from gut bacteria reaching the brain that influence how depressed or anxious a person is. New experiments suggest that Parkinson's disease—previously thought of as a "brain" disorder—may spread from the gut to the brain via the vagus nerve that connects them. People in whom the vagus nerve is severed have a 50 percent less chance of developing the disease!

That said, splitting also has value. In 2012, psychologist Tony McCaffrey described "generic parts technique"—a split-thinking way to overcome roadblocks to creative thinking. With this strategy, he explains, you ask: Can the object I am looking at be broken down further? Does my description of this object imply a use?

In a classic problem, McCaffrey gave people two steel rings, a box of matches, and a candle. He then asked them to create a figure-eight shape that stays together. Most people try to melt the wax to hold the rings together, but the rings inevitably come apart. But using generic parts technique, you make the leap that solves the problem: a candle is made up of both wax and a wick, the latter of which you can use as string to tie the rings together, once you've melted the candle down. People who used generic parts technique solved these kinds of problems 67 percent more often than those untrained in it.

Transcend Normal

"Openness to experience" is a personality trait that has been extensively studied in creative people. People who have this trait have an active imagination, prefer variety, and are intellectually curious. They are sensitive to beautiful things and attentive to their inner feelings. By contrast, "normal" people are agreeable, hardworking, and emotionally stable. Paradoxically, when you are "normal," your brain will likely be less creative—you have little or no openness to new experiences!

In people who have openness to experience, the default mode network operates more efficiently, creating more order than disorder in the brain. In a sense, when you're open to experience, you are going with the flow rather than swimming against the tide in "normal" mode. Stay open to new experiences, and you're more likely to navigate your way creatively through the hustle and bustle of life.

But being open to experience doesn't mean you have to go skydiving or swim with sharks! We're mostly talking about cognitive leaps of faith here, a willingness to loosen your need to control things and outcomes. By most reports, Vik Muniz has this temperament. A freak accident when he was twenty-two (he was shot in the leg trying to break up a street brawl) led to a bribe from the shooter that allowed him to finance a move to the United States, something he had long been wanting to do as a way to open up his creative future. He didn't know what he'd do or what he'd find, but he was open to discovering it. He leaped both literally and figuratively. Discovery consists of seeing new things not only as they are but also as what they might soon be.

Listen to Your Gut

Intuition is the brain's ability to register subtle changes in physiology that have not reached consciousness. As such, hunches are body sensations that have yet to become thoughts. A number of different brain regions form an intuition network that picks up those subtle sensations to give you a gut feeling, an understanding that your thinking brain hasn't interpreted. That gut feeling is vital information, and you shouldn't ignore it just because its explanation is floating outside your reach.

One productive way to manage your intuition (instead of dismissing it!) is to step back and reflect on your gut feeling: What is making you feel excited in the pit of your stomach? Why do you feel nervous? You may even conjecture a hypothesis or two. But if you're at a complete loss to explain your gut feelings, don't give up. When you remain curious, your brain becomes a detective, searching for pieces of evidence to string together to make a case for one of your hunches. In *serial hypothesis testing*, your brain uses intuition to surrender to an internal data search and gradually accumulates bits of information. When you have gathered enough data, you have an insight. Often the insight will occur not when you're looking for it with your thinking brain but when the data threshold for forming an insight is crossed. Progressive insights provide the orientation you need to navigate the edge of brain chaos in creativity.

Another way of managing intuition is *predictive inference*. Rather than looking for evidence, your brain leaps to a conclusion and then tests it out. It is akin to leaping before you look, or making a decision and *then* testing it. An intelligence agency, for example, is collating data about recent terrorist entry points and comes to a dead end. But the agents can't give up trying. They've got to at least infer when and where the next entry might take place. Not knowing exactly why, and at first not justifying their hunches, they may name borders X, Y, and Z as their top three suspicious points—somewhere to start. Then they will see if they can rationalize these hunches with data. If the model does not work, at least they have new data—where the terrorists are likely *not* to be! Then they can reformulate the possibilities and nominate borders P, Q, and R, for instance. When the data and the hunches fit, they execute a border safety plan. Many times this is exactly how intelligence agencies work—they engineer things backward! Sometimes people make relationship choices this way too, first choosing based on gut feelings, then inferring why they made their choice as the relationship progresses. If they collect enough evidence, they might get married. If they can't find any, they might end the relationship.

Here you've already concluded something, but you tinker with the solution to see if it's correct. Then you reformulate your conclusion and tinker with it again. After several reformulations, you arrive at a satisfying conclusion. This is an effective and often time-saving way to create.

When you make both of these intuition management tools part of your mental toolkit, your conscious brain will turn its attention inward, with its roving searchlight looking for data.

MIND POPS

Unfocus helps you loosen yourself from your habits and stimulate new ideas. You won't be aware of the brain doing its work, but when it's ready, an idea or creative solution will surface to your conscious mind. Fragments of knowledge, words, images, or melodies suddenly appear to you as "mind pops," seemingly at random. But researchers can now see that having a mind pop activates the same region of the brain that's engaged when you're open to experience. Unfocused and undemanding activities like doing the dishes or mowing the lawn will often bring them to the fore. Even when they are mixed and conflicted, they are signs of your creative brain in action.

DABBLING YOUR WAY TO EUREKA

Dabbling gets a bad rap. Too often we equate it with something superficial, lacking in depth; people who dabble are dilettantes. When we are not deeply committed to a subject, we are often thought to be wasting our time. But depth is relative, and a certain level and kind of dabbling is clearly beneficial to your creativity and to your life.

Vik Muniz is a living example of the benefits of dabbling. Before he left Brazil for New York, he worked in advertising. Once in New York, he worked as a picture framer. At various points he experimented with sculpting, drawing, and photography. All his creations show the influence of his journey. His background in advertising probably heightened his awareness of everyday objects and the strength of brands; his experience with framing others' work likely gives him an appreciation for balance. Seeing the art of Jeff Koons—famous for his massive, mirror-surfaced, steel "balloon animals"—inspired him to mix media and transform everyday objects into artwork.

The late Apple founder and CEO, Steve Jobs, was another poster boy for dabbling. In his famous Stanford commencement speech in 2005, he told the story of dropping out of Reed College so that he could audit only the classes that interested him. One was a calligraphy and typography class. He had no idea at the time how he might make use of this knowledge, but ten years later, when he was designing the first Macintosh computer, he used what he'd learned in that audited class. If he had not, the Mac might have never had multiple typefaces and proportionally spaced fonts. Dabbling in a topic that interested him—even if it didn't immediately serve him—served him tremendously well in the long run.

And what of creative geniuses like Albert Einstein and Pablo Picasso? They may seem worlds apart creatively, but scientists' and artists' brains respond similarly, especially in regions where complex sensations, thoughts, and emotions are integrated. Both groups display a high degree of DMN activity—demonstrating that it is not just depth of ideas but connections between ideas that matter. That's why you dabble. You're giving yourself one more experience to draw on, one more thing to connect to—and it may be the missing link you were looking for.

Though Einstein and Picasso never met each other, they were

both strongly influenced by Henri Poincaré, a mathematician, physicist, and philosopher. They discussed his theories in their respective "think tanks," Einstein with his study group, and Picasso with avant-garde literati. Einstein extended Poincaré's brilliant mathematical and scientific theories a few steps further to come to his own theory of relativity. On hearing Poincaré's thoughts about the existence of a fourth dimension where you could see everything at once, Picasso was inspired too. His painting *Les Demoiselles d'Avignon* depicts one face simultaneously in front and side view—two perspectives at the same time—the fourth dimension!

Einstein and Picasso both dabbled in many things. Einstein was strongly influenced by aesthetic theory and was fascinated by Freud's work. Picasso was strongly influenced by photography and X-ray technology. Neither man felt he had to become expert in these side interests. Both indulged their curiosity, mulled over their responses, and discussed the resulting ideas with their respective think tanks. The results changed the world.

Deciding to dabble can be a profound choice. It means being willing to try something out and be a student again. In that respect, it is mind-opening, and even though it is unfocused and away from the day-to-day routine, it is a way to take baby steps into "openness to experience"—the sine qua non of creativity. It's also a great way to get out of your comfort zone. Effective dabbling is a bit like taking a dive into the deep end for a few seconds and then swimming away. It may be fleeting, but it can be deep and often invigorating. For a brief life moment, you can lose yourself in it.

ADD COLOR TO YOUR LIFE

Don't settle for a narrow definition of your talents and interests. Don't be hemmed in by a static description of your temperament. Write down several things that describe you—identify your disparate interests. If you can immediately see ways to join these interests in your life, wonderful. If you don't immediately see a way to combine your competencies, use the other creativity-conjuring exercises in this chapter—dabble, nap, daydream, walk—to break down the barriers you've put up between them.

Oftentimes a brief stint of dabbling may be just the glue you're looking for to bring disparate parts of yourself together. Running a marathon, taking music lessons, mixing music, or making pottery can bring color and a sense of satisfaction to people's lives. So dabble in anything of interest to you—see where it goes. But make sure it resonates and feels relevant to who you are.

The Hobby-Creativity Link

Having a hobby is possibly the most socially acceptable way to dabble. Cultivating an interest on the side—a hobby is a side interest, after all—concedes that you know you shouldn't spend all your time with it. But if you've got a hobby (or more than one), you shouldn't downplay it too much. For one thing, engaging in hobbies for one or more hours every day may protect you against dementia later in life. And dabbling helps you in the present too, as two studies by organizational psychologist Kevin Eschelman and his colleagues show.

In the first study, 341 people from different work backgrounds (including managerial positions, education, administration, and accounting) responded to questionnaires about creative activity outside work and also self-rated their at-work performance. People who engaged in more creative activities had a higher sense of their own work.

In the second study, ninety-two active duty captains from the U.S. Air Force completed a similar survey, *and* others rated their work as well. Here too, based both on their own assessment and on that of others, those engaged in more creative activity outside of work had higher work performance.

The important work of physiology professor Robert Root-Bernstein bolstered the value of hobbies. Between 1958 and 1978, forty male scientists had been interviewed four times concerning their work habits, use of time, hobbies, attitudes, and related issues. With access to this information, Root-Bernstein and his colleagues measured the impact of the scientists' work by the number of citations received. The results were telling: hobbies that involved visual thinking, learning from doing rather than just thinking, and art and music were particularly advantageous.

Interestingly, some of the least productive scientists in this study engaged in activities that *did not* make them more impactful. The difference was that the productive scientists saw their hobbies or dabbling activities as having some purpose. They were working on the same thing from a different angle.

BLENDING YOUR INTERESTS

Very often people decide they want to live simpler lives. So they get rid of some possessions or determine to live with fewer luxuries; they whittle things down to a simpler minimum baseline. There's nothing wrong with that. But there is something terribly self-limiting about whittling your*self* down. What if you didn't have to choose between your love of one thing and your competencies in another field? What if you could find ways to marry your talents and interests?

Consider the positive example of Kirin Sinha. In 2012, she was an MIT senior majoring in theoretical mathematics, electrical engineering, and computer science, and minoring in music. For university paperwork she declared science as her major and music as her minor, but both were essential to her sense of self. She was a scientist *and* a musician, and she didn't want to choose one over the other. So she didn't.

Sinha had studied Indian classical dance since she was three, and she believed that learning dance builds confidence and grit, traits that are also necessary for doing well at math. To marry her interests and her belief in their interaction, she launched SHINE, a free dance and math program aimed at sixth- and seventh-grade girls struggling with math. The eight-week sessions were led by MIT students with dance backgrounds. The students learned hip-hop, jazz, and other dance styles. The girls also learned to apply mathematical concepts from dance by writing out their choreographies as formulae, in which, say, x represented a turn, and y a hip pop. Then, Sinha says, "they start to understand things like if you do $3x + 2x$, you're doing the same move five times in a row."

SAYING YES TO WANDERING

The ancient Greeks considered wandering to be a form of regression; it was the opposite of the stability and civilization for which the Athenians were known. Odysseus, the king of Ithaca, said, "For mortals, nothing is more wretched than wandering." And famously Oedipus, the mythical Greek king of Thebes, was condemned to a life of wandering after being discovered as the murderer of his father and lover of his mother.

Now, some 2,500 years later, we do not use wandering as punishment, but we do tend to beat ourselves up for wandering in our heads. In 2008, psychologists Matthew Killingsworth and Daniel T. Gilbert investigated how often people's minds wander and how it made them feel. They developed a smartphone technology to sample people's thoughts, feelings, and actions throughout the day. They found that people spend 46.9 percent of their time thinking about something other than what they are doing, and that it makes them significantly unhappy. We all know that feeling, right?

Involuntary mind-wandering can make you feel out of control and unproductive. And you don't want your thoughts to be wandering while you're driving someplace new or cooking Thanksgiving dinner. But many creative people vouch for the importance of mind-wandering or daydreaming in their discoveries.

The 2006 recipient of the Nobel Prize in literature, Orhan Pamuk, put it this way: "what is a novel but a story that . . . answers and builds upon inspirations from unknown quarters, and seizes upon all the daydreams we've invented for our diversion, bringing them together into a meaningful whole?"

It's not that focus plays no role in creativity. Clearly, Picasso painting *Les Demoiselles d'Avignon* and an entrepreneur trying to make a company profitable both need a certain amount of focus for their creative work. But focus exists on a spectrum. You can be intently focused and mindful (dedicated to your focus), or you can allow your mind to wander. The operative word here is *allow*— mind-wandering and daydreaming are most productive when you're disciplined about using them.

Deliberate Daydreaming

As pleasant as staring out the window at work might be, it's not an ideal way to increase your creativity (or your productivity).

When you fall into daydreaming, it's a sign of cognitive failure or exhaustion—your brain needs a break and takes one without asking. It's like falling off the edge of a cliff. But when you plan your daydreaming, it's constructive and restorative. It's like diving into a pool of water at the cliff's edge. In the first instance, you're not in control. In the second, the daydreaming is not only expected but planned. Called *volitional daydreaming,* this willful and scheduled flight away from the task at hand will help you become more open to experience; it's been shown to help people be more curious, sensitive, and likely to explore their ideas, feelings, and sensations.

In 2012, cognitive psychologist Benjamin Baird and his colleagues tested people's ability to find unusual uses for bricks, toothpicks, and clothes hangers, among other things. The challenge required them to be quick and creative to come up with as many uses as they could. The researchers tested four groups of people in several two-minute periods, then gave all but one a twelve-minute break. During the break, one group engaged in a demanding task, another in an undemanding task (during which they were not focused but allowed their minds to wander), and the third group rested. One group was given no break at all. Guess which group was most creative? The one that was allowed the undemanding, mind-wandering time performed the best.

Some people plan daydreaming time while they're engaged in something that's not at all demanding or taxing—knitting, planting a flowerbed, staring at art in a museum, or people watching. If the task you choose is at all taxing *for you*, it's not going to allow your mind to wander effectively; you'll have to stay engaged and focused to complete it. Scheduling "staring out the window" time can work too—but be deliberate about what you will daydream about during that time (and for how long). If, for instance, you need to prepare for an upcoming speech, set a timer for five minutes and kick back not only to go over it in your head but also to imagine what the auditorium will look like and how the standing ovation will sound and feel at the end.

The Art of Strategic Pausing

If you really give your daydreaming some thought, you will notice that it has a discernible sequence every time. According to neuroscientific writer Rebecca McMillan, daydreaming has three subtle stages. The first stage is the point at which you "decide" to stop focusing (like putting your pen down to start knitting instead); next comes the "decoupling" point, just prior to launching into unfocus (a conscious awareness that you are about to let your mind wander); then comes the moment when you actually drop your focused task and switch to unfocus until your mind is floating in the full-on lightness of a daydream. (You have the full internal permission to let your mind wander, knowing that a calendar reminder or alarm clock will bring you back to reality; you trust this and don't panic when you suddenly realize that your mind is wandering.) Maria Popova, founder of the blog *Brainpickings,* calls finessing these stages the "art of pausing."

Let's say you've been working on a paper for nearly an hour, and you just can't make any headway. You put your pen down or walk away from your computer. Then you pick an activity that is undemanding for you: knitting, gardening, or filing your nails. Give yourself over to it, and use self-talk to let go of your guilt and frustration about your lack of progress on the paper. Remind yourself that you're pausing in order to get back to the problem paper shortly; allow yourself the gift of this short respite. If you find yourself thinking about the paper again, bring your mind back to the wandering state in the undemanding task. When you've practiced this a few times, it will start to become automatic.

WRITER'S BLOCK

Probably every writer at some point experiences the dreaded phenomenon known as writer's block. Sometimes writer's block results from feeling fundamentally conflicted about expressing a thought in writing. You may be torn between plot options and stall for fear of making the "wrong" choice. You may be suffering from paralyzing perfectionism—your inner editor won't let you put something less than polished on the page. Or you may just draw a complete blank! Writer's block is connected with a dysfunction in part of the frontal lobe (a key brain region involved in the generation and evaluation of creative ideas), the same region that is damaged when you can't produce speech after having a stroke and when you're depressed or anxious.

To overcome writer's block, unfocus from your thought loops. Some writers resort to starting in the middle of a sentence to liberate themselves from the tyranny of the complete thought. Others write the ending or conclusion they're sure of first, then turn to the rest of the action or argument. All these techniques attempt to use a little chaos to jar the mind into action. There's nothing like discombobulation to jumpstart the creative brain.

The Body Creative

You can trigger creative thought not only with a wandering mind but with a wandering body.

In 2012, psychology professor Angela K. Leung and her colleagues explored outside-the-box thinking as it relates to literal, physical outside-ness. They built a five-foot-cubed box and asked twenty people to sit inside it. Another twenty sat outside the box. Both groups then took the Remote Associations Test (RAT). In this test, words like *measure, worm,* and *video* are presented, and the subject is asked to think of a fourth word that relates to the other three. The people sitting outside the box were significantly more likely than those sitting inside to come up with the word *tape* (measuring tape, tapeworm, videotape).

To confirm that the position of the body in space matters, Leung and her team tested three groups of people. One group walked around in rectangles while completing a mental test; one group walked around freely; and the last group sat down while taking the test. The free-walking group outperformed the other two groups. Furthermore, walking outdoors seems to be the best creative trigger: another research group has found that walking outdoors increased performance on alternative uses tests (which require calling up information quickly) by 81 percent and on the Remote Associations Test by 23 percent.

What your arms are doing matters too! Compared to jerky arm movements (tracing a zigzag pattern), fluid arm movements (tracing parallel and connected loops with the fingers) have been found to enhance the ability to generate creative ideas, to think flexibly, and to make remote associations. Remote associations are an indication of creativity because they demonstrate that the person can see connections. For example, if I asked you what word is common to *doll, paint,* and *cat,* one answer could be *house.*

So to solve creative problems, go for a walk outside, don't necessarily follow a path, and try to engage in whatever fluid arm movements you can. This technique is useful not just for writing poetry or making music but also for thinking about new business innovations, ways to solve your financial challenges, and even ways to get around bothersome, seemingly unchangeable relationship challenges. A boss who annoys you by micromanaging, for example, may need to be addressed creatively. Coming up with a solution may be easier if you don't walk the beaten path—literally, from your office to hers. It sounds a little absurd, but walking on a winding path or just swinging your arms may yield incredible results.

"TO SLEEP, PERCHANCE TO DREAM"

Though exercise can get your creative juices flowing, almost nothing beats sleep for readying the juices in the first place.

Put simply, sleep comes in two phases. You enter non-REM (nonrapid eye movement) first, followed by REM (rapid eye movement). You cycle through these two phases over the course of your sleep, with the REM episodes gradually gaining in length. During REM sleep you dream more, and your muscles are more relaxed.

When you're asleep, your unconscious brain works its magic in the dark. It puts new ideas together, recombines old ones, and when the conditions are right, it helps you get to that aha moment that is the hallmark of the creative climax. Dreaming—the ultimate tinkering "activity"—is the brain's way of reorganizing memories, shuttling them back and forth across the "dream bridge" that might not exist in your awake mind.

Psychoanalysts have studied dreams extensively. Carl Jung argued that dreams allow for seemingly irreconcilable ideas of the self to come together. If we take his point, it means that dreams not only recombine ideas creatively but also allow for a more coherent *you* when you're awake. This, in turn, makes it easier for you to be creative because you're not battling your contradictions. Paul McCartney reportedly composed the melody for his hit song "Yesterday" in a dream. The song is pretty melancholy, so it's not hard to imagine that his brain might have put it aside during the course of his day.

Dreams allow you to imagine the unimaginable. Just before articulating his theory of relativity, Albert Einstein famously dreamed that he was sledding down a steep mountainside so fast that he approached the speed of light. He also dreamed that time was circular, and that it stood still so that lovers held on to each other for an eternity. When ideas like this come together, there is obviously no focused process. Instead, in dreams, the unfocused brain has the full license to roam around and collect ideas at will. When you awaken, you might have a new insight.

In 2010, sleep expert Matthew Walker from the University of

California and his colleague Robert Stickgold showed another benefit of sleep: the ability to solve anagrams more quickly and creatively. An anagram is wordplay in which the letters of a word are rearranged to form other words or phrases. For example, the letters in *dormitory* can be rearranged to spell *dirty room,* and *Jim Morrison* can be rewritten as *Mr. Mojo Risin* (a phrase from one of Morrison's songs, though we don't know if he was a good sleeper or not). Walker and Stickgold compared flexibility of thinking in sixteen subjects using anagram word puzzles following REM and non-REM awakenings across the night. They found that people awakened after a period of REM sleep solved 32 percent more anagrams than if awakened after non-REM periods. As the night continued, though, problem solving after non-REM sleep got better.

Practically speaking, this means that if you have a shorter time to sleep and need to be creative, time your awakening for just after REM sleep, or ninety to one hundred minutes after you fall asleep. During the interval between going to sleep and the onset of REM, you may be less creative.

The amount of sleep you need is debatable and personal, but common to many creatives is an occasional (or regular) nap. Napping is a great way to activate the unconscious to recombine thoughts in a unique way. It increases activity of the right brain that does some brain housecleaning to help creativity upon awakening. Unlike proper sleep, napping is frequently made up of a shorter period of non-REM followed by mostly REM sleep.

In a 2014 study led by researcher Felipe Beijamini, participants were given a difficult video game problem to solve. Eventually, one group was allowed to nap for ninety minutes, while the other group had to stay awake. The people who napped were almost twice as likely to solve the problem as the wakeful group. But when the investigators looked at brainwave patterns, dream sleep was not involved. Just dozing off was enough to recombine information in the brain and to convert the gist of information into abstractions to allow problems to be solved.

On the other hand, psychiatrist Sara Mednick led a study in 2009 in which researchers used a word analogy test to see how well subjects did after a nap. For example, given "chips: salty: candy: _____" the answer is "sweet." Compared to non-REM nappers and no nappers, ninety-minute REM nappers improved their performance by 40 percent. They were able to make these associations at lightning speed!

Perhaps the jury is still out on whether shorter naps work to enhance creativity, but they are better than no nap. In a 2002 study of sixteen healthy young adult sleepers, researchers created four conditions: no nap, a thirty-second nap, a ninety-second nap, and a ten-minute nap. The clock was started only after the participants were actually asleep, as confirmed by EEG. The ten-minute nap was the only one that significantly improved alertness and cognitive performance.

HOW MUCH SLEEP IS ENOUGH?

In *Daily Rituals: How Artists Work,* author Mason Currey reports that Japanese writer Haruki Murakami sleeps a solid seven hours, from nine P.M. to four A.M. regularly. Benjamin Franklin and Maya Angelou also slept seven hours, from ten P.M. to five A.M. Reportedly, Charles Darwin slept less: from twelve A.M. to six A.M., but he then napped from one to two P.M. If we stopped right there, it would seem that seven is the magic number.

But other creative people did not sleep as much. Franz Kafka slept in spurts—from six A.M. to eight A.M. and then from three P.M. to six P.M. Voltaire needed only four hours of sleep, from twelve A.M. to four A.M. And apparently Thomas Edison also did not need much sleep, only three or four hours a night, plus power naps.

> More recently Jack Dorsey, founder of both Square and Twitter, reported that he works approximately twenty hours every day, which obviously leaves little time for sleep.
>
> From this spray of sleep times, you can see that there is no ready formula for all. You have to do what works for you.

Putting It All Together to Tap into Creativity

Remember that, in your relentless quest for understanding, you may inadvertently shut yourself off from experiences by trying to make sense of them too quickly. Worse, you could deny yourself experiences because you don't understand them or see them as relevant to your life. This denial can compromise the creative process.

Creativity and creative surrender emerge from letting go. As I said earlier, when you let go, you detach from the external world as a guide for a time and turn to your internal stream of attention. There are many ways to do this, as I've outlined in this chapter: positive constructive daydreaming, going for a walk, making fluid arm movements, walking in a circle, improvising music, taking a nap, or dabbling in a hobby. You are in effect removing yourself from your daily routines and activating the DMN, the dream, intuition, and inspiration brain networks, where you will be met by a new and creative mental world.

One of the major obstructions to creativity is a fixed identity. In the spirit of adopting an alternate identity to meet the challenge of conjuring creativity, consider wearing these two hats:

THE TRAINER

Your muscles grow when you move against resistance. Similarly, to build your creative mind, you need to identify your psychological resistance and move against it. This is not simply about being oppositional; not everyone living in a counterculture is actually displaying creativity! Living against the grain is about training your mind to work against its own psychological resistance to creativity.

When you want to be creative, your brain will usually put up a fight, for any of four reasons, visible and discernible, conscious or unconscious: fear of the unknown, intolerance of uncertainty, trepidation at the task's magnitude, or its difficulty. Think of these four factors as the wet blankets to creativity. Which wet blanket is holding you back? Identifying what is holding you back is half the battle. Unfocusing through the many strategies in this chapter will help you periodically throw that blanket off!

Creativity is perspiration as much as inspiration. Vik Muniz is inspired to see unusual connections, but he works hard to bring these inspirations to life. In a sense, inspiration results from generating creative ideas automatically, whereas perspiration reflects the hard work of thought control. To reach the creative goal, they must "balance out" with the right and left brains, and the DMN and executive control network, working in synchrony.

To start this synchrony in your brain, set aside time (fifteen to thirty minutes weekly) for any of the activities outlined above. Go through the different stages of deliberate daydreaming—if you practice this often enough, it will become more automatic. When it does, write down one to three new aspects of your self-concept that came to you. They should not be thoughts that you actively sought but rather thoughts and feelings that were evoked. At the end of a month of this practice, look at the collection of self-related ideas. After six months, you may be ready to write out a new or refreshed set of career goals. Weave all this discovery into your story. Read over your findings as often as you can.

Like Duke Ellington's, your story will eventually congeal into a complete product. When it does, start this process over again.

THE TRICK-OR-TREATER

From time to time, it's helpful to engage in *psychological Halloween-ism,* to define and immerse yourself in a different identity, as perhaps you once did (or still do) on Halloween night. You don't have to notify anyone that you're doing it, and you don't have to wear a costume. Instead, you simply do your best to think, feel, and act like your "mask" identity for a period of time.

Imagine yourself as any identity you want—a programmer, an entrepreneur, a baking aficionado, a teacher, or a librarian. As you immerse yourself in it, challenge the norms of normal, think outside the box, and expand your self-concept. If you want to wear a costume, go for it! Whether you dress up or not, when you imagine in this way, you stimulate many of the brain regions involved in the creative process, including the DMN, the cognitive control network, and the "doing" parts of the brain. You warmed up your creative capacity, and with each new fantasy, this capacity will grow.

You don't have to keep the identity consistent or real. In 2016, psychologist Rosa Aurora Chavez described a specific type of imagery common in creative people, called primordial imagery. They are human yet obviously unrealistic, robotic yet emotional— science-fictional characters brought to life. Think *Jurassic Park, Star Wars,* or *E.T.* When fictional characters come to life, they inspire you to think differently. They guide your mind into an alternate reality, which is how creative ideas are discovered.

You don't have to follow these tips step by step. Let them wash over your mind as you pick and choose the ones you can relate to.

This table summarizes the major mindset shifts that apply to becoming creative. Use it as a guide when you want to check in quickly about changes that you could add to your life.

Focused Mindset	Unfocused Mindset Shift
Focus on having enough energy to work through the day.	Take ninety-minute naps to increase your creativity.
Have a one-track mind.	Dabble in disparate disciplines to stimulate obscure but important connections.
Avoid daydreaming.	Build positive, constructive daydreaming into your day.
Get to your goals as the crow flies.	Meander on your daily walks or hikes to stimulate creativity.
All you can do is be yourself.	Your self is subject to change. Surrender to your creative mind by challenging the norm, your biases about your creativity, and your concreteness.

DYNAMIC LEARNING IN A BRAVE NEW WORLD

Our virtues and our failings are inseparable, like force and
matter. When they separate, man is no more.

—Nikola Tesla

"Fuckup Nights" is a phenomenon that began in Mexico in 2012,
when a few friends gathered one evening to drink tequila and
chat about their businesses. They realized that they had never
really discussed their failures before, but they found the discussion helpful and stimulating. So they launched a monthly program to encourage public discussion about failure—to learn from
the mistakes of others rather than their successes. At each event
three to four entrepreneurs briefly share their stories of failure—
in seven minutes, using up to ten images. Afterward there is a
question-and-answer session and then time for networking/min-
gling (when beer is served), so people can continue the conversation in a more informal environment. The program has proven so
appealing that it has now spread to more than seventy cities in
twenty-six countries around the world.

You wouldn't expect talk of failure to be so open, let alone so
appealing. After all, failure is difficult to own up to and often
embarrassing. Yet it's common—somewhere between 30 and 95

percent of start-ups fail, depending on whether we're talking about complete liquidation versus not meeting projected revenue goals. People seem to feel compelled and relieved to learn they're not alone, and it's helpful to learn from the mistakes of others as well. This is one of the counterintuitive signatures of *dynamic* learning—to own up to, talk about, learn from, and correct errors rather than following a hypothetical "right" way—for which there are many methods, but none that seem to work well for more than a few people. In fact, some experts might even have you believe that there is a "right" way to learn, despite the fact that no two brains are alike. Fuckup Nights helped dispel that myth.

With all that talk of failure, though, you'd expect participants to feel down in the dumps. But that's not necessarily the case. They might have been sad or frustrated (or broke) at the time of the disaster, but American entrepreneurs especially seem to bounce right back.

The current thinking is that failure, rather than being a signal to drop everything and run, is a learning opportunity—as long as you "fail forward," "fail fast," and recognize that "done is better than perfect." When you do, you ostensibly avoid intellectual stagnation and overcome fear of failure.

Put more simply, talk is cheap, so keep on *doing* what you're doing until you get it right. If you fail, tomorrow is another day. Any software developer will likely admit a preference for quickly producing a prototype over endlessly conversing about an ideal finished product. Spend too long researching the next new product for your company, and you run the risk of competitors beating you to market. Fail in a relationship, and you might hear an upbeat "There are plenty of fish in the sea" or "If at first you don't succeed, try, try again." But these failure-promoting turns of phrase seem like glib and disingenuous platitudes—unless you're well prepared and trained to think in a new and dynamic way. It's easier said than done.

In the past, people spent a lot of time learning about their craft or skill before they applied it. But it is becoming increasingly obvious that a quick and dynamic application of learning is the way to succeed. Those who are ahead are beginning to train their brains in this new way already. And in this chapter, you'll learn how to do just that.

DYNAMIC LEARNING

Brightworks School, and its summer camp corollary Tinkering School, is in San Francisco's Mission District. Housed in a nine-thousand-square-foot warehouse, it was founded and is run by writer, computer scientist, and brilliant educator Gever Tully. A self-described "lousy student," no doubt in reaction to his own experience in a traditional school setting, Tully has created a different kind of school—an atypical one, to say the least. It's not one my parents would ever have sent me to, but that's my loss. Brightworks now has schools in Chicago, Los Angeles, Austin, and Buffalo.

Brightworks students do not work by grade—instead, they work in "bands" so they can interact with students of different ages. There are no formal reading or writing classes, and all learning is facilitated by "doing" and interacting. Students are invited to delve into the questions posed in conjunction with a topic, then make something from the answers, then present the findings to the group. If, for example, the theme for the month is "nails," one person might write a screenplay that in some way has something to do with the word (or one of the word's meanings), while another might construct a chair using a hammer and nails, and still another might drop paint-filled balloons onto nails stuck to a canvas to create Jackson Pollock–like art. They form teams, set deadlines, and manage the projects with varying degrees of supervision. They are masters of their own universes.

By all accounts they love it, and by both objective and subjective standards it's a success. Brightworks students are, on average,
two full grades above the national reading and writing levels. One
hundred percent of the parents of children who are trying the
school out want them to stay on. Visitors to the school—like me—
see happy learners and team players. These children are part of a
revolution in learning. They are anti-authority but pro-team, pro–
being guided, and pro-learning.

This is not to say that the schools have no place for traditional
education or that the yardsticks by which we measure it aren't
meaningful. After all, it's hard not to be in awe of the spelling bee
winner, the math whiz, or the child with a steel-trap memory for
dates and data. And what about the valedictorian—who scored
highest across the board throughout his or her academic career?
Surely the valedictorian deserves a graduation day standing ovation. These people seem to have mastered learning processes that
mark them as special and successful.

But are high test scores and grades the be-all and end-all? Does
excellence in spelling, math, rote memory, and writing truly imply
higher intelligence? Certainly most valedictorians have tremendous intellectual capabilities (and I don't begrudge the standing
O's), and clearly even Brightworks cares about test comparisons to
mainstream schools, but just as surely there have always been people who *don't* score or test well who have wildly valuable talents
and deep intellects.

Thankfully, modern cultures and economies have started to acknowledge this. In grade school education there is a trend (on
view at Brightworks, to be sure) toward evaluating mastery of a
topic through means other than test scores: project-based learning, performances, presentations, portfolio assessments, and team
(as opposed to individual) accomplishments. At the university
level too, changes are afoot: Harvard professor of the history of
science and physics Peter Galison asks his students to create films

instead of writing papers—in this way, he feels, science isn't just theory to be rote learned but comes alive. MIT has a "Hobby Shop" in which students are encouraged to tinker; they have produced an intelligent toothbrush that knows when you're brushing too hard, a foldable ukulele, and a spherical robot that rolls uphill and ascends stairs.

And in all kinds of work environments, employers are looking to hire or promote people with skill sets that can't be totally measured empirically—life experience, team building prowess, the ability to motivate others, a head for juggling lots of tasks, an ability to learn from mistakes, and "emotional intelligence." Google's hiring practice, for instance, is to exclude test scores and grade-point averages from consideration—it's less about what you have learned than about your interest in continuing to learn; less about what you know than about how you're willing to use what you know adaptively.

Put in the simplest terms, learning used to be centered on a period of study (our education), and then we mostly switched to cruise control—recalling specialized and specific information and applying it to different tasks and challenges in a timely way. In contrast, the new education is dynamic, giving us the ability to be nimble thinkers and creative problem solvers, to use critical thinking skills to figure out what we don't yet know but need to know. Especially because most people switch jobs multiple times, it's important for young people to learn skills that transfer across disciplines, to think of themselves as capable thinkers and learners regardless of career.

We have to say goodbye to fixed grades (A+, B−, pass/fail), narrow definitions of work identity ("I am a marketing manager for consumer products"), and most of all, our obsessive focus on specialization ("I am a marketing manager for health and beauty consumer products"). We must also embrace the idea that learning takes place all the time outside a traditional (or even nontraditional) classroom, including learning to *not* date the same kind of jerk over and over, or *not* repeat counterproductive habits. Anytime you're engaged in better understanding yourself, other people, or things, you are learning.

Think of the old learning style as a fork that targets and spears specific information. A fork operates through focus—its work is decisive and linear. And it is an essential part of the place setting! But when you learn dynamically, you use a spoon too. Spoons get you to the mélange of flavorful juices and bits at the bottom of your bowl, the ingredients that are every bit as important to the meal even if they aren't clearly distinguishable. Anything that the direct piercing of focus misses is a spooning (unfocusing) endeavor: creative problem solving (lateral thinking), making inferences through associations, predicting the future, and course correcting. (No wonder the DMN is one of the biggest consumers of metabolic energy in the brain!)

To extend the silverware metaphor, consider the power behind a fork and a spoon working together. In 2010, psychologist Jackie Andrade asked two groups of twenty people to listen to a two-and-a-half-minute tape. Beforehand they were told the tape would be "rather dull." Actually, the tape was unbelievably boring. Framed as a birthday party invitation, the message rambled on and on, as the host talked about someone's sick cat, her redecorated kitchen, the weather, someone's new house, and a vacation in Edinburgh, Scotland, that involved museums and rain. In total, she mentioned eight place names and eight people who were definitely coming to the party.

Before the tape began, one group of twenty participants had been asked to shade in some little squares and circles on a piece of paper while they listened. They were told not to worry about being neat or quick; the other group was not asked to doodle at all. But *all* the participants had also been asked to write down the place names, as well as the names of those coming to the party while the tape played, which meant the doodlers had to switch between their doodles and their lists.

Afterward the papers were collected, and both groups were asked if they could remember the places mentioned and the names of the people coming to the party. When tallied, the results were revealing. Doodling (unfocused "spoon" work) during the tape helped that group remember specifics (focused, fork targets): they recalled 29 percent more than the control group. Another way of looking at these findings: the focused brain is like a stiff sponge, while a doodling brain is looser and more absorbent.

Those educated in the old linear way who would like to be hired at a place like Google must first master a dynamic, learning-friendly cognitive rhythm: a deliberate mixture of high- and low-beam flashlight pointing, taking control of challenges and circumstances (focus) while letting go of the need to have all the answers (unfocus). Fortunately, we have the brain bandwidth to make this adjustment.

After all, we now live in a world in which our phones—portable little brains that they are—have relieved us of our duties to remember facts, figures, translations, computations, life events, conversations, and contact information. Modern sensor technology is, in many cases, outperforming our biological capabilities: sensor chips detect food spoilage before your nose can; IBM's Watson trumps human data-processing abilities; and machines are increasingly doing diagnostic work for doctors—an echocardiogram can pick up heart valve abnormalities more accurately than the doctor's stethoscope. In the not-so-distant future, you may not even need to teach your children to tie their shoelaces: Nike's self-lacing sneakers will sense your foot and automatically tighten or loosen to fit. At this writing, self-driving cars are hitting the market, and household robots are on the horizon!

Keeping up with all this technology—adapting to each new evolution, and integrating it into daily or work life (or even competing with it on the job)—can be a challenge. It can make your head spin. But while machines may have taken over old brain functions, their existence has also given us the opportunity to reconnect with ourselves and our own learning capacity. By off-loading whole categories of tasks to technology, we literally and figuratively free up brain space to learn new things and in new ways. We've got more available gray and white matter! Once you recognize that you've got brand-new brain space to develop, you can start the new learning journey.

"EMBRACEABLE YOU"

Before a certain way to do a thing became standard, someone had to invent it. That's the character you want to invite back into your life: the kind of person who takes the first chance. Think of whoever it was who first programmed computers, long before "computer programming" became a course at school. Think of the singer who sang before voice lessons were invented. Their brilliance was not created by knowledge at schools. There was no knowledge in the first place. All they had was the thoughts in their heads. This is the part of you that has been lost to education.

We come into this world with the power to make a difference with our originality, but somewhere along the way, we lose this originality to the knowledge that is given to us at school. This "knowledge" takes over our thinking and becomes our go-to whenever we need to know anything. As helpful as this can be, without our originality, it is far less powerful. Education is best when it helps originality emerge—not when it suppresses it.

I once introduced new software to a group of very smart, educated executive coaches and gave them an hour to figure out how it worked. Most of them got lost soon after the sign-in. Their preconceptions held them back from thinking that they could do it without an instruction manual. We have come to live our lives with instruction manuals, forgetting that we are wired to figure things out on our own.

Consider the One Laptop per Child (OLPC) project. In 2012, the OLPC gave children in rural Ethiopia sealed boxes containing tablet computers that were preloaded with educational software and a memory card that tracked how they managed the new technology. Thinking at first that they would simply play with the packing boxes since they probably had no idea what computers were capable of doing, the project managers were shocked to see the actual results.

Within four minutes, one child opened a box and found the on-off switch and powered up the tablet. Within five days, every child was comfortable with the apps; within two weeks they were singing ABC songs. And within five *months,* the children had hacked into the Android operating system. The OLPC had tried to freeze the desktop settings, inserting software to prevent any changes, but the children worked around it. Somehow, through their own ingenuity, they customized their desktops so that each one looked different.

We are capable of incredible things if we stop behaving like automatons and start trusting ourselves more. The OLPC may not have increased standardized test scores, but its example demonstrates the innate ingenuity of each of us.

A RECIPE FOR SUCCESS

Chef and restaurateur Jonathan Waxman has used the values instilled in him at a traditional cooking school to bring remarkable innovation to the culinary world. But success was not a straight line for him—his career path undulated. He is a dynamic learner.

Born in 1950, Waxman grew up near Berkeley, California. An

accomplished trombone player in high school, he attended the University of Nevada at Reno on a music scholarship. He majored in political science but played his trombone, his first passion, throughout college. After graduation, he played in casino pit bands, most famously with Sammy Davis, Jr., and he joined a rock band called Lynx to support himself.

With his long blond hair and rock-star reputation, a foray into the very disciplined art of cooking might not have been predicted, but when Lynx broke up in 1972 in Hawaii, Waxman quipped that he had two choices for paying his way back to the mainland: selling drugs or working in a restaurant. He chose the latter and loved it.

When he had earned enough money to return to California, he didn't jump back into kitchen work immediately. At first he sold Ferraris by day and tended bar by night. But soon he was introduced to Tante Marie's cooking school in San Francisco, which led to his signing up in 1975 for the La Varenne cooking school in Paris, where he received the *grand diplôme*.

At first, the transition from musician to chef may seem like a leap, despite both requiring an artistic temperament. Yet Waxman once said, "There is a strong correlation between music and food. You spend a lot of time woodshedding, just chipping and chopping and butchering, before you get to the real thing." Tinkering was at the heart of his enjoyment of both art forms. To emphasize the importance of tinkering in cooking, he once compared the process to the creation of the little black Chanel dress. "How many times did she have to cut it to get it perfect?" he reminded us. "A billion times, right? It's the same thing for food." That's how you get things right—and as close as possible to iconic (much like his signature roast chicken!).

Two years later Waxman returned to the United States, first working at Domaine Chandon in Napa Valley, where he put his French technique to the test. But a short two years later, he moved on to Chez Panisse to work with Alice Waters, then became executive chef at Michael's in Santa Monica, where he merged his school-taught talents with the freshness of his California roots. The resulting cuisine was delicious and revolutionary—so much so, that Dorothy Hamilton, founder of the International Culinary Center in New York, referred to him as "the Father of Modern American Cuisine."

If you had met Waxman at that point in his life, you might have predicted that a successful life was in the cards, and to an extent you would have been right. When he moved to New York in 1983, he brought this unique cuisine—clean and fresh California ingredients with a hint of French sophistication—to the East Coast, and in 1984 he opened up a restaurant called Jams on East 79th Street. It was a hit—a "culinary comet." The pièce de résistance was a grilled chicken–and–fries entrée, but the red snapper ceviche, the crab cakes with corn and tomato salsa, and the tiny pancakes served with smoked salmon, crème fraîche, and yellow whitefish caviar also caused a sensation. The food was so tasty (albeit expensive!) that Andy Warhol ate at Jams once or twice a week. Waxman recalls entering his dining room and seeing Woody Allen and culinary royalty James Beard, Wolfgang Puck, and Julia Child too. The musician had transferred his creative skills to cooking, and "the Eric Clapton of chefs" looked like he had made it.

But that was not the way the cookie crumbled. As time went on, Waxman caught the celebrity bug—he bought a Ferrari and became known for wild nights out on the town and financial indulgence. When the market crashed in 1987, his expensive menus became less desirable, and he could not maintain his lifestyle. He closed shop, sold his Ferrari, and moved back to California, where he fell in love, got married, and had three kids. He was finished with the wine, women, and song. And had you known Waxman at that time in his life, you might have thought he was finished with cooking too. He went about five years without a restaurant of his own and seemed to fade from the culinary scene. It's conceivable, though, that he had just been storing up ideas and waiting for the next "right" time to try again.

In 1993 he returned to New York. Seeing his past as a series of valuable lessons to learn from, he jumped back on the restaurant-creation bandwagon. He explored cooking beyond his classic French training, worked as a consultant with the Ark Restaurants Corporation, and opened the Bryant Park Grill and other restaurants, including Washington Park and Table 29. In 2004, he opened the now famous Barbuto. Described as "a bit of French, . . . a bit of Italian, a smattering of Greek" with a "California sensibility," the restaurant has been enthusiastically reviewed and raved about: the roast chicken became almost as legendary as the one at Jams; the lemony spaghetti tossed with sweet Maine shrimp was labeled a "knockout"; the buccatini earned praise as "perfectly al dente"; and the creamy, sharp chocolate pudding was hailed as "the rightful coda to the chicken."

Although the restaurant also gets critical knocks—a seasonal dabbler, Waxman changes the menu constantly, and not every dish is critically embraced—he remains an icon in the eyes of many who celebrate the art of cooking. As a testament to his love for both cooking and music, he opened Adele's in Nashville, now a bustling epicenter of the music industry. That's how life comes together when you tinker and dabble. Without warning, profound connections arise.

Waxman is the quintessential dynamic learner, a rock star turned classically trained chef turned improviser who dives head-first into his passions and gets lost but never gives up. Such a dynamic learner, with all the menu tinkering and restaurant dabbling, always has a place to go. A dabbler, even when staring at failure like a deer in the headlights, will somehow find what's needed inside and jump out of harm's way in the nick of time.

Whether you're making a soup or a satellite, you as a dynamic learner don't focus on immediate perfection. Of course, you'd give it your best shot once you had enough information to start. But after a first version, you'd examine it. Making a soup, you'd trust your taste buds and intuit that you should make the next batch with less salt or more stock. In the case of a satellite, you might discover a design flaw, and you might build the next version with slightly different programming. Between versions, your mind would collate the experience of the prior version and come up with more subtle changes. In either example, you'd likely not present the finished product until you'd tinkered through a few early iterations.

In the dynamic learning paradigm, mistakes are not only par for the course—they're essential for progress. It's not that excellence is not your goal—you're just so much more determined to not let mistakes get you down. When you unfocus to iterate, you tinker with the result, making adjustments that will keep you competitive and relevant as you go along. Each mistake is a clue to the next step, no matter how rugged the terrain of your learning journey.

QUICK ON THE DRAW, STRONG TO THE CORE

Jonathan Waxman seems to have proceeded under the guidance of his own genius. Despite the vicissitudes in his career, he trusted his innate ingenuity to navigate his path forward. The question then becomes: how did that ingenuity speak to him?

Just as you have a physical balance point—a center of gravity (COG)—that keeps you upright and prevents you from falling, you also have a psychological balance point, a psychological COG. Your originality (your own true voice) grows from this place, as does the mechanism for emotional self-control. In real-life contexts, you tap into this inner compass when you're unsure about where to go, how to respond, or what to do next. Self pep talks keep you buoyed in the face of overwhelming emotional or intellectual input, be it commentary from well-meaning advisers and teachers, anxious investors, or vocal critics. In other words, your psychological COG keeps you grounded and true to yourself as you make your way through the learning journey called life.

Jonathan Waxman seems to have a well-developed psychological COG. He created his own type of food—food that he liked, appreciated, and defended. Before farm-to-table food became all the rage, he waxed lyrical about its superiority. When people complained about his expensive chicken dishes, he justified the price by referring to the fresh quality of the meat. And when he opened a Table 29 restaurant in Napa in 1991, he knew he hated it, listened to his gut, and moved back to New York. Indeed, only when you're self-connected, operating outside traditional learning and educational boundaries, can you fully express your greatest strengths.

A case in point: my clients from a very different profession, stock brokers. Some investors do well when the market is volatile, and just as many tank in a tumultuous economy. Given my proximity to their inner dialogues (or what they tell me in therapy, anyway), I have noticed a discernible pattern: investors who perform best choose stocks that they understand well. They stick to their own investing style, and the more volatile the market gets, the more deeply they stick to that style. Activating their psychological COG gives them the stability to avoid making bad decisions in the midst of stock market change. (In his best-selling book *One Up on Wall Street,* the hugely successful Fidelity fund manager Peter Lynch recommended a similar strategy to nonprofessionals: stick with investing in companies whose products you use and think are great, he advised. The operative word here is *you.*)

Investors who do poorly tend to be overwhelmed by market volatility. When the going gets tough—or even blurry—they are unduly influenced by the opinions of others. They go whichever way the wind is blowing, following the latest investing trend. Sometimes they get lucky, and an investment pays off. But more often than not—and certainly over the long run—their lack of self-connection to the idea, to the trend, yields lower returns.

When great investors go deep inside themselves for gut guidance, it's not that they lose their connection with reality. On the contrary, they find an inner compass to navigate the sea of change. And they incorporate and integrate deeply everything they learn, gaining that much more understanding and confidence in the face of the next rough patch.

The lesson here is that if you are in focused, old-school learning mode—following the leader, studying the facts—you're less likely to hear what your COG has to say. The best way to tap into your COG, to hear it, is to activate your DMN. Meditating, listening to music, and, perhaps no surprise, vacationing have all been shown to improve the brain's ability for COG-connected original thinking ("self-circuits") and emotional control. Exercise is both a great way to refine DMN activation and an example unto itself. Almost all exercise requires engaging the abdominal muscles. Warming up this key area by lying on your back and lowering your legs from 90 degrees to the ground or by doing some planks engages these muscles—your core. Similarly, you invoke unfocus to get your psychological COG firing.

Though many people have learned to connect with their psychological COG automatically and unthinkingly, you have to commit to cultivating this sense of self and catch yourself whenever you are operating outside it. Simply wondering if you are or are not connected to your COG is a surefire way to locate it. Try this when you're lost in an argument, or are arguing yourself into a corner. Or when you find yourself at a fork in the proverbial road, at a decision point in your career or personal life, ask yourself—literally, using second-person self-talk (see Chapter 1)—"Are you operating from your COG, or are you being swayed by someone else's opinion or needs?" It's quite amazing how this deliberate pause and self-questioning will build confidence and optimism in whatever path you choose. And remember that it'll reduce your stress too.

COG MANEUVERS: REFLECTING AND RELATING

In 2016, psychiatrist and brain researcher Christopher Davey and his colleagues looked at which brain circuits are active when people self-reflect, the first step toward self-understanding and *hearing* their psychological COG. They asked ninety-six participants to say whether an adjective applied to them or not. The adjectives were not particularly favorable or unfavorable and were likely to elicit self-reflection: e.g., *skeptical, perfectionistic, lucky.*

When participants reflected on themselves, it activated their DMN, which showed up on brain scans. Though science can tell us which specific DMN regions are responsible for different parts of the self-reflection process, the big-picture takeaway is that hearing yourself grows from unfocus.

Connect to your psychological COG through unfocus, and all of a sudden you may better understand not only yourself but others too. Three discrete circuits within your DMN "light up" when you're trying to understand how someone else feels, how you are different from them, and how they see the world. In other words, you are using the same parts of your brain when you listen to your COG as when you're negotiating, forming teams, or anticipating another person's next move.

THE BOUNCE BACK:
TALKING (TO) YOURSELF OUT OF FAILURE

When you fail at something, you've got to pull yourself up by the bootstraps and keep going, proceeding with the valuable lessons from the failure itself. This is easier said than done, especially when your brain is largely conditioned to hear and remember the negative, to respond to the crisis and not the lesson within it. Indeed, for every Jonathan Waxman who is able to learn from his mistakes and move on, far more people who have made a mistake or failed at something are beaten down by it. They discontinue their effort and settle for something else. Whether it is a small issue like finishing an office project or cooking a new dish, or a larger issue like making a career choice or beginning a relationship, only a blessed few are able to truly feel inspired when they fail. Psychologist Martin Seligman has referred to the deflation felt with repeated failures as "learned helplessness." In 1988, psychologist Carol Dweck explained that the magnitude of a person's failure matters less than their mindset about it. If you think you're doomed and forever stymied by your failure—if you have a fixed mindset—you won't try again. But if you believe that intelligence is malleable—if you have a growth mindset—you will rebound much faster.

To demonstrate that the brain is wired to rebound from failure, engineering professors David Franklin and Daniel Wolpert pinpointed the five basic mechanisms on display in the brain when a person bounces back from failure. These mechanisms help the brain regain the spring coils it needs to bounce back. Self-talk is the activating agent for each of these mechanisms, and the result is more energy and enthusiasm. Because we know which brain regions correspond to each mechanism, we know what you need to ask yourself to make the spring coils come back. To that end, I have included a key self-talk question for each mechanism discussed below.

This five-step system of brain "spring coil regeneration" (my own phrase, not a scientific one) gets you switching from the low beams of focusing on failure to the high beams of attention. Wondering, *What updates does my brain need?* is the way to fail forward intelligently. When you're learning under stress (e.g., after failure, while slowing down, in confusion, or upon hitting a wall), one of these might get overstretched. Asking these questions will put the spring back into every step of your brain's learning process.

1. Fight the Feedback

We get feedback all the time and from all kinds of sources. People respond, machines beep and screech, new mail piles up in our in-boxes. The feedback we get (or give ourselves) from having failed can be overwhelming and stressful. Unfortunately, a stressed brain has trouble deciding what's important; it thinks *everything* is important, including negative (unhelpful) feedback. You need to help it out—to manually tag information as relevant (helpful) or dramatic (unhelpful). Tinkerers and dynamic learners are experts at this kind of feedback control.

One way to tinker with feedback, rather than just accept it at face value, is to ask yourself questions about it. At Brightworks, for example, one of the teachers told me a story about a girl who was painstakingly making a chair. Every time she thought she'd finished it and made it stable, it came crashing down whenever any weight was placed on it—she got feedback about her design and building prowess from the thing itself. Dismayed, she looked up tearfully at the teacher. But the teacher didn't dwell on the drama of the chair breaking—he focused on the process. "You're one step closer," he said, "almost there. I wonder what could fix this?" Given this nonstressful feedback, the child recognized that she was not breaking chairs so much as making progress. The spring returned to her cognitive step: she ignored the drama of the broken chair and looked to why it was happening. With this attitude she eventually built a chair that anyone could sit on.

That lucky girl had a wise teacher to help her fight the negative feedback. But you can easily do this for yourself. For every obstruction you encounter, ask yourself, *Is this relevant or is it dramatic?* It'll help you separate the wheat from the chaff when your brain has too much to handle. Often you won't even recognize what's making you feel bad. But when you realize that your brain is unconsciously dramatizing recent feedback, you can tag it appropriately and put it aside.

Especially if you're trying to create something (whether it's a recipe, a novel, or a chair), try keeping a re-routing journal—a notebook or computer file in which you document your changes in your process. Review the journal regularly to discern the progress you're surely making. This can be a great way to tinker your way forward, as it will help you remember each point of change. It also helps you see the feedback traps before you fall into them again.

Self-talk question: What dramatic feedback am I mistakenly considering relevant right now?

BELIEVERS BOUNCE BACK

In 2006, Columbia psychologist Jennifer Mangels and her colleagues studied what happens in the brain when people with fixed versus growth mindsets receive feedback. They found that in people with a fixed mindset, the brain tends to dwell on negative feedback, whether expected or unexpected. Worse, it ignores the corrective suggestions that arise as the brain tries to figure out what to do.

For this study, the researchers first determined the mindset—fixed or growth—of forty-seven participants. They then asked a slew of general knowledge questions. The test takers typed in their answers, then rated their confidence in being correct. Then they were told whether they were correct and given the correct answers—all this while their brains were hooked up to machines recording their brainwaves. After eight minutes, they were asked to return for a surprise retest on all the questions they had answered incorrectly. They knew this only just before they started again.

Despite similar performances on the initial tests, people with a growth mindset performed much better on the second test. They believed they could bounce back, so they did! In the fixed group, the brainwave responses to negative feedback were correspondingly greater, indicating that they had wiped out these mistakes faster, without giving themselves a chance for correction.

2. Remove Resistance

Do you know that feeling when you just can't seem to get ahead? No matter what you do, something is stopping you, but you can't tell what. The universe of obstacles that can impede your progress can be divided into three categories: people, places, and things. Once you understand which category you're dealing with, you can institute the *resistance rebuttal* (more formally known as *impedance control*), the second mechanism that Franklin and Wolpert described. Over time, as you work out what's in your way, the roadblocks become surmountable because they lose their power to silently terrorize you.

Say you're trying to learn how to use a new team-building software platform at work, a technology that will allow you and others to report on what you're doing. But you just can't get your head around it. What's the real issue here? Is the technology itself really difficult (the thing), is your office too loud or busy to allow you to concentrate (the place), or are you intimidated and distracted by how quickly everyone else seems to be learning how to use the program (people)? Let's imagine that you recognize that it's the people. Now that you know the real problem, your stress and negative chatter will start to dissipate, and you can pivot to the solution.

For starters, consciously designate a longer period of time to learn your way around the new software—give yourself the whole day instead of just the ten minutes it seems to be taking everyone else to get the hang of it. Now go a step further and divide the designated learning time (the day) into phases: perhaps before your morning staff meeting, you will try to learn the basics of logging in and navigating the main tabs. Before lunch, you will learn how to enter your own information quickly and discern how to send it to specific others. After lunch you'll try to actually send a message to the group. In between each phase, build in an unfocus period to let your mind synthesize and consolidate the information you just mastered. Fifteen minutes of consolidation time is enough to go out and get a coffee or read the front page of the newspaper or play solitaire on your computer. In this unfocused downtime your resistance to using the software will diminish, and you'll regain the energy and optimism you need to overcome it. If you're a procrastinator, this time away may seem like more wasted time—procrastinators tend to want immediate rewards because their brains can't stand the wait. Yet exactly this kind of deliberate unfocus will give you time to overcome the resistance to your learning.

Self-talk question: What's stopping me (people, places, or things)?

3. Use Your Predicting Power

Your ability to predict the future is probably better than you think. *Systematic forecasting,* as some people call it, is an ability to estimate the likelihood of things happening by collecting data in the present and applying it to the future. Even if you're using the prediction algorithms of machine learning in a business, at some point being able to predict where to apply them or where new markets exist will prove a valuable skill. Researchers call it *prediction control.* It's like learning how to jump the gun intelligently.

In 2009, neuroscientist Moshe Bar wrote a helpful paper explaining how the proactive brain works. Even if you have done something many times over, he reminds us, every moment is actually a brand-new experience. For example, every time you get into your car, you see a driver's seat, and even though you've seen the seat before, this new moment has never existed previously. Though the process is opaque to you (you just get in and drive, after all), seeing that seat sets off an amazing cascade of thought.

For starters, you know this is a driver's seat because by analogy your brain matches the visual input (what you see: the seat) to a known entity. Once your brain has figured out that this is indeed a seat, it associates for you, based on your memory and your understanding of driving logistics—for example, you will expect to find a cup holder or steering wheel close by. Based on these associations, you can predict various aspects of your ride: that you will be able to steer on the road and that you will have somewhere to put your cup. Your brain is constantly engaged in making analogies, then associations and predictions. But when you're learning something brand new (or difficult, especially in a nonlinear, fact-based way), or when you're uncertain and need to clarify things, hypervigilance and overfocus use your brain resources to pay attention only to things you can see. It shuts down the process of prediction, and you're stalled or stumped.

If you think about it, we unfocus to predict all the time. We use satellite images to predict weather patterns, volcanic eruptions, rains that trigger mudslides, or even infectious disease outbreaks. In these instances, we literally unfocus to view patterns from above earth.

But you can unfocus to look into the future too. When you dare to predict, it's not just an empty guess. The act of predicting is based on subtle unconscious clues that come together to form the prediction. With it, you can predict bad investments, the consequences of going into a mosh pit, or even relationship success. Simply ask yourself what the future will be like, then look around in your head to find evidence to support that view.

By first predicting the future, you set up a signpost for your brain—a target for it to hit. Entrepreneurs, for instance, will often have a BHAG (bold, hairy, audacious goal). It acts as a guide for the brain to devise conscious and unconscious plans. To start, you don't have to be reasonable, and sometimes when you're stuck, you unfocus to go for the big goal. Your brain will figure out the rest.

Life is a series of successful experiments that can be tweaked as each new finding sheds light on prior ones. Your brain is wired to do this if you dare to be the principal investigator—the futurist— of your life. So go ahead and set up hypotheses and test them *after* you predict what will happen. It'll shake things up in your brain and allow you to jump right over the obstacles in front of you.

Self-talk question: What can I infer from the information I have so far?

4. Balance Brain Equations

We like to think we are aware of the pros and cons of our efforts, but in fact our brains are not wired to judge them if they are fruitless; we see our futile efforts only if we consciously ask, *What am I getting for what I am putting out?* When you're focused and determined to make a situation work, you assume that that focus and determination justify the effort, when they may actually be obscuring the fact that you're doing a lot for close to nothing in return. Often we forget to ask this question overtly and so might stick around a relationship or organization even if it has been going downhill for years. If you have even a glimpse of hope for a situation, you will stay stuck in the familiar rather than cutting your losses and moving on. Of course, in other instances your brain does abandon ship, as when you're not that psychologically invested in something. But that kind of overreaction can be a misstep too.

Here again the ballast is self-talk—literally ask your brain if your efforts are worthwhile or if you should change course. Don't always assume that the pros and cons are obvious. Always ask yourself this overtly, especially if you're slowing down or not reaching your goals.

Whether you're trying to come up with a new idea or to make a relationship or business work, you're always learning. Every so often, while following your initial strategy, ask yourself what is working and what is not. You'll be surprised by how wasteful you are about personal energy, often doing things for which you get nothing in return.

Thinking overtly about the pros and cons of your behavior will keep you out of mind-traps like *I already bought the unhealthy food—I should just eat it* or *I might as well stay for this entire horrible movie because I've watched half of it already.* Understanding the pros and cons of continued actions can help you make more fruitful decisions.

In terms of the old-learning paradigm, you might spend time memorizing information, being overly comprehensive in collecting supporting data to launch a new idea, or even hiring someone who is cheap at the outset but will cost you tons of money later on.

In each of these situations, asking yourself about the pros and cons can save a lot of wasted time and money.

Self-talk question: If I keep on doing what I am doing, is my effort worth it?

5. Learn by Feeling and Doing

Learning by touching prototypes and doing things is called *sensorimotor learning*. Every time you act, you advance by learning in real time through real experience rather than by thinking. At medical school, for example, when we were understaffed and needed to learn new surgical procedures, the common aphorism was "See one, do one, teach one." We wasted no time in endlessly reading or observing. Doing was the pathway to learning. It was the only way to ensure improvement too.

When Jonathan Waxman invented California cuisine with a French accent, the idea didn't just fall into his lap. He worked at it. He learns from his mistakes. He sees limitation as an opportunity and is noted for saying that for professional chefs, the word *sabotage* does not exist—you work with what you've got. And in his typical experimental style, he's not willing to stick with older traditions—instead, he'll tinker with them. He took what he learned about nouvelle cuisine—the ever-so-small portions of French food—and adapted the idea to the American palate: lighter fare but still classic American dishes. He adapted the traditional BLT by sautéing shrimp in the rendered fat of the cooked bacon and slapping the shrimp on top for perfection! At the core of this approach is what Waxman calls a reactionary and revolutionary attitude—he didn't accept things at face value. And he values doing too.

When Hunter Lewis (now editor in chief of *Cooking Light*) was a food journalist, he approached Waxman to learn about cooking. Waxman asked him to work in the kitchen for a day, but seeing that Lewis was all thumbs, he suggested a longer internship to hone his skills. Lewis worked in Waxman's kitchen for a year, immersing himself in cooking to truly understand it. To his credit, Lewis stuck it out, and Waxman was satisfied that he had had the experience he needed to become an informed journalist.

Learning by doing replaces learning by overthinking. Even making mistakes can help you discover new things. It's also more practical, because you learn to envision the future from concrete iterations rather than through thought iterations.

Self-talk question: What one action can jumpstart my brain?

Putting It All Together for the Love of Learning

Here's the shorthand for dynamic learning. The four C's are Change direction, Be Curious, Curate advice, and, lastly, Co-construct learning.

CHANGE DIRECTION

In your brain, attention exists on a metaphorical pivot. When you're focused on learning within a traditional classroom or when you have set your sights on a specific goal, you're externally focused. You are using your "fork." There's certainly a time and place for that, but don't forget the "spoon." Pivoting inward, by listening to your intuition and your psychological COG, reconnects you to your original self and expands your learning beyond the facts on the page. This switch of focus allows you to bathe in the sea of memories, aspirations, values, meanings, and purposes that make up the complexity of you. And that's where the magic lies!

Pivoting inward happens when your mind wanders spontane-ously. But you can also plan your unfocus, be more deliberate about it: known psychological vehicles can help you make this switch.

One such unfocus vehicle is mental simulation, or imagining what it might be like to do or be something. You can simulate what it would feel like to be in your ideal job, with an ideal partner, or in an ideal life. This unfocus uses your predicting power too.

This fantasizing should not be brief or casual. Set aside time to do it. First, think of what you want to learn, like using the new software program I discussed in Remove Resistance. One way to prepare yourself for this removal is to simulate what you actually want. Imagine how you would get there: call a colleague to find out how to do it, set aside one hour twice a week to do it, and imagine what you might want to truly collaborate about. You don't just think out the steps; you simulate them in your mind as if they were actually happening.

You might want to do some or all of this mental simulation out loud—either to yourself or to someone willing to listen. You can also pick a time when you're alone to walk through your learning goal mentally: in the shower, walking the dog, or when you're feel-ing bored or have nothing to do. Every time you actively simulate a situation, you activate your psychological COG.

When you mentally simulate situations, you activate the DMN. The more specific your visualization, the more meaning you'll get out of it and the more you will activate your psychological COG.

Whenever you get lost while learning, whether you are follow-ing an instruction manual to build a cabinet or developing an email list for your business, simulate the result you want in your mind. Be as specific as you can (visualize the finished cabinet or the audience that is responding). This will pivot your attention to engage your COG and predicting power and will help motivate you to get to the finish line.

BE CURIOUS

We are all born curious. We explore as babies by putting all kinds of things in our mouths, we play make-believe as children, and we ask challenging and often countercultural questions as teenagers. As we mature, however, our innate curiosity takes a backseat to a more concrete view of the world.

But learning clearly improves when you're curious. In 2014, neuroscientist Matthias Gruber and colleagues asked nineteen students to examine more than one hundred trivia questions. The students had to rate how confident they were that they knew the answer, as well as their general level of curiosity about the topics. Some of the questions stumped them; they were curious about some but not all of them.

Then the researchers used fMRI to look at the brain blood flow of all the students. While lying in the scanner, each participant was shown the same set of trivia questions followed by a lag time and then the answer.

As the students anticipated each answer, a photograph of a stranger flashed onto the screen. It was meant to be an incidental stimulus, which they were not supposed to notice particularly. Then after a few seconds passed, the answer appeared. This sequence was repeated 112 times.

After the fMRI scanning, each student took a quiz on the answers to the trivia questions and recall of the faces. Unsurprisingly, the students recalled 71 percent of the answers that really piqued their curiosity compared to 54 percent of the answers that didn't. Curiosity about the trivia questions activated the brain's reward center and probably facilitated learning. When the questions did not elicit curiosity, they were easily forgotten.

But the more surprising finding was that the students were able to identify even incidental facts—the strangers' faces—more when they were curious than when they were not. This effect persisted a day later. Long-term memory (the hippocampus) was more engaged when students were curious, thereby helping them remember the incidental faces. The mere sense of anticipation was enough to get their memory jazzed.

When something interests us, we are more likely to remember it. When you're curious, your brain rallies to make sure that you remember not just what you're curious about, but anything else you come across around the same time. Many innovators take advantage of this fringe benefit—they remember and connect surprising parts of their discoveries because they are fueled by curiosity. And they can handle the tension and surprises that come with curiosity because they are connected to their psychological COG.

CURATE ADVICE

We live in a world of advice-givers. Parents, teachers, self-help experts, financial gurus, personal shoppers, and spouses all willingly offer their views and opinions. You probably offer it to others as well—it's human to opine and advise. Giving and getting advice is, however, less benign than you might think.

First, giving advice. In 2015, Columbia psychologist Dean Mobbs and his colleagues studied the brains of advice-givers. They found that when people give advice that is accepted and leads to others' lives improving, the reward centers in the advice-givers' brains activate. However, these same advice-givers' brains are not rewarded when the advice they have given is rejected or when someone else gives advice to the people they advised. We seem wired to want our own advice to lead to the success of others. But even unconsciously, we care more about people accepting our advice than about their winning as a result of it. Well-meaning though it may be, you should take advice from others with a large pinch of salt.

How about responding to advice? In 2009, Emory University neuroeconomist Jan Engelmann and his colleagues used brain imaging to examine what happens in the brains of people making financial decisions. Participants had to choose between financial puzzles, where the chances of winning were clear, and lotteries, with different probabilities of winning. They had to figure out the probability of success prior to making a choice. In half the trials, an expert economist gave them his economic advice. When the subjects got that advice, the regions of the brain involved in the valuation process were inactive. But when the expert did *not* give his advice, the "valuation" regions of their brains actively were involved as they tried to figure it out themselves.

Lo and behold, expert advice replaces active valuation by the brain! When you give advice to someone, the person passively listens but does not actively process or absorb your advice. In other words, blindly accepting advice does little to stimulate thinking. It is the opposite of discovery. So by all means listen to advice, but make sure you tinker with it. Put your own discovery process first.

Rather than take advice, it's preferable to tinker, like the girl who built the chair, or even like Jonathan Waxman learning through doing (and messing up) in the kitchen. When you control feedback and commit to "feeling and doing" thinking, you will learn far more effectively. Activate those spring coils in your brain rather than deactivate them!

CO-CONSTRUCT LEARNING

Machines are gaining traction in the workplace, and it's not just mobile devices and faster computers. Robots are being made to take over countless jobs, probably even your own. This impacts how and what you choose to learn and how you define yourself professionally too.

Vinod Khosla, co-founder of Sun Microsystems, believes that

machines will eventually replace 80 percent of doctors. Machine learning, he points out, is a far finer integrator of extensive data and provides much more accurate diagnoses. Of course, people may prefer the warm touch of doctors, but this may not always be the case. In 2016, the Australian researcher Matthew Winter found that people who are preparing for kidney stone surgery prefer watching a video animation in which a doctor narrates a preparation procedure to having a face-to-face consultation. This has implications for how doctors learn and think about their profession. Doctors in training should perhaps deemphasize diagnostics and learn to assess machine errors or augment machine diagnoses instead. And rather than focusing on their bedside manner alone, they may want to learn to record clear messages to prepare surgical patients. A physician-entrepreneur with a dynamic learning mindset may realize that compiling these kinds of video libraries may become an important business opportunity too.

It's not just doctors who will be impacted. Oxford University researchers estimate that in the next two decades 47 percent of U.S. jobs will be automated. The World Economic Forum predicts that by 2020 robots will replace five million jobs, many of them in the "office and administration" category, although other sectors will be affected as well. So what will you do when "administrative assistant" positions are no more, and how else might you apply your organizational skills? You will be more likely to switch jobs and invent a new one if you keep your work identity looser and your learning more flexible—if you connect with your ingenuity and your psychological COG.

Other service jobs will be affected too. Tech-No-Logic has made a robot that can cook: it picks up ingredients from separate containers and whips up a meal by following recipe instructions from an app. Momentum Machines has made a multitasker bot that can make and flip hamburgers in ten seconds. Soon it will be able to replace an entire McDonald's crew. That's why there is so much talk about the need to "upskill"—machines will take over the easier jobs. Dynamic learning for new roles using all of the brain's spring coils will be key.

Learning to live with and develop alongside machines will require a new learning frame of mind—one that will compete with machines where relevant and also work together with them. Your ingenuity—your original intelligence, not learned skills—will be crucial and helpful. But your ingenuity will have to be applied in the context of the community of machines that are becoming increasingly connected to one another and to you.

British entrepreneur Kevin Ashton coined the phrase "Internet of Things" to describe how in our brave new world machines are increasingly connected to us. You can control your garage door from a remote location, and you can watch your kids at home while you're at work. Distance, once an obstruction to connection, is no longer relevant in our wireless world.

More than ever, you must realize that your brain is part of the Internet of Things. After all, it's wired with electrical circuits like any other device. It can be activated or made to rest. With its buzzing electrical circuits and information systems, it is set up to connect with the world of devices and external information storage. And just this fact is changing our brains and how we think and act.

In 2010, one of Google's co-founders, Sergey Brin, said, "We want Google to be the third half of your brain." Be assured, he hasn't invented a new kind of math in which *hemi* means "three"! He meant that he wanted humans to think of Google as a way to relieve the stress of storing so much in our brains. He was suggesting that we off-load information storage to the sites that Google will take you to and free up our own thinking machines—our brains—for other things.

In other words, use your newly freed-up head space to use your brain's spring coils more effectively, or to connect with your psychological COG and ingenuity. Take the lead, and be in charge of the relationship. Ask yourself what you can automate (how you can team with machines), what you can off-load to technology (what you can delegate to machines), and what kinds of technology you can stop overly relying on (how you can manage your time better with machines). Also, notice how machines are connected as a community. Are you as connected with other people as machines are to each other?

By applying the principles of dynamic learning, you will adapt to the speed of change, course-correct when necessary by using your brain's spring coils, and most of all, use your internal compass and substance to activate your inherent ingenuity. Machines will always be better at being machines, but when it comes to being human, you have the edge.

Learning in a Focused Mindset	Learning in an Unfocused Mindset Shift
If lost while learning, focus on external cues to get back on track.	When lost, turn to your inner compass and ask, "Who am I?" Your own ingenuity should be your primary guide.
Respond to feedback, both positive and negative.	Carefully consider feedback with a growth mindset; challenge its relevance.
To be agile, fail fast, and fail forward.	You can't fail forward or fast without reactivating your brain's spring coils, so build in self-talk to stay agile.
Base your next action on evidence and data.	You are as much a creator as a follower of data, so simulate and imagine solutions as well.
Machines are separate from you.	Your brain is part of the "Internet of Things."

MASTERING MULTITASKING

Simultaneity . . . is the property of all great poetry.

—LeRoy C. Breunig

When you're doing two or more things at the same time—reading email and speaking on the telephone, for example—you're multitasking. When you're trying to accomplish multiple tasks on the same day—like finish a report while tending to the needs of a sick spouse—you're also multitasking. You could even describe multitasking as doing two things over an extended period of time, such as working at your current job while starting another business on the side. Both might demand your attention equally, requiring you to constantly split your attention between them.

Though many people wear their multitasking "ability" like a productivity badge of honor, the short-term accomplishments themselves are often dubious. Even if you actually finish the multiple tasks you start, more often than not multitasking leaves you frazzled and spent; your brain's attentional flashlight runs out of batteries, and as a result, the path ahead can seem confusing or dimly lit. I call it *wobbly brain syndrome,* in which you become effectively disconnected from the calming influence of your DMN.

Doctoral student Kep Kee Loh and cognitive neuroscientist Ryota Kanai recently described this phenomenon when they studied media multitaskers—people who, say, text while watching TV and browsing the Internet at the same time. In the multitasking people, the brain's conflict detector—the anterior cingulate cortex, or ACC—had less gray-matter density than in people who used just one device at a time. It was as if multitasking had gobbled up brain tissue in that region. To make matters worse, the more people multitasked, the less the DMN was connected to the ACC. As a result, a big task load created unbearable conflicts. In lay terms, the result was confusion, discomfort, forgetfulness, and as much as they tried to stay focused, *less* attentiveness.

For a real-life example, consider a short-order cook, who must simultaneously hold multiple orders in her head, keep an eye on a rapidly growing stack of order slips, while cracking eggs, flipping pancakes and hash browns, chopping vegetables, frying bacon, sausages, and burgers, and in the infrequent lulls, even ordering supplies. Any Thanksgiving host knows that keeping even half as many balls in the air can lead to rapid burnout (and a vow to let someone else host next year). No wonder the stereotypical short-order cook is short-tempered.

But some short-order cooks are *not* flummoxed by the barrage of things to do. If you've ever taken a peek through a diner window or through the swinging doors behind the counter, you've seen them—as mesmerizing as magicians, they seem at one with every task that comes their way. They may be a little sweaty, but they are emotionally unperturbed, taking the frenzy in stride as they transition seamlessly from one task to another.

This is the same skill you will see in the nurse who calmly triages patients in a chaotic emergency room; it's on view with many first responders, people who work on site in disasters. And the same multitasking skill is needed to direct live, multicamera television: managing many monitors at the same time, making sure the teleprompter is working, deciding which angle to highlight in any given moment, when to add graphics or information at the bottom of the screen, all the while listening to feedback in an earpiece and giving directions through a microphone!

So what's the difference between a short-order cook, a nurse, a first responder, or a director who is drained and depleted at the end of the shift, and one who might even whistle his or her way to bed at the crack of dawn? The first type is the classic multitasker— they may get things done, but they do it all with their "hair on fire." The latter, on the other hand, is a *supertasker*—their neurological juggling is more fluid, and as a result, the action is more productive.

Some people seem wired to supertask. Psychologists Jason Watson and David Strayer studied two hundred people in a driving simulator. Participants had to drive behind a car that constantly braked, so they had to be on high alert to avoid a collision. It was like being in stop-and-go highway traffic.

Then in the multitasking portion of the study, participants had to solve simple arithmetic problems while they were driving. And in between problems, they were asked to remember two to five words they were shown. Imagine actually doing this while you're driving in highway traffic! It requires more attention than speaking mindlessly on a cellphone!

Not surprisingly, this research showed that for most people doing two things at once is close to impossible. However, 2.5 percent of the group separated themselves from the pack. Not only was their driving unaffected when they were multitasking, but some of them even drove better.

Whether one is born with the necessary neurological connections or not, however, it's clear that a certain amount of practice can breed supertasking ability. You know this from your own life— the more you have to juggle the same two (or more) responsibilities, the better you tend to get at keeping those particular balls in the air. Or not, and you (and the cook, nurse, first responder, or director) realize a career change might be in order. But what if you didn't have to put in hours or months or years of practice to become so neurologically facile?

"THE MASTER OF TINSELTOWN MULTITASKING"

Even in Hollywood, where the pace is frenetic and the spotlight never fades, Ryan Seacrest stands out. His work is widely respected throughout the industry; he's been nominated for Emmys several times, and at this writing, he has even won one. As busy as popcorn on a hot skillet, he has been called "the master of Tinseltown multitasking." TV host Jimmy Kimmel summarized it best when he joked, "I know why unemployment is over eight percent—it's because of Ryan Seacrest."

On most days, Seacrest hosts a radio show, *On Air with Ryan Seacrest,* from six to ten A.M. Over the course of the rest of the day, he attends to his duties as executive producer of eight reality and scripted television shows, and up until 2016 he was also the host of the live vocalist search competition *American Idol.* In addition, he has launched a clothing line, and he keeps tabs on his philanthropies for seriously ill and injured children. Somehow he is also seemingly in very good shape and reportedly finds time to date as well!

At first glance, Seacrest's life sounds enigmatically unachievable and inconceivable. Yet research shows that learning how to supertask can put his facility for doing many things within arm's reach.

We know what is working right in a supertasker's brain. In essence, the supertasking cook, nurse, first responder, or director has learned to "staff" their brain with just the right capacity to remember, filter, and manage conflicting information. They use a variety of brain training strategies to make neurological connections where there were none, to avoid redundancies of thought and action, to become a more efficient and less exhausted multitasker—a supertasker. Cognitive rhythm, we know, provides the best conditions for supertasking regardless of the specific tasks to be juggled. The common strategic denominator is that all invoke the power of unfocus.

DISSOLVING STRESS

Stress isn't always a bad thing. A little stress—called *eustress*—is always going to be necessary to motivate you to get a job done. But after a certain point, eustress becomes distress, creating chaos in the brain, disrupting DMN functioning, and throwing you out of cognitive rhythm.

A recent study compared two groups of medical students: one group was applying for residency, a particularly high-stress juncture in a medical career, and the other group was not yet at that point and therefore was less stressed. (They were no doubt tired; that's par for the course!) Compared to the less-stressed medical students, those applying for residency had a DMN that was not well connected to the rest of the brain. It was out of the loop. Furthermore, their brains' conflict centers perpetuated the internal chaos. When you're always on—waiting, nervous, anticipating, wondering—chaos and fatigue are the result. That's a classical pattern for the multitasking brain, not the supertasking one.

You can do numerous things to reduce your stress—exercise and meditation are popular and effective, and both have been shown to normalize DMN function so the brain can get back into gear. Alternatively, you could use self-talk to reframe your tasks as "an intense period that will soon be over" or "an intense period and time to practice being a supertasker." This will deactivate your amygdala and revive your DMN, the recipe for getting back into cognitive rhythm.

But when you already have a million things to juggle, one counterintuitive thing you might not think of doing is to *add* another task to your day. Here's the (happy) rub: this added task should be playful and joyful; it should take your mind off your growing to-do list. When you give yourself over to it, your brain will respond with a metaphoric sigh of relief. (This is why companies like Google provide games, sports, and workout equipment for their ambitious and supertasking employees. Management knows that having unfocused time can help employees manage their days much more effectively.)

If video games are your thing, consider research by cognitive neuroscientist E. L. Maclin. He and his colleagues trained people to multitask while using a video game called Space Fortress and found that playing the video game increased the participants' alpha wave power, one of the unfocus frequencies. Once they were in alpha, their multitasking became easier. It's like trying to swim in calm water rather than stormy waves. Being more in alpha mode replenishes the brain, enabling you to switch your attention more easily—a hallmark of supertasking.

There's no hard and fast rule on how often to do such play. For me, in medical school, a short, playful break (to walk outside or chat with friends) after a sustained forty-five-minute study period proved stress-reducing. You will have your own limit of focus, and it will change a bit depending on what exactly you're doing. A good rule of thumb is that stress is like dehydration. Just as sipping water all day can keep you from getting parched, giving yourself small breaks can prevent stress from taking its toll on you.

To be clear, I'm not suggesting that you abandon the counter when you're a short-order cook or drift off into a stupor in the middle of a workday. But before you arrive and during the course of a multitasking day, add an unrelated task that requires little effort. It will help warm up your DMN and relax you. With your relaxed brain, you then take your cruise control to a different level.

THE ADVANTAGE OF AGE

If you're thinking that supertasking training is for the young and nimble, you're in for a nice surprise. Your age does *not* necessarily limit the effects. In 2013, kinesiologist Joaquin Anguera and his colleagues used a three-dimensional video game, NeuroRacer, to train people at supertasking. Results showed that men and women between sixty and eighty-five became better at supertasking than twenty-year-olds who were untrained in the game. Sure, training a twenty-year-old would probably place them at an advantage, but the point is that with training you can reverse age-related multitasking deficits.

CALLING ON YOUR SILENT PARTNER, THE UNCONSCIOUS

Your unconscious brain is a silent but powerful partner to your conscious brain in dealing with the world. This alliance of the conscious and unconscious mind occurred to people long before the current era of information-processing psychology. For example, in the late nineteenth century, educated public figures were fascinated by the phenomenon known as "automatic writing," during which people could allegedly write prose while carrying out other tasks. Like George Hyde-Lees, wife of poet William Butler Yeats, they claimed to feel as if they were owned by something else, and in this state of dissociation, this "outside" force would compel them to write. Even Sir Arthur Conan Doyle—creator of Sherlock Holmes—thought of this spiritualism as genuine. But psychologist Wilma Koutstaal explained that this very real phenomenon is probably related to automatic brain processes, in which one switches from conscious intention to a state of awareness in which memories and understanding are automatically activated in one's brain—with one less task to "do," you can focus on other things!

The idea of voluntarily switching your state of mind so that something automatic can be activated may sound challenging, to say the least, yet actually you do this all the time, even if you aren't aware of it. When your eye sees a colleague's hand outstretched so that you can shake it, your brain registers this image but it also guides your hand to do the actual shaking—you don't merely stare at the hand. A conscious process allows you to *see* your colleague's hand and an unconscious process *guides* your hand so that you don't have to actually look at its destination—your colleague's grip.

The seeing and guiding in that scenario are handled by different visual wiring systems. *Seeing* is a conscious act involving the ventral visual stream (a bunch of neurons that go from the eyes to the brain). *Guiding* is an unconscious act handled by the dorsal visual stream (a bunch of neurons that also connect the eyes and the brain behind the ventral stream). Both of these wiring systems go to different parts of the brain so that you see and guide at the same time. Too much seeing and no guiding would make you stare at your colleague's hand. (That would be strange, to say the least!) Too much guiding and no seeing would make you miss the hand. People who are unable to supertask lack the right balance between seeing and guiding—specifically, they don't trust their guiding neurons. They get caught up in the details of a task (metaphorically staring at the outstretched hand) instead of loosening up enough to let the unconscious do its job.

FEAR OF THE UNKNOWN

Your unconscious brain contains a mixed bag of intimidating emotions and experiences. Anger, fear, sexual impulses, loneliness, neediness, feelings of abandonment—things you don't really want to be too visible—live in your unconscious. They are neighbors of your unconscious guide system, the "less controversial" part of the unconscious mind. Knowing that these things sit next to each other tends to make us reticent to let go of focus. If we let go and thereby stir the unconscious mind, we may inadvertently open that mixed bag of emotions. But if you don't take that chance, the "conscious you" will try to supertask. That's like braking around a corner rather than putting your foot on the gas. Not only will it wear down your brakes, but it could also cause you to skid off the road. You absolutely have to dare to dabble in your whole unconscious pool—good *and* bad—as it will help make your supertasking more fluent.

One way to activate your unconscious brain and release yourself from the clutches of focus is to doodle. As we have previously seen, it activates the DMN and gets your focused, conscious brain out of the way.

When you set aside time to doodle, you will find yourself drawing seemingly random things that are probably not as random as they seem. Psychoanalyst and pioneer of introspective journaling Marion Milner finds that doodling overrides conscious obstructions and allows the unconscious self to kick in. The symbols that you draw reflect the goings on in your subterranean brain.

Psychologist Robert Burns has also studied doodles for much of his life. In an interview published on the *Register*—a British technology, news, and opinion website—he said doodles reveal much about the mind's inner workings. Much as an EEG, when connected to your brain by electrodes, records brain activity with a stylus, he pointed out, a doodle can reveal brain activity because it is connected to your brain by your hands.

If you hesitate to doodle on the job in order to supertask, consider that by 2007, twenty-six of forty-four U.S. presidents were self-admitted doodlers. If there's any job where you need to be a supertasker, that's it, right? The painter, printmaker, and theorist of the German Renaissance, Albrecht Dürer, also doodled, as did the prolific Russian writer Fyodor Dostoyevsky.

In fact, Dostoyevsky noted how the conscious mind can get in the way in *Winter Notes on Summer Impressions:* "Try to pose for yourself this task: not to think of a polar bear, and you will see that the cursed thing will come to mind every minute." As long ago as 1863, he recognized that conscious, focused thinking could fail us. More than a century later, social psychologist Daniel Wegner's research proved that if you think *Don't drop the ball* when you're juggling and stressed, you're more than likely to drop the ball. Your conscious brain gets in the way and takes up energy, leaving no energy for the unconscious brain to guide you.

THE POWER OF MUSIC

Even in older adults, just four months of musical training can improve focused and unfocused attention. It can increase your overall IQ and improve your ability to spell as well. Brain scans show that musical training lights up the regions that make your fingers move and that are involved in listening. That's no surprise. But relevant to unfocusing, it beefs up the brain bridge that connects the hemispheres. Adding more lanes to the brain bridge allows thought traffic to flow more easily.

When you play the piano, you use both hands: the left and

right hands play separate parts. Their patterns of movement often differ as well. You can't focus on one hand at a time—you have to focus on both. To do this, your brain unfocuses—deactivates—and your attention deepens as you let go of focus on either hand, especially if you're playing a concerto as opposed to a simple action like musical scales.

Focusing on one task at a time, or *serial processing*, makes bottlenecks worse. By contrast unfocus, by activating parallel brain circuits and deactivating focus, allows your brain to share its energy to attend to both hands, making supertasking possible.

GETTING THROUGH BRAIN BOTTLENECKS

When you need to respond to an email while you're on the telephone, you have to read, write, and listen at the same time. But your brain can often do only one task at a time properly. It's as if there's one checkpoint, and tasks that must be done have to arrange themselves in a single file in your brain.

When many tasks try to squeeze through a bottleneck, the results can be disastrous. Think of driving from an on-ramp onto a jam-packed highway. That's what every new thought faces. It slows down, and eventually the brain becomes a parking lot for thoughts! That's when you drop the multitasking, when instead you should see this as a signal to switch to supertasking mode.

In 2015, neuroscientist Omar Al-Hashimi and his colleagues looked at how certain people's brains overcome bottlenecks—how they deftly switch brain lanes and somehow find a way through. They used the video game NeuroRacer, which is designed to have players perform single- and then multi-component tasks. For example, players have to keep a car within a target box while responding to various road signals; the signals increase in number as the game gets harder. As the number of things they have to pay attention to increases, an information bottleneck is created in their brains.

Some of the players had superior multitasking performance: they had faster response times, made fewer errors, and were more accurate. The researchers noted that the *superior parietal lobe* (SPL) was key, helping them quickly switch between tasks by loosening the grip of focus. The SPL also efficiently manages brain resources by keeping things for a longer time in the short-term memory cup so that the person can, effectively, pick up where they left off more easily.

Another way to reduce bottlenecks is through *redundancy reduction*—combining one or more tasks to save time. If you have to pick up a friend and on the same day go to the supermarket near that friend's house, you focus and notice their commonality— both require you to drive through the same neighborhood. Even though stopping to consciously think through ways to reduce redundancies might take time at first, taking the step of unfocusing on your separate goals and tinkering with them to see which ones can be combined will decongest your bottleneck in the short term. With practice, it becomes much more automatic.

GETTING PHYSICAL

You aren't conscious of it necessarily, but your body supertasks all the time. Walking is supertasking 101—it uses many leg and abdominal muscle groups and requires you to look where you're going.

Certain physical exercises enhance neurological supertasking. At your local gym, you can probably find a piece of equipment called a ViPR. It's a rubber cylinder about belly-button high on a six-foot person. Spaces are cut into the cylinder like a jack-o'-

lantern so that you can put your hands through to get a grip on it. To practice multitasking, get down on one knee and rotate your upper body to the left. Place the cylinder vertically on the ground with two hands inserted into the jack-o'-lantern holes. This is the first move. Then lift the cylinder with both hands, swing it to the horizontal position, and take it with you as you rotate your upper body all the way to the right, keeping your lumbar spine stationary and moving only your thoracic spine as you extend your arm at the elbow to lift the ViPR up horizontally. This simple lift and twist requires you to think of multiple things at the same time. It warms up your supertasking brain and helps you train your brain to overcome bottlenecks. Called *embodied cognition,* this technique relies on the fact that changes that you make with your body can translate into cognitive improvements as well.

You can also use your cognitive flexibility (rather than hunkering down with focus) to integrate the tasks on your to-do list and manage bottlenecks. Cutting yourself some slack mentally will allow your brain to conserve energy so that you're less tightly wound up, and you have enough energy for the various unconscious unfocus processes. Your brain will start, pause, switch, and restart tasks all the way. Believing in unfocus will allow you to do this.

I recently saw cognitive flexibility in action while having dinner at a friend's home. As I stood with her in the kitchen, I watched her put a casserole in the oven, put leftover roast chicken and vegetables in a frying pan on the stovetop, fry some bacon, and warm up leftover mashed potatoes in the microwave. She did all this while talking to me and attending to her ten-year-old daughter, who came in intermittently to ask some oddly (but nonetheless charming) existential questions.

Cool, calm, and collected, my friend got into the rhythm of each action, not doing one thing at a time but starting and stopping at will. I could see her cognitive wheels turning.

The casserole went in first. Intermittently, she checked on it and changed the oven temperature when she needed to. Halfway there, she put the chicken and vegetables in a pan over medium heat. She left them for about ten minutes, turning and sautéing them respectively every now and then. A few minutes before everything was ready, she put the bacon on.

When I finally saw the roast chicken, bacon mashed potatoes, delicious vegetables, and a casserole on my plate, I realized that she was the bottleneck master. In and out, back and forth, tinker and wait—cognitive rhythm saved the day. Like a short-order cook, she smoothly switched between tasks in a way made possible not just by practice but by being willing to leave things halfway in the process and then return to them. The climax is at the end when everything is put together, but before that, you have to be flexible and trusting enough to let the oven, microwave, and frying pan do their respective and differently timed work. You need to be flexible and go back and forth between multiple things without obsessing about completing each dish first.

FINE-TUNING FEEDBACK

Although my friend's dinner came together swiftly, she would not have cooked the food so perfectly had she not continuously sought feedback—prodding the chicken, checking on the casserole.

Without feedback, your brain loses track of its own results. That makes multitasking more difficult. But it turns out that the "scope" of feedback that you allow yourself to consider is meaningful.

Cognitive science researcher Hansjörg Neth and his colleagues compared local and global feedback in the context of multitasking. They used a computer program called Tardast, aptly named after the Persian term for "juggler," to investigate multitasking behavior, complex system management, and constant supervision.

During the experiment, the researchers presented the participants with ten trials via a computer screen. For each five-minute trial, the participants had to manage six tasks.

Performing a "task" meant pressing a button to fill up a vertical white bar with black. Pressing the button raised the level, while releasing the button caused the level to fall. The participants' goal was to get the black to rise to the highest level within each vertical bar. They had to press the button quickly to get the level to rise, and they could press buttons only one at a time and in quick sequence. But some bars were more difficult to fill than others, and all the bars increased and decreased at different speeds. After each five-minute trial, participants received feedback on how they had done.

The researchers found that *any* kind of feedback improved multitasking. But local feedback (how the person did on the last trial) was superior to global feedback (how they had done all day) for multitasking.

Back in the kitchen, as my friend cooked dinner and prodded the chicken to check for doneness, she was getting feedback that helped her determine how much longer to cook the bird. Had she prodded the bird and then considered all her previous prods— previously gathered information about the slowly evolving doneness of the chicken—she would have gotten caught up in feedback analysis. As it happened, her quest for feedback was not very deep or far-reaching. She kept her mind on the present texture of the chicken and moved on. And that served her (and me) well.

Without feedback, your brain gets overwhelmed. If you feel like you have a billion things to do in the course of a day, dipping into conscious feedback is a way of taking stock. Don't just take it for granted that your brain is updating information as you go along. Give it local feedback. Stop and think about what you just did and how it relates to what you have to do next. This momentary period of unfocus from your task will allow you to tinker with your approach to make it better.

But asking the right questions—ones that bring local feedback to bear—is key. The emergency room physician who is inundated with trauma-related procedures might say to herself, *Three down, seven to go.* That is global feedback—an emphasis on the full day's work. Or she might say, *That last one went well,* which is local feedback, emphasizing just the last task. The ER doctor who gets a little more specific with her local feedback—*That last one went well, but next time make sure all the dried blood has been cleared so there's not even a speck before you suture*—allows her work to improve. Taking time to give this feedback may stop the flow of her work in the short term, but it allows her to tinker with the lineup of sutures so that each successive one is better yet requires that much less conscious brainpower the next time. When you practice thinking this way, it trains your brain for supertasking.

SEEKING INTERCONNECTIONS

When you're in supertasking mode, your brain helps you remember half-completed tasks while you move on, so that you can return to them. It helps you remember not to leave something on the stove when the phone rings. It also helps you restrategize about pending goals as you go along.

The brain region that helps you do all this is your frontopolar cortex. It acts as your "personal shopper." Think of it as standing by with a shopping bag containing clothes you're considering buying as you try them on. It seems to become active specifically when you need to keep recently completed tasks in mind as you do other things.

Say you open an email just as the phone rings. You pick up the phone, and just then your boss comes in and drops a note asking you to complete an urgent task. You might take the call, then complete the urgent task while remembering to get back to the email. Your brain's personal shopper stands by, holding the message from the email while you complete the urgent task. Studies show that damage to the frontopolar cortex makes multitasking much more difficult.

Your brain's personal shopper is also a great connector. It likes to match similar things and makes leaps of connection even between things that have *semantic distance,* or distance in meaning. For example, a bird and an airplane both have wings, but they are otherwise different—they have a medium semantic distance. But an airplane and a fox have a greater semantic distance. Your personal shopper looks for connections between concepts. The greater the semantic distance, the more innovative it will make you in connecting two things. It might, for example, suggest that an airplane and a fox are both on a mission. It might suggest that pilots should learn from a fox's attentiveness to know how to navigate difficult terrains. The more you think about it, the more similarities you will find. Your brain's personal shopper will use its extraordinary matching abilities to help you do so.

To train this region, set aside time to make different kinds of connections. Start with fifteen minutes a week, then incorporate this into your day in the shower, when you're bored, or when you can't find something to do. It's a great replacement for crossword puzzles or Sudoku. Start by comparing items in your bedroom, then in every other room. Looking for connections is a way of doodling (while you wait) and tinkering (fiddling with concepts to find connections). It's not a focused mental journey but a journey of discovery as you realize what the connections are.

Your personal shopper is part of the DMN. It turns on with unfocus as you search for connections, wait to see them, or tinker with objects so that you can see them another way. But if you plod right through your day, you'll barely have any time to make connections.

SEEKING SIMILARITIES

Ryan Seacrest was once asked how he managed to keep ten jobs at the same time. One way, he explained, was "consolidation." He looked for ways to consolidate tasks and places he needed to be at any given time. His radio show studio was just across the hall from one of his TV show studios. To a large extent, his brain bridges semantic distance, looking for connections where they are not immediately apparent.

Finding connections is a type of thinking called *analogical reasoning,* and although it can happen spontaneously, it helps to make a conscious habit of it. People who perform analogical reasoning well have greater fluid intelligence—they are more flexible thinkers. This kind of mental flexibility allows you to connect with your cognitive rhythm.

So if, on a particular day, you have to cook, clean, lead a team discussion at work, complete a report, and meet your best friend, allow your personal shopper to help you find ways to simplify your life by connecting things for you. You just have to ask yourself out loud, "How are all these things connected?"

FILTERING DISTRACTIONS AND ELIMINATING INTERRUPTIONS

When you supertask, you have to manage distractions. They have the potential to stop the flow of your focus/unfocus choreography and bring about cognitive mayhem rather than cognitive rhythm. The key to managing them is to develop a filter—a way to identify distractions and lose them!

In 2010, brain researchers Todd Kelley and Steven Yantis found that it is possible to train attention to filter out distractions. Stuff still comes at you, but once you've learned Kelley and Yantis's techniques, you can filter out what does not belong and allow in what does.

In their experiment, they showed people a square, but it was not made of four lines. Rather, each line was a series of dots, and the space within the square was filled by dots as well. Some of the dots were red, and others green. Participants had to quickly determine whether the red or green dots were more numerous. Meanwhile, distracting images surrounded the square, making it more difficult to concentrate. However, when the participants were trained to concentrate by practicing attending only to the square over and over again, they did much better in their red-or-green-dominant determinations.

The middle frontal gyrus, a chunk of tissue on the left and right sides of your frontal lobe, midway between the top and the bottom, is the part of the brain that you can train to be a filter.

You can filter distractions in two ways: proactively and reactively. With proactive filtering, you prepare to ignore anticipated distractions. This is what Kelley and Yantis taught their subjects to do. With reactive filtering, you swat aside unexpected distractions as you encounter them. You need energy and brain resources for both. So rather than tensely completing each task on your multitasking list, you limit the intensity of focus so that you have the energy to flexibly deal with unanticipated distractions.

Inhibiting irrelevant information can allow you to achieve greater brain synchrony of alpha and beta waves. Focus and unfocus waves become more aligned. Filtering out distractions literally activates cognitive rhythm. So it's useful to consciously label your distractions in your day. If you're kept from your work by the regular *ding* of your Facebook feed—a modern-day distraction, to be sure—you can anticipate the noise and remind yourself that the *ding* is a distraction that will keep you from your work. Or better yet, turn the sound off on your phone so you're not aware of the notification. In so doing, you free up attentional resources to be able to supertask.

Not all distractions are created equal. Some, better described as interruptions, can't be filtered out in the same way. In 2010, neuroscientist Wesley Clapp and his colleagues found that distraction occurs when you're presented with irrelevant stimuli. Suppose you're reviewing an important email at work, when your sister sends you a funny cat video. That's a distraction, irrelevant to the current email—you can save it for later or never. But suppose your boss sends you an urgent email about a new deadline. That's an interruption, because it requires your attention, and you need to take care of it.

Distractions and interruptions have unique impacts on your brain. While both can shake up your short-term memory cup, making you forget what just happened, interruptions are far worse than distractions. Distractions disrupt the connection between the middle frontal gyrus and the seeing brain (visual cortex), but they don't obliterate it, so your brain still remembers whatever you were doing, and you can come back to it easily. When you're interrupted, however, switching tasks derails you, and this connection falls apart. Although distractions can reduce your productivity if you do not tag and filter them, interruptions can be even more disruptive.

Nobody can stop all interruptions to their day, but sometimes you have to make it a priority to eliminate interruptions that are not on your supertasking list. To do this, label your tasks "interruption-free" if they are, and engage in them in places and ways that will reduce the likelihood of distraction and interruption (e.g., don't just turn down the volume of the dinging phone—turn it off for a while). As a doctor, I protect the time I allot to filling out medication prescriptions. Same thing for when I'm driving somewhere new. For me (and my patients, in the first example), answering the phone or talking to others could be disastrous.

Putting It All Together for Easy, Breezy Supertasking

As with any area in which you want to improve, it helps to dedicate some time every day to practicing supertasking techniques. Suppose you set aside time each morning to get yourself into a supertasking frame of mind. Practicing all the techniques I outlined above might take about half an hour. You don't have to do them all at once, of course, and you may not want to do one or two of them at all. But whatever amount of time you give over to unfocusing will repay your efforts by enhancing your ability to supertask.

As you explore your supertasking capabilities, keep two ideals in mind:

THE HAPPY, PLAYFUL JUGGLER

If you're used to being methodical and sequential, juggling may seem like a nightmare. Just the thought of it may make you break into a sweat. Yet your brain is wired for juggling tasks, so why not use part of every day to find and train that part of yourself?

Start with being playful. Metaphorically, you should not look to your juggling with dread. Rather, be the one who juggles in the square with a smile on his face and a hat at his feet, expecting that people will reward you for your efforts. It's all about dissolving the stress in alpha!

Contrary to what we think, play helps your brain become less distracted. In fact, in animals, play helps the frontal lobe of the brain mature. Also, when (human) children play, it helps them become less impulsive and inhibits random behavior.

In 2007, neuroscientist Jaak Panksepp suggested that ADHD might occur as a result of children not playing enough. He explained that play—of the rough-and-tumble or fantasy variety, not play dates and organized sports—has a vital role in regulating the brain and allowing children to focus. You could call it an attitude of inventiveness. He also pointed out that our "no child left behind" curricula emphasize regimented functions like arithmetic, writing, and reading, at the expense of natural play. Play is to education what unfocus is to cognitive rhythm.

Pretend or forced play does not help. Instead, play should satisfy a basic need to survive and grow. If it doesn't, you will become more obsessive and distressed. But if you have a passion for your chosen game, it will improve your well-being.

Some people feel that life is serious, and there is no time for play. Life can certainly feel that way when you have work to do and bills to pay. But in this context, seriousness amounts to worry, and worry is rarely as necessary as we think it is. In fact, people often worry in order to create a buffer when something negative happens. The emotional switch from worry to sadness or loss is smaller than the more precipitous shift from happiness to sadness. That being the case, why not learn to manage the switch, rather than prevent yourself from enjoying the playfulness and happiness that you can?

Somewhat paradoxically, the serious philosopher Plato offered one of the best-known definitions of play. He described it as "those natural modes of amusement which children find out for themselves when they meet." Play is discovered, invented, enjoyed, and then made into a pattern until the children run out of steam. Run out of steam though they may, children are still more likely to stay engaged in play than in the drudgery of homework. Children constantly reinvent this kind of play with local feedback, tinkering with different aspects of the game they are playing. And they dabble in different forms of playing until the game is exactly what they want it to be. Try interrupting a child's game when he or she is engaged in it. You'd have a better chance scaring an intruder by making a funny face!

If you're a leader, you can infuse the mentality of play at work. If you're a homemaker, you can add this mentality to chores. Either way, finding a path to playfulness can lighten the burden of the tasks at hand. You don't have to fake a playful attitude. Find the right fit for you, the way children try out a few different games before they settle on one.

THE OPTIMISTIC CRUISER

Ryan Seacrest dropped out of the University of Georgia because he felt he really needed to follow his heart and give Hollywood a try. As he said to his parents, "I'd like to give it a shot. But if I'm not supporting myself within one year, I'll come back to school." So he packed his Honda Prelude and drove 2,300 miles to Hollywood. He hasn't looked back since.

What made Seacrest decide to drop out of school to make his life a success when the majority of people struggle to find their way forward? It probably wasn't just a rational decision. He admitted that it was about *trying*—testing out a hunch. He planned to return if it did not work out.

Hunches can be like tailwinds that propel you forward fast. Once you learn how to fly, supertasking will be that much easier.

Initially, your hunch may be vague and unclear. But it doesn't have to stay that way. Examine it more closely, tinker with it, and it will shake off the dust, reduce the vagueness, and give you more data to consider.

In 2011, psychologist Arie Kruglanski explained that learning to examine hunches is an art. Your unconscious brain has a set of rules that it follows, which are really tinker tools, formally called *inferential devices*. When you don't know what to do, you can mimic these mental tools consciously.

Put yourself in Ryan Seacrest's shoes. You do not know the possibility or probability of your success in Hollywood. One tool you could use is to categorize the decision: How important is it? Would you regret not trying this move? And you could estimate the consequences. In the worst-case scenario, you'd lose a year of school, but you'd probably also learn a lot about yourself and about life. When your brain registers, *This is important—I will regret not trying—there's not much to lose,* it will quickly make a decision that you're not even aware of, and it will start planning your path forward and look for ways to reach your goal faster.

Of course, your brain has lots of other rules like associations or comparisons with the past. But as Kruglanski points out, rational and intuitive thinking use the same rule systems, and they work hand in hand in the brain. The key is to have an "optimizing" attitude that drives your intuition to find the right rational rules. You aim for the finish line with grit and determination, learning all along the way by pleasurably tinkering. When you do this with a positive mood, it will make your intuition that much more accurate.

To further understand this concept of optimization, think of a baseball or cricket player who has to run to catch a flying ball. As he chases the ball, he adjusts his speed, looks at the ball, and prepares to catch it all at the same time. When he does catch it, it's because he and the ball were always connected despite its changing speed and his own changing speed and position. He's not cal-culating the trajectory or running ahead to where he thinks the ball will land. (That would be a mental distraction, which, if he tried it in practice, he could tag and ignore subsequently.) He fol-lows it until he catches it. No book can guarantee that he will catch the ball. Only repeated practice can help him know how fast to run, how much to slow down, and how to connect his gaze with the catch. As he runs, his brain calculates that he might miss the ball, so he slows down—but if he slows down too much, his brain has him speed up again. Each adjustment is a part of the optimiza-tion strategy.

We marvel at these moments because they involve rational ac-tions like a cupped hand, and intuitive actions like speeding up or slowing down. They both happen at the same time. This is cogni-tive rhythm in action, and it's supertasking too. Learning to make quick adjustments to fine-tune your hunches may even become your primary strategy when you're learning to thrive in a super-tasking world. When you apply unconscious rules and optimiza-tion strategies, you know full well that you could drop the ball. But you will eventually learn to become comfortable with the course correction and focused execution without feeling sick to your stomach due to your supertasking speed.

The supertasking mindset requires many steps, so you have to be careful not to overwhelm yourself. As with the other chapters, let the information in this one wash over you, and then come back to institute one or two things first. The table below summarizes the major mindset shifts that apply to supertasking. Use this guide when you want to check in quickly about changes that you could add to your life.

Focused Mindset	Unfocused Mindset Shift
Take a serious and focused attitude when supertasking.	Be more playful and self-forgiving as you start to supertask.
It matters most to stay alert, conscious, and focused on the tasks at hand.	Practice relaxing into your automaticity from time to time— explore your unconscious frequently by doodling.
Be superrational as you plan.	Practice being intuitive and see if tasks can be joined to be done at the same time.
Complete tasks as you initially planned.	Do tasks when they best fit into your day and provide local feedback as you do so.
You can learn to supertask only by thinking more clearly.	Moving, functional exercises, and video games can all help to develop your supertasking brain.

GETTING UNSTUCK

What we usually consider impossible are nothing but engineering problems . . . there's no law of physics preventing them.

—Michio Kaku

February in Boston can be quite depressing. The promise of the
New Year has worn off, and the cold has taken its toll. The roads
are an ugly mix of sand and slush, and you can't really get anywhere without having to negotiate snow banks, black ice, and
crawling highway traffic. If you've lived here awhile, February
gives you an excuse to kvetch about something—if not the weather,
then life in general. Yet as I sat across from Jackie during her therapy hour, the tone in her voice signaled more than the customary
winter blues.

"I feel exasperated," she protested. "I don't know how I ended
up here, working like a dog, lugging around groceries, and endlessly driving the kids to their activities. My life feels like a stuck
record. My husband is a good man, but our relationship has
reached an all-time low. We're just stagnating. I don't even do
things I really love—playing the piano, gardening, or even walking on the beach. And to cap it all, I think I've hit the glass ceiling
at work. How did I become a prisoner in my own life?"

Jackie's story was familiar to me—I had heard many versions of it over the years. Regardless of the context, routines—once comforting and safe—can gradually become ruts. Stability in your relationship, once a prized goal, can become a buzzkill. The monotony of even a secure and somewhat fulfilling job can wear you down (and not just in February!). As a result, you procrastinate more than usual. You feel ambivalent and therefore have a hard time making decisions. A general lack of motivation often leads to unhealthy lifestyle choices—eating junk food, sleeping less, stressing more—which only make you feel worse, more stuck. It's a vicious cycle. Nobody is immune.

Regardless of how we're stuck, when we hit that breaking point, we try to jolt ourselves out of our doldrums by various constructive and destructive means. In a marriage, we might introduce romantic date nights or have an affair. The individual feeling generally stymied might make an effort to find "me time" or "work-life balance" without knowing what the best me time or balance actually is. At work, you might try to avoid contentious situations and just try to do your job well, or you might quit. Some of these strategies may work for a while, but because they are static solutions—singularly focused on prioritization, recalibration of duties, or hunkering down—you get mentally exhausted quickly.

Furthermore, these attempts at steadfast focus usually don't last. In every case, you're trying to change using conscious strategies against a far stronger unconscious pull. There's no point in Jackie having a date night when her intuition has given her the sinking feeling that her marriage is going down. Work-life balance lasts until the next hurricane of tasks sweeps you off your feet. And hunkering down to get the job done is useless if you take two steps back for every step forward.

In all these scenarios, a focused mind rarely brings lasting and authentic solutions. Eventually your stuck mind returns to conveyor belt mode, moving your psychological baggage around and around; the more you focus on the problems you're facing, the more stuck you might actually get.

Of course, stuckness isn't always about big, life-altering dead ends. It can also manifest in small ways. You can't conjure up a specific word you need when you're in midsentence or remember a name when you run into someone. It's on the tip of your tongue, but it just won't come. Your mind seems frozen.

Neurologically, setting aside early Alzheimer's or a minor stroke, what's happening when you can't remember a word or a name is similar to what's happening when you feel malaise or stagnation in your life. Intensely focusing on remembering it rarely does the trick—instead you often end up feeling *more* at a loss for the word or name! Like a fly furiously and repeatedly butting against a closed window, your mind is stuck. Searching for a way out is futile. As your angst escalates, your brain's cacophony reaches an all-time high. (You may remember from Chapter 2 that this is a hallmark of writer's block too, but that's a creative issue.)

Then minutes or hours later the word or name pops into your head. It seems miraculous, but known psychological and neurological processes have actually brought it to the fore. And what's more, those processes—the cascade of small psychological and neurological shifts—are reproducible. The fly needs you to open the window for it, and figuratively you can do that for yourself as well.

THE POSSIBILITY MINDSET

Empowering your mind to get unstuck begins with shifting perspective.

Instead of thinking about your predicament—which will only incite anger, anxiety, or sadness—you need to get more emotionally neutral (unfocused) about your situation. I call this *shifting to the possibility mindset*. When you can't find a word or a name, sometimes just releasing yourself from the focus on coming up with it, the *need* to find it, and allowing yourself to believe that it'll come to you any minute is enough to jog the word or name into view. That's the possibility mindset in action.

Possibility is the proverbial key to the ignition of your mind; you can't drive (to your destination, unstuckness) without it. When you have a possibility mindset, you actually increase your brain opioids, relax and reward your brain, and make it more possible to move. You can't move against the resistance of a belief in impossibility.

When I recommended this to Jackie, she rolled her eyes. "I don't want some super optimistic nonsense that's all inspiration, no destination," she said doubtfully. The vice president of human resources at a large corporation, she felt some urgency to get back on track or get on another one—she had neither the time nor the patience for platitudes.

Steer Your Brain Toward Possibility

Manufactured optimism is, by definition, false. False optimism tells you to "look on the bright side" or reassures you that "things are going to get better." Authentic optimism, by contrast, comes from a subtle shift in your self-messaging: you simply tell yourself, "getting unstuck *is possible*." That small tweak of phrasing significantly alters the message and begins to galvanize your brain toward change. Just as, after buying a white car, you suddenly start seeing white cars, when you "buy" this message, your brain will look for things consistent with the possibility of a solution. Such *attention shifting* is simply steering the brain in another direction.

So say it out loud, say it to yourself, but send this message somehow. Let this new message capture your brain's attentional network and begin to work its magic.

Your stay in the possibility mindset will not be uninterrupted, of course. You'll have moments of doubt and foggy patches—times when just relaxing your brain into the idea of possibility seems too structureless and free-floating. When you're feeling that way, you'll revert to focusing on what is right in front of you. But your earlier efforts to imagine possibility will not have been for nothing: when the fog clears, you may be able to look further ahead; your ability to relax into possibility will also be incrementally improved and useful when you encounter the next foggy patch.

"Buying" into this idea is a process; it doesn't happen overnight. Once possibility steers you in a new direction, you may still need to take steps to calm and neutralize the anger, anxiety, or sadness you've been feeling.

To get your feelings under control, you can try *affect labeling,* a fancy term for naming feelings. Look at your anger, frustration, or sadness from as many angles as you can, and try to describe it accurately. Jackie, when she got mad, rather than stewing, learned to say out loud, "I'm really angry." And when she was anxious, rather than sighing in frustration, which just made her more anxious, she learned to call her anxiety out. Naming your feelings may seem like a child's strategy, but it serves a very sophisticated purpose: it is effective at putting up a barrier between your brain's anxiety center, the amygdala, and your thinking brain, the prefrontal cortex. This barrier acts as a kind of ballast; by setting the course for possibility, you give yourself some protection, and your undefined emotions won't feel like a tidal wave about to consume you.

CHANGE YOUR BRAIN LENS

Affect labeling can also help you *reframe* your emotions, applying less judgmental descriptions to them. Whereas you might be flat-out angry at how stuck you're feeling, the reframed, less negative way to put it would be that you're feeling "emotional intensity gone awry." And rather than being annoyed by your frustration, you can see it as a "signal to change." This isn't only semantics. And it's different from taking a deep breath before acting or responding—common advice for calming your emotions. Taking the proverbial deep breath is an act of *suppr*ession, but introducing the idea of possibility—simply saying *getting unstuck is possible*—is *pr*ogression, or forward thinking, so to speak. And it is an all-important first step. Many studies have demonstrated that reframing emotions calms the amygdala, the brain's anxiety processor; reframing trumps suppressing them when you're trying to reduce stress.

Ask Solution-Based Questions

Armed with a new mental calmness and simply stated sense of possibility, you're ready to start asking yourself productive, solution-oriented questions. The operative phrase here is *solution-oriented*. That is, don't ask open-ended *What should I do?* questions of yourself, but shift to *How can I make this happen? What specific things can I begin to do?* Instead of asking, *How do I change my life?*, which is so daunting that it might make you feel more stuck, ask instead, *How have others successfully navigated this impasse?* By being solution-oriented, you're using focused techniques to navigate a very unfocused sense of possibility. In your brain, focus and unfocus are working together in a more productive cognitive rhythm. You don't default to either extreme.

Jackie looked around at other marriages—those she admired as well as those she thought were problematic—and also at those who had broken through the glass ceiling at work. Seeing how others had navigated these waters gave her a template to work from and tailor to her own situation.

Think of being solution-oriented as "playing to win" rather than "playing not to lose." Consider the case of my tennis hero, Serena Williams. In the 2012 U.S. Open, she was tied with Victoria Azarenka, one set each. In the third set, Serena found herself down by two games at 3–5. Victoria was looking strong, but Serena did not prepare to lose. Slowly but surely, and rather amazingly, Serena marched back from her deficit and won the last set at 7–5. In a postmatch interview, she said that rather than focusing on the high probability of losing the tournament, she shifted her mind to consider a different question: What would it take to *win*? Calculating that all she needed was twelve more points, she used possibility thinking to guide her point by point to the trophy. In other words, she switched from "probability" thinking (*what are my chances here?*) to "possibility" thinking (*twelve more points and I'm there!*).

Use Belief to Maintain the Journey

Without possibility, your brain cannot plan or learn. Believing in possibility may feel like a gamble—too much empty hope or wishful thinking—which is why many of us maintain a dose of self-protective skepticism even while giving lip service to possibility. But skepticism and doubt can lead you astray. Doubt will add to the neurological frenzy of distraction. It will make your thinking shaky. It will stymie your progress toward change. Belief, on the other hand, is a panacea to an exhausted brain. It will reenergize your thinking. In that state, your mind will have permission to live outside the norm.

REALLY?

Reality, as you see and experience it, is not written in stone. To the visionary, in fact, "realism" is a blindfold. It is an unnecessary and limiting distraction to a mind working on becoming unstuck. Your aim is to construct a vision of what you want—unrestricted, unedited, and unrestrained. You can shape it to fit reality later on. Stretching your mind outside the life that is facing you can be lifesaving. Yet even the best of us may be tempted by the reassuring lure of apparent pragmatism.

These proclamations reflect cases of succumbing to that temptation. In 1929, Irving Fisher, a Yale economist, was quoted in *The New York Times* as saying that stock prices had reached "what looks like a permanently high plateau." This was three days before the stock market crash that triggered the Great Depression. In 1957, the editor in charge of business books for Prentice-Hall said, "I have traveled the length and breadth of this country and talked with the best people, and I can assure you that data processing is a fad that won't last out the year." Following an audition by the Beatles in 1962, a Decca Records executive said to their manager, Brian Epstein, that they had no future in show business. Epstein recalled that the executive didn't like their sound, and that he believed that groups of guitars were on the way out. Fast-forward to recent years and this pattern of "expert" and "measured" predictions remains questionable too. In 2016, the majority of Brexit polls were wrong—the United Kingdom ended up separating from the European Union despite widespread predictions to the contrary. And in that same year, Donald Trump's victory over Hillary Clinton in the race for U.S. president was missed by the Upshot section of *The New York Times* and the Princeton Election Consortium, which put Mrs. Clinton's chances of winning in the 70–99 percent range.

It's tempting to believe authoritative people who are certain. Their clarity may be reassuring. But they *can* certainly be wrong!

Scientists know that a belief in the possible and a rejection of only one right answer is at the root of scientific progress. Scientists use hypotheses—by definition, the possibility of an outcome—to justify their path forward. They look at past evidence and, based on it, make a prediction about the future. Then they test their prediction with an experiment. If their hypothesis proves inaccurate, they look for why their prediction might have been wrong and go back to the drawing board. A really dedicated scientist is fueled by curiosity and the desire to find an answer. Mature scientists realize there is never a final answer. There is always more to learn. That's a key attribute of the possibility mindset.

Seemingly impossible things have been made possible by science. Smallpox, an infectious disease caused by the variola virus, is estimated historically to have killed 300 million to 500 million people. In the Elephant War in Mecca in A.D. 568, it decimated Ethiopian soldiers. In 1713, it obliterated Hottentots. In 1738, it killed off half the Cherokee Indian population. And in 1776, it wiped out a significant portion of the Continental Army.

After the discovery of a vaccine, however, smallpox declined. After World War I, most of Europe was smallpox free. After World War II, transmission was interrupted in Europe and North America. In 1950, the Pan American Sanitary Organization decided to undertake eradication of smallpox throughout the northern hemisphere. In 1959, the World Health Organization decided to eradicate it *world*wide. In 1980, smallpox was eradicated following a global immunization campaign.

What a feat—and what a dazzling example of the possibility mindset in action! Every step of the way—from discovery of the vaccine, to hemispheric and then global eradication—a declaration of possibility was followed by experiments, *trying,* and victory. It pays to expect good things and to allow the possibility mindset to pave the way for further actions.

When your brain expects good things, this positive belief leads to a feeling of reward and anxiety reduction. And this is not just wishful thinking—it's actual physiology. In 2007, psychologist Tor D. Wager and his colleagues at the University of Colorado showed that when you expect pain relief from a pill, a placebo releases opioids, the pain-relieving neurochemicals in your brain. He and his colleagues applied uncomfortable levels of heat to participants' skin, then gave them either of two creams: a placebo cream that they were told was pain-relieving, and a control cream that they were told had no effect. In fact, the two creams were identical. In those who received the placebo cream—and so expected pain relief—their brains were bathed in natural opioids.

A 2015 study led by pre-med researcher Sonya Freeman further illustrated this point. Participants were given three tubes of the same cream to relieve physical pain. One was labeled "lidocaine," so they expected pain relief; one was labeled "capsaicin" (the active ingredient in chili peppers), so they expected the pain to get worse; and the third was labeled "neutral," so they expected neither positive nor negative effects. Freeman and her team found that in people who expected worsened pain, the brain regions that process "disgust" and "anxiety" were activated. However, in those who expected relief, the brain's reward center was activated. It pays to believe—physiologically.

Stay True to Yourself

A crucial ingredient in adopting the possibility mindset is being true to yourself. Persistence is important, but persistence for its own sake—because you believe that it will get you to your goal—is about as effective as false optimism.

Whether on the home front or at work, when you choose authenticity over goal-focused pitching, you inspire people to meet you where *you* are. The difference is subtle, but the combination is winning. Being mindful of your audience—the spouse or business colleagues you are trying to convince—will help you adapt your message to be of greatest interest to them. But without an authentic message in the first place, it's easy to fumble or end up where you don't belong or even where you really don't want to be.

Especially when you're frustrated, it's tempting to adopt someone else's message or, worse, a canned mantra like "I deserve better" or "I don't need to tolerate this." Yet there is always something slightly disempowering about these insistences. I call them *emotional pouting*. They do not come from authentic pride.

In 2010, psychologist Charles S. Carver and a colleague asked students at the University of Miami to fill out multiple questionnaires related to pride, missed goals, and self-control. The study measured two kinds of pride: authentic pride—where a person feels a genuine sense of accomplishment or a heartfelt desire for something—and hubristic pride, which comes from arrogance or self-importance ("pouty" pride). Participants with greater authentic pride reported themselves able to feel energized happiness when they achieved a goal, and their responses revealed that they had greater self-control and control over their attention. People with hubristic pride were angrier and impulsive.

When you get what you want, your brain feels rewarded, and its reward system activates. But this reward system has two parts—one registers rewards that come from within, called *intrinsic rewards,* and the other registers rewards from others, or *extrinsic rewards.* When your pride is authentic, you get an intrinsic reward. You stop focusing entirely on external benchmarks and on other people for pats on the back, or for anything else you want, and rely more frequently on your own sense of accomplishment and pleasure as your beacon. Hankering after extrinsic rewards (compliments, money, promotions, gifts) can undermine your brain's intrinsic reward system—it activates less, and the good feelings you get from the extrinsic rewards are not as long-lasting.

When you're in possibility mode—moving forward bit by bit as your goal becomes clearer—you have to find a way to stay committed to your path despite great uncertainty. During times of uncertainty, the intrinsic reward system—feeling good and true to yourself—will keep you on track. Intrinsic rewards are your brain's compass under such conditions. But you can't be in uncertainty mode the whole time. From time to time, you will necessarily revert to and rely on old behavioral and psychological habits. That's where extrinsic rewards play a role. Getting praise or a raise can feel very good indeed, and even advantageous, but the moment things become less certain, the praise and the raise lose their power and may even turn your intrinsic motivation off. You can *focus* on external rewards, then *be guided* by internal rewards. Switching back and forth between both is cognitive rhythm in action.

It's a little like going for a jog. You may like the extrinsic reward of appearing healthy, but the jog needs to help you *feel* healthier today, for the goal of "health" to be motivating over the long term. Both intrinsic and extrinsic rewards can orient and motivate you to get to your goals. The key is to strike a rhythm between the two and to check in with yourself from time to time to assess your real level of satisfaction.

Understanding authenticity and internal rewards was important for Jackie to get unstuck. She started to speak from her heart. She suspended the need to convince her husband and her boss to help her and shifted instead to a heartfelt understanding of what she truly wanted. She learned that when the brain is stuck, the heart will come to the rescue.

In therapy, Jackie allowed herself—in fits and starts—to look away from her stuckness and embrace the idea that things could be different. Freed up to imagine and invent a future in her mind, her zigzag train of thought led to unexpected realizations and convictions. She would have missed memories and feelings that were tucked away if she had focused only on what was obvious. In one session, she talked about how she wanted her husband to be more engaged in their marriage, but then she reflected on the fact that her life in general felt increasingly devoid of passion. And in seemingly unrelated nostalgia, she recollected how she had climbed the ladder at work much faster than she had anticipated. It wasn't because of some kind of strategy or external goal. It was because she was driven from within.

As she talked, she began to realize that her relationship, money, and work issues were really not her primary concerns. The thing she most cared about was reigniting that spark within *herself.* Your spark is your greatest ally when you can find it. It is the best guiding light you could have. As the Carver study above found, it gives you more self-control.

Fully in the possibility mindset, Jackie had transcended the distraction of specific unhappiness. Instead, she started to get inspired—filled with purpose and autonomy. Her mind was no longer stuck. It was intent on wandering further, ready to explore the field of possibilities that unfocusing had ushered into her life.

YOUR MIND AGLOW

To imagine what is happening in your brain when your mind wanders, think of the default mode network that we discussed in Chapter 1. Imagine the DMN is an octopus curled up into a ball. Releasing focus makes it glow, a phenomenon we can actually see in functional brain imaging studies.

The DMN aglow reaches out its "tentacles" to connect with the tentacles in the past (your memory bank brain) and future (your visionary brain). These "tentacles" are nerve fibers that connect brain cells in different regions. The more you unfocus, the brighter the glow, and the better your recollection of the past and imagination of the future.

When the past, present, and future join "tentacles," your life makes more sense because your identity—your internal story about yourself—is less disjointed. And information starts to flow spontaneously. This flow of information is called *autonoetic consciousness*—think of it as spontaneous thoughts or automatic knowledge.

When you're stuck, spontaneous thoughts are such a welcome intrusion. They are a sign that you have activated your un-conscious brain. And that's a good thing.

Your conscious brain processes information at sixty bits per second at best. Your unconscious brain crunches information much, much faster—some have said at eleven million bits per second. Despite the debate over the actual number, most experts would agree that the unconscious brain is a much, much faster processor. It works under the radar, but it forages for data that your conscious, focused brain won't find.

FIFTY SHADES OF COGNITIVE GRAY

The downside to having such a turbo-boosted unconscious brain is that it is prone to jumping ahead of the logic of your conscious brain. In these instances, your unconscious brain can be less ac-curate too. As determined, passionate, and possibility-oriented as Jackie now was, the big leaps that she made sometimes spooked her. Indeed, the questions she started to ask herself—When would she confront her boss? What if she and her husband could not resolve their conflicts?—showed that she had unleashed possibil-ity and was tapping into her authentic desires, but the ramifica-tions were also unsettling.

Especially after Jackie developed confidence with her initial progress, an all-or-nothing attitude was alluring, yet intimidating to her. It's fine to want to "go big or go home" and confront situ-ations head-on. There's a time and place for that. But black-and-white thinking can sometimes be all show and no substance—and it can be too much, too fast. When you're stuck, the answers often lie in the many shades of gray—in minor tweaks in your thinking rather than a complete overhaul. You don't have to pursue every possibility that your wandering mind produces. You can tinker with the options, mull them over, and modify them. That's a spirit, as well as a process of doing things.

Tinkering as Spirit

As journalist Alec Foege writes, "Contrary to popular opinion, most great American innovations have been happy accidents made by serial dilettantes and dreamers, not trained engineers or professionals." He points to Benjamin Franklin—who invented the lightning rod, bifocals, the Franklin stove, the odometer, and the U.S. Postal Service—and Thomas Edison, who spent enormous amounts of time trying to find the right combination of materials to make a lightbulb. Perhaps their tinkering mentality, Foege says, came from the rich pioneering American *spirit* of their era.

American or not (and of course there are countless examples of innovation through a tinkering mentality from around the globe), what's interesting about this observation is the idea that tinkering is a spirit in addition to a process. Common to all people who invent things or plan cities or build websites is a pioneering spirit—an embrace of tinkering and possibility. It's not that planning is not part of their process, it's that the plans are not untouchable. They are open for tinkering and change, small or large.

Jackie's tinkering spirit came from her curiosity and her urge to make her life better. It came from a spirit of nonacceptance of life at face value. Even when she was down, she would say, "My friends all tell me that my life is great and I should just get over my silliness. But I don't see it that way. I feel that it's helpful to wonder about how I can make my life better, even if I don't immediately know how. Just this openness has kept me going."

That's the spirit of tinkering. And it's the type of spirit you can find in yourself if you start out with possibility thinking.

THE POWER OF ITERATION

In 2011, Nassim Taleb, professor of risk engineering at New York University, described why "tinkering outperforms design." Contrary to the concept of intelligent engineering, wherein you focus on building (a business, a technology, a recipe, a marriage) with a fixed plan, tinkering allows you to find unexpected solutions and to respond to unexpected surprises. This, he explains, is the basis of modern technological inventions: each version was designed to improve on the prior and to beat the competition as well. In fact, Taleb regards tinkering as the basis of "antifragility"—the ability to remain resilient and relevant in an ever-changing world. You remain flexible and change with the times.

Tinkering as a Process

Switching from focusing on your problem to seeding the idea of possibility involves many complex processes, but unfocus is necessary to help your brain stay on track in the possibility mindset. Rather than thinking no solution is in sight, you replace "not knowing" with a new *hypothesis:* a solution is possible! You activate your *imagination* to design possible experiments to discover a solution. Along the way, you may abandon an experiment because it's not working out—as when Jackie tried talking to her husband about work and all he did was give her advice rather than listen. Or you may see a better way of addressing the problem—as when Jackie realized that she needed to revisit what she truly wanted out of work at a deeper level, to see what she might be willing to give up, so that she could approach her boss with greater conviction.

When you experiment like this with thoughts, you're tinkering with them. And when you're imagining solutions, you're tinkering and unfocused too. In 2013, brain researcher Luigi F. Agnati and his colleagues explained that imagination is a result of tinkering with old ideas and thoughts based on unique experiences to create newly recombined ideas. Switching tracks between one experiment and another, or going back and forth to old ideas before you find the right ones, is an unfocused process.

Think of it this way: every skyscraper was first an idea, then a sketch, and then a formal design. At each of those essential stages, there were redrafts and adjustments along the way. To reach the heights of your own life—to become unstuck—learning how to become an intelligent tinkerer is indispensable. A tinkerer's path is not wild meandering; it's well-considered freedom. Tinkering with your planned course of action is always wise, and tinkering along the course is probably even wiser.

Tinkering with possibility—with a number of ideas for the future—is like "thought sketching" until you get the picture right. When you're afraid to take big leaps, you can and should examine the fear that the big leaps inspire. A big leap will feel more manageable if you tinker with smaller, incremental steps.

It's not just about taking small steps, though—it's also about looking at things from as many angles as possible and indulging your curiosity. Curiosity activates your cognitive rhythm. It takes you out of focused goal-*targeting* into unfocused goal-*discovery*.

In 2012, cognitive psychologist Marieke Jepma and colleagues conducted a study to see what happens to brain blood flow when participants are curious. The researchers induced curiosity by showing them blurry pictures that aroused curiosity, then analyzed their brain blood flow. Later, they relieved the participants' curiosity by showing them what those pictures actually were—and again did brain blood flow analysis. Then they compared the analyses.

In the state of curiosity, they found, blood flows to brain regions that process arousal and conflict. Relieving the curiosity activates the ventral striatum—an intrinsic reward center. When your tinkering is fueled by curiosity, you are in unfocused, activated search mode, and when it is relieved by focused discovery, you feel good again. Each act of curiosity—tinkering with a single question at a time—gives rise to a short-term reward when you resolve it. Building in short-term rewards in this way can be motivating and gives you the energy to make it through the day.

There is no one-size-fits-all solution for stuckness. The possibility mindset will empower your wandering mind, but tinkering with the ideas and feelings it stirs up is the most productive way to consider your options.

STRATEGIC MENTAL MEANDERING

Figuratively and literally, unfocus works its magic on your mental patterns best when you strategically set aside time to let your mind wander. Many successful people have built what I call *strategic mental breaks or meanderings* into their lives at times when they're lost or stuck.

Steve Jobs, founder of Apple and Pixar, never completed college. He said he "decided to drop out and trust that it would all work out okay." Notice that he trusted—that is, he had a sense of possibility. In 1974, he spent time at an ashram in India, meditating, ruminating, and walking around nearby villages. In 1976, he founded Apple.

When Facebook hit a rough patch in 2008, founder Mark Zuckerberg followed Jobs's advice. He took time off to mull over the future of the company. After that he turned around his fortune.

Bill Gates still takes a secluded "think week" twice a year to ponder the future of technology. In one week in 1995, he was inspired to write a paper, "The Internet Tidal Wave," that led Microsoft to develop its Internet browser and beat out its competitor, Netscape.

Successful visionaries understand the benefit of taking a break to chew on ideas. When you let go of focus, amazing things happen in your brain. Your wandering mind becomes a detective in search of more elusive thoughts. It helps you put two and two together, when prior to that you were stuck. A wandering mind in a state of inspired possibility is actively in search of something. You don't get in its way. But you don't have to be a capital-V visionary, drop out of school, or go to an exotic destination to muse on things. You can activate your visionary capabilities right where you are.

UNDERSTANDING YOUR PERSONAL
NOOKS AND CRANNIES

As energizing as it can be to tinker with your thoughts and explore them from many angles, you may lose steam after the initial burst of excitement. Especially if you feel you're going nowhere fast, you may want to give up believing and simply do something more "realistic" or "concrete." This is understandable—nobody wants a brain that is aroused and conflicted 24/7. It's not that pleasant. You need an intrinsic reward so that you can feel energized to pursue your goals even when the solution is not obvious. You have to refuel your brain so that more of *you* is present.

Just by mentioning the word *present,* I had Jackie's eyeballs rolling skeptically. But a brilliant paper about how the mind works, by philosophers Bryce Huebner and Robert D. Rupert, gave me the means to keep her engaged.

Fundamentally, Huebner and Rupert explain how people motivate themselves to get from point A to point B. A goal may be what you aim for, but it does not by itself motivate you. Jackie, for instance, could not maintain in her head a motivating picture of what her relationship and work life could look like. The goal was too vague to motivate her. You can be motivated by some sense of tangible personal reward, as in the jogging example, but often even that is not enough to *be* motivated.

Instead, to pursue *your* goals, *you* have to show up to life—to be present as fully as you can be. And when I say "present," I'm not referring to the level of your attention. I'm referring to the number of "self" circuits that are activated in your brain. A critical number must be activated for you to be motivated to keep going.

Goals activate your beliefs and your past—metaphorically, they hang up pictures in the gallery of your brain's memory centers, bringing as much of you "online" as possible. When enough of the right pictures are hanging, you feel juiced. When there aren't enough or the pictures are a mixture of things you like and dislike about yourself, you may feel uninspired. I call the right number of representations that you need to feel juiced *critical psychological mass* (CPM). CPM is the minimum number of facets of you that need to be alive for you to feel motivated to do something. And they're not always obvious.

For Jackie, one representation meant restarting piano lessons. At first you might ask what piano lessons had to do with Jackie's current goals. The answer—everything. When *you* want to reach a *goal*, it is not just the goal that matters—you matter too. For Jackie, the absence of music in her life made her feel psychologically numb. Resuming piano lessons added the inspiration that she needed to tinker with other, unrelated goals. When I first met her, I thought her longing for piano playing was a side-thought of little significance. But when she talked about how playing the piano used to make her feel, I realized that this dormant part of her was a powerful force that truly moved her. More important, it was a part of who she was—without it, she felt less energized.

There are umpteen vice presidents of human resources in large corporations who are married with two children. But there was only one Jackie. Similarly, regardless of your age, race, job, and family situation, there is only one you. When you're trying to honor the complexity of your originality, the small puzzle pieces of your past matter. The devil is in the details. And tinkering is the only mental tool small enough to get into the nooks and crannies that make up all of you.

The smell of your grandmother, that crisp fall day when you played ball with your dad, the shame that you felt when you brought home your fifth-grade report card, the joy of a cue stick in your hand, and the thrill of losing yourself in a game of Power Rangers are all memories that are stored in your brain but inaccessible to a focused mind. Tinkering unearths this nostalgia. It allows your predictive brain to use your memories to fill in the gaps in your mental picture of yourself so that it can construct a different picture of your future. It also makes you feel more complete and whole. This authenticity fuels your path forward.

When possibilities start to reveal themselves to you—the byproduct of letting your mind wander—you necessarily develop version 1.0 of your plan, then update it as you discover more. This planned development and revision is a form of tinkering. It pays to allow the process to unfold over time. Think of it as savoring a piece of quality chocolate. As the square melts in your mouth, subtle and delightful flavors emerge. You would miss them if you gulped the chocolate down in one or two quick bites. Similarly, savoring your thoughts can reveal subtle information. The key is not to be discouraged by your 1.0 plan if it doesn't hit all targets. Have you ever compared how an old landline looks compared to a smartphone? It's hard to believe that one form led to the other, but it did.

You don't have to obsess about being perfect either. The less you obsess about the tinkering, the more likely you will proceed with speed to the first version of your solution. You will learn for the next version, and then you will feel even less stuck. When you regard every decision as a version that precedes the next, imperfection matters less. Life is more like playing with Legos than a concrete construction. You can move stuff around.

As Jackie tinkered with her options, she got better at pinpointing them over time. When she concluded she should talk to her boss, she didn't jump to do it. She deliberated over it. Soon she realized that she would be better served if she were armed with more information. How fast were others promoted? Were men at an advantage? How much were others paid? Would her promotion help or hurt others?

Before she learned to tinker, she had thought of opening that conversation with "I'd like to talk to you about a raise." After tinkering with other possible scenarios, she opened the conversation with "I've observed a pattern of who is being promoted. I'd love to understand if I'm correct in recognizing that I fit the criteria."

Lao Tzu once said, "When I let go of what I am, I become what I might be." Possibility is about being and letting go; tinkering is the process of becoming. Jackie's tinkering allowed her to become more informed, self-assured, confident, and motivated. She worked up the nerve to talk to her boss, and the result was positive. She got the raise!

Since she was on a roll, she thought she'd approach her husband, Bob, next, about improving their marriage. But when she broached the subject, he thought that she was being unrealistic. He was already pulling twelve-hour days. Shifting gears and pandering to some Hollywood ideal of a youthful romance seemed ridiculous to him, when they were both working so hard to save for their kids' college education. She partly agreed. So she left that discussion disillusioned and about to give up.

I reminded her that this was his first response. What if it were not his final one?

MAKING LEMONADE FROM LEMONS—
NEUROLOGICALLY

Most people—and certainly most corporations—prepare for errors by trying to prevent them. When we do this, however, we miss the potential upside of errors, the things we can learn from them and the way we can use them to transform our lives.

Have you ever forgotten a piece of cheese in the fridge that subsequently became moldy? Or perhaps you let the dishes pile up in the sink, only to find some strange green stuff growing on them? Your natural instinct was probably to block your nostrils and throw the cheese out, right? And if you didn't throw the dishes out, you likely quickly transferred them to the dishwasher and pressed WASH as fast as you could.

Well, thank goodness Scottish biologist Alexander Fleming was not squeamish or eager to dispose of vile and smelly things. One August, he took a vacation from his lab where he was investigating staphylococci—the kind of bacteria that 25 percent of people carry around in their noses, mouths, and anal and genital areas without much consequence. Staph, can, however, cause pus-filled acne, cellulitis, and even heart valve inflammation. When Fleming returned from his vacation, he found a strange fungus growing in the staph cultures in his lab. Rather than automatically toss the petri dishes out, he noticed with interest that the fungus had killed off the surrounding staph. This led to the discovery of penicillin. If he had seen the fungus, blocked his nose, closed his eyes, and thrown it out, we might have seen much slower progress in the treatment of infectious diseases.

And then there's another famous drug example. Angina pectoris is chest pain that arises due to blockages in the heart's arteries. The drug company Pfizer developed a pill called UK92480 to relieve this kind of chest pain. Although the drug was a hopeless failure, Pfizer noticed an interesting side effect—it seemed to cause erections. Instead of ignoring the side effect, they investigated it. Later called Viagra, the drug was approved for erectile dysfunction.

What if some side effects in your life had a use? A focused mind regards unintended consequences as irrelevant. An unfocused mind stops to think, tinker, and ponder the possible opportunities. As with Alexander Fleming and the Pfizer scientists, the possibility mindset in action is not just reactive but responsive; not just error aware but opportunity seeking—and willing to unfocus from what is right in front of your eyes.

Think of all of the things you've chalked up to a bad day and ask yourself, "What if I *didn't* throw the baby out with the bathwater?" What if you had had the inclination to metaphorically doodle while sitting with your errors? We prefer to forget our mistakes and obliterate any trace of them. Yet they may offer a fruitful opportunity.

LAUGH A LITTLE

In 2015, cognitive psychology professor Henk van Steenbergen and his colleagues conducted an experiment to examine the impact of humor on the brain. Did it affect the brain by softening the impact of stressful situations?

Participants were asked to complete a task that puts stressful demands on their thinking. In the arrow-flanker conflict task, an arrow symbol appears on the screen, pointing left or right. The participant is to press the corresponding arrow key on the keyboard as quickly as possible. However, on both sides (flanks) of the target arrow are other arrows pointing in the same or different direction. If the arrows on either side point in the same direction as the central arrow, it's easier for the brain to respond. If they are incongruous, most people need to pause to take in and sort the options, then press the key.

Prior to doing this task, participants saw neutral or funny cartoons. The investigators were trying to see if seeing something funny helps the brain.

It does. When participants saw the funny cartoon, they had to use less mental effort to get the arrows right. In the brain, humor helped the conflict detector in the frontal cortex. It dampened the demands on this brain region and allowed the brain to be more flexible.

Errors do, however, create stress, and in the process of getting unstuck, humor plays a huge role in moving on. When you're faced with what you think is a horrible mistake, it can be your greatest asset, because it allows you to think differently and often more clearly.

When Jackie next spoke to Bob, she laughed with him about how unnecessarily serious she had become. Her less intense approach made him more receptive to discussing changes, and together they devised ways to build different experiences into their lives. They didn't jump into the high-pressure date nights—command performances of romance that they seemed presently incapable of feigning (at least on a schedule). They didn't expect each other to falsely care, be deliberately intimate, or not acknowledge that they were distracted. Instead, they started small: every evening, they set aside thirty minutes to reflect on positive issues like how their marriage had improved their lives or how their kids made them proud. They also introduced a weekly "cocktail night" at home and made it into an event that even their kids inquired about by that name because they looked forward to their mocktails. Trying new things was not earth-shattering for them—nothing changed overnight—but the process of considering and living the options together made them feel more alive and connected.

And they tinkered with their successes and their failures. When the weekly cocktail night started to feel like forced fun, they switched to every other week. When their nightly chats started to feel like positive psychology hype, they decided to be more mindful and spontaneous, but not forced about their positivity. They spread it throughout the day—called each other—not every day but when the thought arose. It took a certain effort to get there, but once they realized how good this made them both feel, they did it increasingly.

"Getting real" can be the greatest dream for the busiest of couples. It relieves the pressure to be something you're not. You can also change things up from time to time. And you can laugh about the things you take too seriously in life too.

Putting It All Together to Ease the Friction

Most people listen to advice and make the corresponding changes, to little or no avail. That's because they change their thoughts and actions without changing their fundamental philosophies or belief systems.

Think of your mind as an aquarium. Your thoughts and actions are the fish; your philosophies are the "mental medium," the water, oxygen, and food that feeds those fish. You need to work on changing your mental medium before you try to change your thoughts and actions. From now on, every time you hit a wall in your life, make mental medium changes first.

SILENCE THE EXCUSE-MAKING MACHINE

In 1956, psychologist Jack Brehm conducted an experiment in which he asked people to rate the attractiveness of household appliances like an electric sandwich press, a desk lamp, a stopwatch, and a transistor radio. Many people rated two things equally. When that happened, he asked them to choose one of the two things they had rated equally to take home with them. Twenty minutes later they were asked to reevaluate the appliances. Somewhat surprisingly, they rated the gifts they had chosen to take home more highly, even though they had previously rated them the same. For example, if they had chosen to take the sandwich press home instead of a stopwatch, they downgraded the rating of the stopwatch. They convinced themselves that they had made the right choice.

In 1968, psychologist Robert E. Knox and his colleagues asked people to rate the chances of a horse winning a race. Before they bet, on average people rated the chance of winning as 3.48. After placing a two-dollar bet, the average rating was 4.81. Again, when you're invested in something, your brain considers it more important. The same principles apply to how you rate a vacation choice before and after you make it. And research actually shows that this bias can persist two or three years; you tend to remember what you value and value what you remember.

In other words, your brain is wired to rationalize or excuse your choices, and this will work against your best efforts to get unstuck. Even the thought of changing course or the slightest unfocus will cause brain chaos. The technical term is *cognitive dissonance.* Your brain rebels against change, even if it is good for you, and irrationally tries to stay stuck. Stuckness can feel safer than change.

The first step toward silencing this excuse-making machine is to simply recognize that it could be happening to you. Since self-talk in the second person will decrease your stress more effectively than in the first person, the self-talk here needs to be "You do not accept any excuses. The goal is to become unstuck."

Of course, sometimes your excuses resonate with the core of your being. You might say, "This is just not for me," deferring to your "insight" about yourself. You might rationalize the choice to accept the status quo by saying you're not a born adventurer. Thoughts like this are signs that your brain's excuse-making machine is interfering, so intervene with self-talking.

(Much research has been done to isolate and identify an "adventure" gene. While several studies have reported that a dopamine D4 receptor gene [DRD4] may be associated with novelty seeking, a slew of other studies have been unable to replicate this finding. Even when your genes contribute to this behavior, they account for only 4 to 6 percent of the total picture. Suffice it to say, if you're currently not much of an adventurer, it's not a death sentence. You're not a prisoner of your genes or your habits. You have the ability to change your mental philosophies if you so choose.)

ADD "STRESSLESS SEGMENTS" TO YOUR DAY

Stress is an undertow that pulls you away from the shore of calmness that you want to reach. It keeps you stuck in your habits. It's hard to change your thoughts, emotions, or habits when you're stressed.

Life stress rarely goes away, but you can learn to manage it better. For starters, it's helpful to set aside time that you vow to protect from your daily stress. However difficult it may be to carve out this time for yourself, know that if you can manage it, the benefits will be great. To wit: physician burnout is a growing epidemic—it's a serious consequence of stress. In 2014, internist Colin P. West from the Mayo Clinic asked physicians to take one hour of paid time off, every other week, to join a discussion group. During that time, they engaged in mindful reflection, shared experiences, and learned from one another. After nine months, their engagement, empowerment, burnout, depressive symptoms, quality of life, and job satisfaction significantly improved. The same stresses still came their way, but they felt better overall.

I know it's challenging to find an hour every month, let alone every week, but an uninterrupted, protected weekly hour is what you should try to build up to. The goal is to throw your troubles away for that hour, to take your psychological baggage off your mental conveyor belt. Whether alone or with someone you enjoy, choose an activity that is most likely to bring some calmness to your day, whether it's painting, walking the dog, or staring at the ceiling from your favorite chair.

An internist colleague recently told me a story that I found shocking. While she was talking to a patient on the phone, the patient appeared to be having a heart attack. My colleague said to her, "I think you're having a heart attack. You'd better come in." The patient politely declined because her son had an important game, her husband was coming back from a long trip, and a million other reasons. She wanted to postpone the visit to the doctor by a day at least, she said. Absurd, yes? Yet if you have built no deliberate off or stressless periods into your schedule, you too may miss the signs and absurdly undermine your health.

LIVE A BELIEF-DRIVEN LIFE

Beliefs are a biological gateway to incoming sensory information. They tend to direct your senses. Change your beliefs, and you change the things you see and hear as well.

The literature is replete with examples of illnesses appearing and disappearing based on belief. In 1988, psychologist Nicholas Spanos and colleagues did a study in which people with warts underwent hypnosis to make their warts go away. The effect of this intervention was compared with receiving a placebo as well as with no treatment. Hypnosis was associated with wart regression, especially if participants imagined it vividly.

How this works is still debated, and like most interventions, it probably doesn't work for every kind of wart or in every situation.

But more than twenty studies, some controlled and some anecdotal, have shown this effect. People who have seen it theorize that belief activates "biochemical battle strategies." Chemical messengers help immune cells kill microbe-induced warts, or they cause small arteries to be selectively constricted, cutting off the vital nutrient supply to warts. Belief has an underlying biochemistry. That's why it may also help when you're feeling stuck.

Don't be afraid to rationalize this belief to your brain—to explain (out loud or just by thinking) that you need it to reward your brain. Remind yourself of the pain relief and placebo studies that I mentioned earlier.

If one person has done what you want to do, then it's doable. At least one person who was dirt-poor has found financial freedom. Many people in the world who were single into their later years found love at last. Remember, we're not concerned with how likely it is, but whether it is possible. When you recognize this deeply, you're on your way to becoming unstuck.

LOOK TO THE HORIZON

Think of limits as horizons. Rather than letting them paralyze or deter you, keep going and tinker along the way. When you do, you'll see that like horizons, limits can shift. What seems like an end is often not so if you keep exploring.

With this concept in mind, try to think of your ideas and even your roadblocks as dots on the horizon. Know that they will shift—perhaps they'll get bigger, perhaps they'll recede—as you approach them, turn them over, and consider them as options. Take this principle to heart—take one small step a week for the first month, then twice a week for the next month. The steps don't have to be progressive or connected.

Say you want to switch jobs but can't for practical reasons.

Rather than do nothing, start looking for another job anyway, knowing full well that you're flying in the face of practicality. Spend thirty minutes browsing the Internet for job offers. This will expand your idea of what's possible and potentially stimulate your brain to consider new possibilities.

Think of how Jackie first mulled things over, went back to them, and reexamined them, even after Bob flat-out rejected her proposal to change how they spent their time together. Increase this behavior gradually over time. Think of every step as tinkering, and be a sculptor of your own life.

OPEN THE DAYDREAMING DOOR

Living a "whole brain" life means making time and space for your unconscious, which works in unfocused ways under the radar. Deliberately build waiting and wandering times into your day so you don't keep metaphorically banging your head against the wall of stuckness.

In the 1950s, Yale psychologist Jerome Singer identified three kinds of daydreaming: *positive constructive daydreaming,* a process relatively free of psychological conflict, in which you imagine things playfully, vividly, and wishfully; *guilty-dysphoric daydreaming,* driven by a combination of ambition, failure, and aggression, or by an obsessive reliving of trauma; and the kind you might call *poor attentional control,* which is typical of the anxious and those having difficulties concentrating. It's the first kind you want to shoot for—positive constructive daydreaming.

When you allow yourself to daydream, your reflections help you plan better for the future and pay attention to the multiple things your brain is processing. In addition, these daydreaming breaks give you a chance to detach from habit—a great way to start becoming unstuck.

It's vital to set aside time for mind-wandering every day. Some people do it when they first wake up—before getting up for the day. You could also daydream while staring out a window, sitting in a waiting room, or going for a walk. As paradoxical as it sounds, a life without waiting time is inefficient; your brain battery will quickly run out of life. There's no hard and fast number to easily turn to, but if you start with fifteen minutes a day and then build in fifteen to thirty minutes three or four times a day, you'll likely see a change to your level of stuckness.

If you're thinking that sixty minutes of daydreaming is far too much to schedule into your day, you're probably kidding yourself. Many studies show that we probably already spend at least half of our waking time daydreaming. Instead of letting it creep up on you, why not make it constructive by entering it into your tinker-table and doing it deliberately, at times when you're most likely to be fatigued or bored? You may need an alarm to help you remember to daydream at first. Over time, it should become second nature.

VISIT WITH YOUR HEART

Your brain's emotional centers are connected to your thinking brain. This is not as esoteric as it sounds. Think about it: If you saw a fox on a hike, your *anxiety* would make you *think* to avoid it, right? If you saw your best friend at a shopping mall at the top of an escalator, your *excitement* would make you *think* to rush to the top. When I put it this way, can you see how thinking and feeling are intricately connected? In fact, neurologist Antonio Damasio wrote an entire book on the subject called *Descartes' Error*. He asserted that neurologically it's incorrect to say, "I think, therefore I am." Instead, thinking and feeling circuits are interwoven in the brain.

Operating from your heart when your head is stuck makes good sense. (Of course, your brain is very much involved in what we call "heart" as well—it processes intuition, love, and instinct—but I'm speaking metaphorically here.) When you're lost, it's important to go back to what you truly want and believe, a place where you don't need to convince yourself of what truly elevates you.

John Cassavetes, the Greek-American film director, was regarded as one of the most influential moviemakers of our time. When asked how he decided on the movies he wanted to make (often on a shoestring budget or loans), he replied that he had a one-track mind. All he cared about was love, so he made only movies about love. Exploring love was his passion. What makes *you* feel in your element? Admit it. Embrace it.

To incorporate "heart" into your life, once a week schedule a "heart visit" to do the thing you love by yourself or with someone close to you. It doesn't have to take much time, but it's an important way to keep you on track. If your element is cooking, then set aside one evening a week to prepare something masterful or that makes you feel nostalgic. If music is your thing, make a point to play or listen to it. If you feel in your element when reading, make time for it. If writing poetry is what feeds your soul, try to write a line or two a day. The point is to do something emotional. More studies than I could ever mention now point to our emotions as guiding lights when we're lost.

During this check-in time, ask yourself, *What is my guiding philosophy? What do I truly care about? How has it changed?* Answering these questions will activate strong feelings that will help you fit together the puzzle pieces of your life.

When focus holds you captive, you're stuck. But when possibility is your compass, you can't possibly be stuck! By adding new unfocused philosophies and principles to your focused day, you can

tap into your cognitive rhythm. You will no longer be in a stale-
mate with life. In fact, life will feel less like a chore and more like
an adventurous game.

The table below summarizes the differences that focus and unfocus bring to your mindset. Refer to it when it all seems overwhelming. It's always helpful to have a bird's-eye view.

Focused Mindset	Unfocused Mindset Shift
Let external reality guide you.	Let your beliefs shape external reality.
Create strategies and execute them.	Wait within and between strategies.
Accept that life is stressful.	Make stressless periods a rule during the day.
If you can't reach your goals, think about a foolproof strategy before acting.	If you can't reach your goals, think of every new action as chipping away at the sculpture that you eventually desire.
A solid thinker is rational and goal-directed.	A solid thinker always connects with the heart as well.

FROM DISENCHANTMENT TO GREATNESS

> I think it is possible for ordinary people to choose to be extraordinary.
>
> —Elon Musk

In January 1964, a son was born to a newlywed teenage mother in Albuquerque. Barely a year and a half later, the mother decided she could not stand her inattentive and alcoholic husband, so she filed for divorce. When her son was four years old, she married a Cuban immigrant, and they moved to Houston, and when he was a teenager, to Miami. The boy never saw his biological father again.

Despite the disruptions to his childhood, the young boy was curious and driven. As a toddler, he felt he was too old to sleep in a crib, so he took it apart with a screwdriver. He rigged an electric alarm to keep his younger siblings out of his room. He made an automatic gate closer out of cement-filled tires. And from an umbrella and some tinfoil, he made a rudimentary solar cooker. Eventually, his parents made him move the clutter of his invention and experimentation to the garage, which became his laboratory. When he was twelve, he was featured in a book on "bright minds," which described him as "friendly" and "serious" but also as "not particularly gifted at leadership."

As a teenager, the boy became preoccupied with computers, and while still in high school, he started an educational summer camp with his girlfriend. Called the Dream Institute, the camp promoted creative thinking for fourth, fifth, and sixth graders. So much for not being a leader! He graduated as valedictorian of his class and went on to Princeton University and an undergraduate degree in computer science and electrical engineering. Then he held jobs at Fitel, Bankers Trust, and the investment firm D. E. Shaw, where he became the company's youngest vice president.

But the financial promise of working on Wall Street was not enough for him. The real "Dream Institute" was in his head. It had yet to emerge. So in 1994, despite his extremely lucrative career, secure job, and the promise of a big bonus, he quit and moved to Seattle. There in his garage, he began to develop software.

In July 1995 he started the online bookstore now known as an online everything store: Amazon.

Jeff Bezos would become a great devotee of books, education, and people. In 1999, he was voted *Time* magazine's person of the year. In 2008, *U.S. News & World Report* selected him as one of America's best leaders. In 2012, *Fortune* named him businessperson of the year. In 2016, *Forbes* listed him as the fourth-wealthiest person in the world, and *Harvard Business Review* named him the second-best CEO in the world.

When you think of all Bezos has achieved, it's easy to confuse "greatness" with accolades or money. But the kind of greatness Bezos embodies is about more than just accumulated wealth or power. What makes him remarkable is his faithfulness to his own vision—and his willingness to act upon it and even change his mind if the results start to go south. In fact, he is noted for saying that consistency of thought is not a particularly positive state of mind; he believes that people who get things right may even have contradictory ideas the following day. His example teaches us that greatness is not only an exceptional state of mind—it is a translation and constant iteration of that state of mind into an act of profound meaning.

Given that such profundity is often abstract or difficult to achieve, many might think that "greatness" is an artificial goal. Just the thought of aspiring to greatness may turn you off. But it's less off-putting if you think about it as rearranging your brain's cells and circuits so that you become the best that you can be—a capacity that every human being possesses. Your brain can change—and the beautiful thing is that *you* can change it.

Focus is undoubtedly part of the formula for greatness. But more important, the origin of this focus will determine your success. In this chapter, you will learn how unfocus is actually the fertile ground from which focused actions arise, and to that end, greatness is only as far from you as your willingness to build unfocus into your daily thinking.

When it comes to unfocus, it's not just "rest" and "time away" that are important. In the context of greatness, unfocus will help you express different sides of yourself, immerse yourself in a sense of purpose, examine past experience from different angles, think outside logical sequences, and imagine and then express your vision of the future. In every instance, you have to finesse your relationship with rational thought so that it is not a burdensome obstruction.

YOUR TWO-SIDED SELF

The very essence of human nature is paradoxical, and so greatness is paradoxical too. In many instances, you have to be cruel to be kind, naïve to be smart and curious, and vulnerable enough to explore the strengths that lie alongside your weaknesses. But the conventional habit of defining your identity one way or another forces you to focus on only one aspect of yourself. It's the same with defining yourself by your professional title. When you express only one side of yourself, being "great" is like trying to catch a ball with one hand tied behind your back. Focus amputates the other side of you, and your greatness.

Every story has at least two sides. For instance, the uniqueness of an original artwork is cheapened by reproductions that anyone can hang on a wall, but these replicas also allow people access to what might otherwise be unaffordable. Genetically modified foods may be toxic to the body, but they also require fewer insecticides and provide a sustainable alternative to feed the world. Capitalism, for all its associated excesses and exploitation, also provides an opportunity for economic and political freedom. And even though we complain that gadgets distract us during conversations, we revel in the connectedness that technology affords us.

More often than not, we form opinions about one side or another of an argument, swayed by a *focus* on our own preferences. Sometimes this focus leads us to take strong positions. We may even join social causes—political rallies, veganism, anti-GMO organizations, or Occupy Wall Street. There's nothing wrong with taking a position. But when you focus on only one side of an argument, you run the risk of being narrow-minded. And you lose the galvanizing tension inherent in conflicts, paradox, and contradiction. Oversimplification frequently breeds a false sense of satisfaction. You have to learn to unfocus to see the big picture from time to time, and you have to be a dynamic tinkerer to dispel disenchantment.

Jeff Bezos, for example, is known as one of the more generous CEOs of our time, but he is also notoriously temperamental and harsh with his employees. And even though he comes across as very serious at heart, he is reportedly also quite playful; at his wedding, he had outdoor playtime for the adult guests, including water balloons. Also, one of his pieces of advice is to be stubborn and flexible—stubborn so that you don't give up on experiments too soon, and flexible so that you're open to different solutions. The ability to be different at different times is a license that great people grant themselves. You don't have to be one thing only.

When it comes to making decisions, Bezos loves data to help, but he will sometimes sell something that research "proves" customers won't buy, because he believes that short-term research is not a great predictor of something's long-term viability or popularity. That is, he unfocuses from the data in front of him to look at the longer-term ramifications. His high beams are back on!

Complexities, not sterilized personality traits and opinions, are what great leaders are made of. And for you to reach your own greatness, it would help to unfocus from your supposed identity— to look at the other side of who you are. When you do, unfocus will help you feel more integrated and give you the power you need to activate your greatness.

EMBRACING PARADOX

In your brain, pain can lead to the release of "pleasure" chemicals. Stress can direct your attention in a timely manner, but if you don't manage it, it can throttle you. Parallel brain circuits of love and hatred can run at the same time. The DMN, when it activates to allow great self-connection, also connects you with others more profoundly. You are wired for paradox—so why not acknowledge it?

One unfocused way to understand your paradoxical nature is to think of any self-defining attribute that you have as being on a spectrum rather than crystallized at one end of it. Then on any given day, or in a conversation, reflect on this spectrum. For example, rather than calling yourself an introvert, reflect on situations in which you behave like one and those in which you prefer to let your hair down. You might also write out three characteristics that are true of you, then look for an example for each where you did not stick to this rule. Do this every week, and soon you will see that your personality and beliefs have many colors that focus can never capture.

The tinkering mindset challenges you to explore uncomfortable assumptions and manage paradoxes: to focus, but also to unfocus; to daydream in a planned but not accidental way; to supertask, yet not multitask; to be so intensely engaged that you can surrender. These apparent contradictions reflect the actual complexity of who you are. The tinkering mindset acknowledges it and is supported by it.

Life is not about *finding* the time to do what you love—it's about *making* the time because your life matters. If you manage your contradictions and show up to your life as "you," you increase your engagement and productivity because you can be all that you are, and not a sterilized and disempowered version of yourself.

FUEL FOR THE DREAM

Achieving greatness requires being the most empowered version of yourself. And this "power" often comes from having a sense of purpose, even when the going is tough.

A sense of purpose is neither a thought nor a feeling but an often imperceptible, spontaneous, and recognizable drive that fuels your ambition. And it confers an intelligence—a way of making things happen—that frequently defies purely rational explanation. Your brain's reward center is activated every time it makes an appearance.

People who have a sense of purpose are "on a mission" (as Bezos was when he packed hundreds of books by hand before he raised the necessary funds to put together a warehousing system). They are driven and inspired by the continuous reward that that mission provides. At its core, having a sense of purpose means that people "feel moved," *after* which they may consider their impact on the world or their legacies. *Time* magazine's one hundred most influential people of 2016 range from Adele, the singer, to Caitlyn Jenner, the reality TV star, Olympic athlete, and transgender activist, to Stephen Curry, the NBA star. You may balk at associating these people with a group that also includes the pope, Aung San Suu Kyi, and Angela Merkel. But they are there for a reason. These people made it to "center stage" with unforgettable and influential "performances" because they are plugged into their sense of purpose and drive. They did not all start out trying to change the world. Their journeys now afford them a global platform to be able to change the world if they so desire, but it all starts with a sense of purpose. In my practice, people who try to hitch themselves to social goals up front rarely connect with a sense of purpose, although they do experience a temporary reprieve from a social conscience. Also, soapboxes, rather than being effective vehicles to express a sense of purpose, frequently provide a venue for those who are disenchanted.

A doctor who loves her job, for example, is not usually driven by wanting to save lives, although this is frequently the enjoyed and desirable outcome. Rather, she is most frequently fueled by a sense of living as her highest self. That is an abstract feeling. The goal—to save lives—is a way of reaching that feeling state. But it's the feeling that drives her, not the goal. If you've ever tried to connect with your sense of purpose (not your goals!), you'll know that it's like trying to catch a butterfly with your hands. It's elusive and won't land until it really wants to. Focus won't get you very far, no matter what great cause it connects you to. Instead, unfocus, like waiting for the butterfly to land on your hand, is what will get you there.

If you ask the luminaries mentioned above about their sense of purpose, they are unlikely to say that they wanted to serve humanity. More likely, they would say they wanted to be their best and as true to themselves as they could be. That's your first priority in the order of operations. The problem with this direction is that it's vague, and you can't really focus on being your best or "most true"—you have to discover it, and it's an ongoing process. Moreover, embarking on an uncharted journey of self-discovery can be anxiety-inducing. Yet it is precisely this discomfort that will help you become self-actualized.

Many of us, when faced with this tension, run out of fuel. When we do, we are tempted to lower the bar of our ambitions to reduce our anxiety. Called *self-handicapping*, this decreased effort or *not trying* may allow us to avoid our fear of failure, but as tempting as it may be, it is the last thing we should do. Make self-handicapping a habit, and you may well develop more gray matter in a brain region that suppresses negative emotions—the conflict detector. But while protecting your self-esteem, this prevents your access to a sense of purpose and greatness too. On the contrary, when you're anxious, you should consider upping your game. And upping your game requires unfocus—exploring yourself and spontaneously responding to what you find.

Positive disintegration: Kazimierz Dabrowski, a Polish psychiatrist and psychologist, developed the theory of *positive disintegration* to explain why anxiety and tension are necessary for self-actualization. They shape your personality, he argues, but more important, without them, you cannot grow. They light a fire under you. As tennis great Billie Jean King has famously said, "Pressure is a privilege." You simply have to know what to do when you come apart. Changing your brain for greatness is all about reconstruction.

As the name implies, in positive disintegration, you come apart in a good way, only to build a bigger and stronger version of yourself and your life. It is not a one-time process; it's a lifelong labor of self-love, rebuilding yourself to progressively higher and higher forms of greatness.

THE DYNAMIC DRUMMER

Development to your full potential depends on three factors—your ability to thrive in the extremes of life, your current talents and ability, and your drive toward growth and autonomy. There is no "right" path to greatness, and it is anything but focused and well demarcated.

Gifted students often experience positive disintegration. Given their emotional sensitivity and propensity to march to their own drummers, they are often misdiagnosed with ADHD. But they are not inattentive—they've simply shifted their attention to a better version of themselves and are adjusting to this emerging mental state. Despite frequent disintegrations as a result of their emotional sensitivity, they subsequently reintegrate.

The disintegrations are frequently referred to as "dynamisms" because they are states of emotional flux. These students intermittently take themselves apart with self-questioning and, on every occasion, put themselves together in an altogether different way until they reach a version of themselves that is acceptable to them. People will tell them to focus, choose, or settle down. But gifted students will sacrifice the peacefulness of never coming apart because for them, the suffering of stagnation is far worse.

In every human, this "gift" awaits. Your greatness relies heavily on your willingness to unwrap it.

To achieve positive disintegration, Dabrowski explains that you have to first address (not *resolve*) conflicts *within* yourself, then *between* your current self and your desired higher self. He calls conflicts within yourself *horizontal conflicts* as they arise at your current level of self. The conflicts between your current level of self and your higher self are *vertical*—they call for an upward movement into a higher or greater version of the current you, your greatness.

In horizontal conflicts, you are trying to figure out whether you should stay at your current job or change, whether you should stay in your current relationship or move on to another one. The choices are not clear. You can't make up your mind easily. The conflict tears you apart, but you don't panic. Instead, you learn to tolerate the tension welling up within you, much as you might hold up a dumbbell until you have to bring it back down again. Each anxious moment, like a heavy lift, gives rise to pause. When it becomes too much, you let it go.

You may at first wonder what good all this will do. Why not just end the discomfort and make a quick decision, right? You don't, because that would be like not working out and mistaking your lack of emotional exercise for productive relaxation. They're not the same.

Also, as you practice this anxiety-tolerance, tinkering with the different levels of anxiety (like increasing weights as you get stronger), you enter the vertical conflict phase. Here you simply ask, *Am I living as the highest version of myself?* Most of us are not. And when we think of the time we've wasted, we might freak out. Here again, rather than running away from this anxiety, it's advisable to welcome it, little by little, letting go of it to breathe when it feels like too much. Over time this anxiety becomes the fuel that allows us to take off to our higher selves, propelling us to our greatness.

Anxiety and tension may tear us apart, but if we're patient with them, if we let them activate our greatest fury, determination, and strength, we are more likely to activate our greatness.

Resolving our horizontal and vertical conflicts is difficult because we fear that we might inadvertently make the wrong choices. Our brains are supersensitive to error. This is not just an adult fear—it's present from birth. In 2006, psychologist Andrea Berger showed six-to-nine-month-olds two arithmetic equations, one correct and one incorrect: $1 + 1 = 2$ and $1 + 1 = 1$. She also showed them one or two puppets, depending on the equation. When she offered them the answer options of 1 or 2 (together with the corresponding number of puppets), the children stared longer at the wrong answer than at the correct one.

As adults, this sensitivity grows. When you do something wrong, your brain's conflict and anxiety alarms go off. Ideally, you'd want them to light a fire under you, but if you're not in a positive disintegration frame of mind, you freeze or flee. In some cases, that's the right reaction, but when *regret* freezes you and you ruminate on it rather than examining your mistakes and correcting them, you can quickly become stuck in self-flagellation.

You can see this in competitive sports when a person under pressure goes off their game, gets defensive, and loses. They start to come apart! But then all of a sudden, they realize that they are choosing between defensive options (are stuck in horizontal conflicts) rather than being the truly aggressive competitor that they can be. With all the practice they've put in, they should be playing at a higher level—that is, they should be thinking of their vertical conflicts. They make new conscious choices, leaving behind the defensive ambivalence and reaching a whole new level of play.

In everyday life, it helps to navigate career choices this way. For example, if you are a doctor who really wants to be at the nexus of technology and medicine, you might give up your regular practice and academic medicine, then reintegrate a new career in medical technology. Or if you're a homemaker who wants to work part-time, you might rearrange your caretaking duties to make that happen. The time for rearrangement is often the most distressing, disintegrating. You know you're on the right track when you start to feel in charge of your own destiny.

Spontaneity: Spontaneity is a gateway for your purpose to emerge—a moment of relaxation when the truth will show itself. When you're spontaneous, you don't overthink things, so your sense of purpose is likely to feel more authentic and less contrived.

Being spontaneous is easier said than done, yet it is of immense value in discovering and expressing your sense of purpose. When you're spontaneous, it's as though your brain's control regions relax the door of the memory vault and allow memories to come out and mix with the rest of the brain activity. Spontaneity also activates the improvisation circuit—your willingness to make mistakes and "not know" because you will explore and create a solution in the moment. Jazz musicians, for example, do not focus in the traditional sense; rather, they submit to the unpredictability of the musical information coursing through their brains.

HOW THE EXPERTS LET GO

Spontaneity, when it works well, is particularly useful in life. It mixes together and productively confuses the sensory and motor aspects of your mind. At all times, both parts of your brain are active. You move, and while you move, you see, hear, taste, touch, or smell. Focus limits us by forcing the primacy of one or the other aspect of our mind. Unfocus, in the form of spontaneity, taps into a deeper, more automatic, and integrated intelligence.

Perhaps that's why, in so many experts, the brain switches into "purring" mode—a low level of activity but very, very present. Professional race car drivers recruit the task-related brain regions less than do amateurs, and the information integration between the regions is greater. Similarly, expert archers' brain activation is less widespread than in novice archers, indicating that conscious activation is in a lull. In elite Ping-Pong players as well, the focus circuits in the brain are less activated.

We like to be in control all the time, so spontaneity may be counterintuitive. It requires deep self-knowledge and the conviction that you will recover. You don't get to this point in one fell swoop. You can't induce spontaneity, but you can progressively practice being spontaneous so that you get used to the anxieties and fears associated with it. Choose one day a week when you will call up an old friend, go on an unknown hike in a local park, or say no to work when you can. Ironically, "practicing" spontaneity this way will help you feel less intimated by that rapid heartbeat that comes with venturing out of your normal routine. Your physiological reaction (the rapid heartbeat) likely won't dissipate with practice, but your comfort with it will increase, and that can eventually lead you closer to your greatness.

To discover a sense of purpose, you can't focus on it. Instead, to achieve this state of positive disintegration and spontaneity, embrace the core values of these states of mind and remind yourself from time to time about an idealized self, the relentless curiosity to discover it, the willingness to be anxious, tense, and wrong, and to pay attention to what makes you "overexcitable." All these factors will help you reinvent yourself.

THE PAST THAT NEVER HAPPENED

Experience informs us. If you've done a certain something before, you've gained the experience to do that same task the next time with greater ease. Even when you're trying to do something new, you can draw on a *similar* experience for help. But past experience can also turn out to be a trap. In 2009, business consultant Andrew Campbell and his colleagues studied why good leaders make bad decisions in the moment and found two culprits: emotions were incorrectly tagged due to past experiences, and prior patterns were incorrectly imposed on current ones. Your very own past could be your prison too!

Our memories are like a house of mirrors. Our brains, by randomly inserting information, can fictionalize the stories that we "remember." That's what psychologists Chad Dodson and Lacy Krueger found in 2006 when they conducted a study to explore misremembering.

The study participants watched a video about a burglary and a police chase. Then they were given a questionnaire. Some of the questions related to the actual video, but others referred to related things that were not in the video at all. For instance, they were asked about "the police shooting" or burglars having a gun. Neither event had been shown in the video.

The researchers then asked the participants to remember which things occurred in the video, on the questionnaire, in both, or in neither. To add an element of uncertainty, the researchers explained that not everything on the questionnaire actually happened in the video.

The result? Participants in the 17-to-23 age bracket misremembered things when they were uncertain. They mixed up the video and questionnaire information. For example, they described a police shooting in the video that had never happened there—it had been in the questionnaire. Older adults (60 to 79) also misremembered things, but they did so when they were confident about them. In both situations, every new related event distorted a prior memory. The information got jumbled up.

We may not only distort information, but also invent things that didn't happen at all. In these *memory illusions,* your mood can strongly influence what you remember. Researchers study this phenomenon by using lists of related words (e.g., *nurse, sick, medicine*) and ask people to later recall them. Among the actual words shown later are distractors called "lures" (e.g., *doctor*).

Funnily enough, when you're in a negative mood but not so down that you're depressed, you'd be able to remember that *doctor* was not part of the original list. That's the one upside of being in a funk! But when you're in a positive mood, you are more likely to "recall" the word *doctor* even if it was never presented to you. Your stress level as well as your level of arousal or excitability can also distort memory recall.

And it's not just memories, but timelines that can be distorted. In 2014, psychologists Youssef Ezzyat and Lila Davachi described how very shifty and inaccurate our recollection of timelines could be. We regularly miscalculate the timeline of seeing people's faces on any particular day, depending on the emotions and memories that are intruding.

The long and short of it is that your memories are not reliable. They may be a broken compass when you're recalling breaking up with someone, reflecting on a job interview, or thinking about a big leap in your life. So why focus on them? Rather, tinker with them. Dabble in alternative possibilities. Break up your coherent narratives—reexamine them and make them whole again in a different way. Playfully retell yourself a different version of your life. Of course, memory has a place in day-to-day activities, but overinvestment in memory does not.

YOUR FUTURE LIFE IS WRITTEN IN SAND, NOT IN STONE

Logic, like memory, is both helpful and misleading. We couldn't do much without it, yet there are reasons to temper our blind faith in it. Great thinkers always question the apparently inevitable. They are skeptical of logic alone, even when the focus that it provides is comforting.

Many years ago, for example, doctors believed that stomach ulcers occurred when hydrochloric acid (HCl) ate into the very lining that secreted it. We also believed that eating spicy foods would cause more HCl to be secreted. Based on this information, we advised people who had stomach ulcers to avoid spicy foods. It made sense at the time. Besides, who would believe the opposite, that eating nonspicy foods might put you at risk of ulcers?

In 1995, led by gastroenterologist Jin-Yong Kang, researchers in Singapore questioned 103 Chinese patients with stomach ulcers about their chili-eating habits. Compared to people with ulcers, the group without ulcers ate chilies three times *more frequently* every month, and also ate close to three times *the amount* of chilies. Chilies, it seems, have a protective effect against ulcers!

Subsequent studies explained that the active ingredient in chilies, capsaicin, inhibits acid secretion, stimulates alkali and mucus secretion, and promotes gastric mucosal blood flow, all of which help prevent and heal stomach ulcers. Capsaicin also protects against the current "real" cause of ulcers, the bacterium called *Helicobacter pylori.*

Great minds like Dr. Kang's refuse to accept the apparently obvious. They question it and then tinker with their hunches. They realize that when someone says something is inevitable, they may simply be tired of trying to change it. Great minds frequently pause, unfocus, and look at things from another angle.

When we are trying to change an old belief system, a problem arises when we use focus to justify our biases. In 2012, brain researcher Martijn Mulder and his colleagues found that people tend to believe in choices that they think are more probable and that have a larger payoff for them. When they do, the frontoparietal cortex—the brain's focused flashlight—is to blame. Focus keeps your eye on one line of logic only, but great minds know that this is a trap because logic and truth are not synonymous.

When we are thinking, we regularly take shortcuts to avoid mental effort. Stereotypes are one such shortcut. They can be helpful when they are conscious and true, and when they describe people rather than evaluate them. But at other times stereotypes make us think inflexibly, and frequently they are inaccurate. They compromise our greatness.

Take age, for example. Most people would say that their age is the number of years they have been alive. But what is a year? It is the time it takes for the earth to revolve around the sun, right? Someone, at some time in the distant past, decided that the age of the human body is somehow linked to the movement of the earth around the sun. Doesn't that sound a little random? Until recently, we just accepted this system of thinking. As surely as the earth keeps moving around the sun, we expect that we will keep on aging until we die. But progressively, this connection between our bodies and the earth's movement around the sun has come into serious question.

Even though the earth keeps on moving around the sun, we can make it seem, cosmetically at least (through plastic surgery and Botox), as if our skin is resisting aging. Now we've advanced even further. In 2011, Ph.D. researcher Mariela Jaskelioff and her colleagues were able to reverse aging in mice by reactivating an enzyme responsible for keeping tissues young. The results were dramatic—the aging process reversed! In December 2013, David Sinclair and his colleagues discovered a naturally produced compound called NAD that rewinds aging-related death in mice. When mice are younger, NAD helps their cells stay young and energetic. But as they age, levels of NAD drop.

One researcher found, however, that giving mice a substance that could be converted into NAD could reverse aging. The result was astounding. In human terms, it was as if specific cell functions in a sixty-year-old person were like those in a twenty-year-old. By tinkering more deeply than the skin, Sinclair and his colleagues were able to further disrupt our assumptions about age. Studies with humans are now in progress. Renowned Harvard geneticist George Church explains that aging is just a program that can be rewritten. Soon our bodies will likely be able to resist the passage of time even more.

You don't need to change genes to change the effects of aging. In 2015, psychology doctoral student Daniela Aisenberg and her colleagues studied two groups of elderly people. One group believed that eighty-two-year-old people still had strong cognitive skills, whereas the other group thought the opposite. They found that when you think of the elderly as being sharp, and you are elderly, you are able to perform a task that challenges flexibility in thinking more effectively than if you carry a negative bias. Similarly, in 2015, doctoral student Deirdre Robertson and her colleagues found that negative ideas about old age make people walk more slowly.

Our stereotypes can clearly alter our perceptions. But luckily for us, our stereotypes can be reversed, as long as we don't just continue with blinkers on, and as long as we unfocus to question our assumptions.

In 2013, psychologist Malgorzata Gocłowska and her colleagues conducted a series of experiments to see whether forming impressions opposite to a stereotype would increase flexibility and creativity in thinking about matters unrelated to that stereotype. In one experiment, they asked the subjects to produce adjectives to describe a female mechanic (counterstereotype) and male mechanic (stereotype). Then the researchers tested the participants' cognitive flexibility by asking them to generate three new names for pasta.

First, they were given examples of pasta names. Prior experiments show that when subjects are given examples, the first names they come up with are related to the grammatical structure of the examples (e.g., *linguini,* ending with an *i*). But those who are flexible in their thinking depart from that structure. The researchers found that participants in the counterstereotypic condition were more flexible in their thinking.

In another experiment, after the counterstereotype and stereotype portion of the study, participants were asked to generate novel ideas for a themed night at a university nightclub, first in writing, and then by sketching a poster advertisement. Their ideas were then rated using standardized measures for creativity. Here again, participants in the counterstereotypic condition were more creative in their thinking.

Great people are more flexible and creative than others. They think outside focused categories. One way to train yourself to do this is to reflect on the stereotypes that you hold (e.g., narcissistic men and overemotional women). Then consciously reverse them. Say out loud or write the opposite of that stereotype. Then try solving an unrelated problem—you may just find a new solution!

THE NEED TO KNOW

Sometimes we resist being unfocused because it is disorienting. The natural human tendency is to focus and to wish to put an end to openness in thinking. In scientific terms, this desire is called *need for cognitive closure* (NCC).

In 1994, psychology researchers Daniel Webster and Arie Kruglanski pointed out five characteristics of people with high NCC: discomfort with ambiguity, preference for predictability, preference for order, decisiveness, and closed-mindedness. On the surface, these attributes sound rational and clear-headed—perhaps ones you want in a leader—but in a world where things are constantly changing, these attributes do not serve anybody. The list is a formula for mediocrity.

High levels of NCC make it difficult to adapt to conflicts when incongruent tasks present themselves: there is less connectivity between key brain regions such as the short-term memory cup and other thought control regions. That means that your brain's ability to switch things up is stymied by your underlying NCC. Just having this trait of wanting things to be done can hamper your mental flexibility when you need it.

To train yourself away from a need for cognitive closure and toward flexibility in thinking, create time in your week for low-NCC activities. What are some safe chances that you could take where you would definitely not know the end result? You could go for a walk for no more than fifteen minutes in a direction you've never walked before. That way, if you do get lost, you can find your way back. Or you could choose a topic that really interests you and look it up and take notes on it, even though it has no actual relevance to your life right now. These kinds of activities will get your brain used to the idea of low NCC and will help you become more alert and mentally flexible.

IMAGINING WITH THE BRAIN IN MIND

Great people don't just intend to be great—they imagine it, with precision, and tinker with their imaginations until they get it right. Committing to your imagination is committing to unfocusing from reality. Rather than aiming for goals, you create them. Rather than following a focused path, you make one in your imagination.

As early as 1995, neurologist Marc Jeannerod and others pioneered the study of how imagery impacts the brain. They found that imagining moving actually stimulates vital movement circuits in the brain. Imagery warms up the brain to take action. It offers a leg up to intention. Since then, numerous studies have demonstrated that imagery can help people move again after a stroke has impaired their movement: simply *imagining* improved mobility or use of a now-useless limb helped these people move better again. And in 2015, brain researcher Chang-Hyun Park and his colleagues confirmed that imagery stimulates the "action brain." Because the action brain is involved in actual movement, it helps people move—whether a senior needing to gain better mobility or a healthy young athlete wanting to improve performance.

When you imagine, your image may not be fully formed at first. You have to tinker with it. One method of seeing what your brain is up to when you're imagining is called a *brain-computer interface* (BCI). BCIs work by conveying electrical activity from your brain to the computer via electrodes. As you change what you are imagining, the feedback on the screen changes. This allows you to change what you are thinking until you see the pattern you are aiming to see. The specific pattern depends on what you are trying to achieve. For example, if imagining generates a pattern that corresponds with moving your arm, you learn to imagine at that level of intensity and clarity to generate the same pattern.

In 2015, physician and neurophysiologist Floriana Pichiorri and her colleagues studied twenty-eight patients who had recently been severely physically impaired following a stroke. They were divided into two groups. Both received motor imagery training (training to imagine moving their limbs), but only one had the visual aid, the BCI, as well. The group with BCI showed significantly greater improvement in movement. The more they tinkered with their images by looking at the computer feedback and making small adjustments, the more their poststroke movement improved. The nontinkering group did not improve as much. To be sure, you're unlikely to walk into a lab to try out BCI, but whenever you develop an image, try to draw it out, and then keep on working at it. As you work on your image, your brain biology will likely change.

In other words, when you imagine moving, you stimulate the same parts of the brain that would be stimulated if you were *actually* moving. The reason you do not move is because imagination is sometimes a weaker activator, or because other regions put the brakes on your movement. When you give your brain the go-ahead, it will let go.

Try this: choose one to three images that represent a goal you want to achieve. If you want optimal health, imagine yourself running a marathon and crossing the finish line. If you want a fulfilling relationship, imagine yourself satisfied as you are lying next to someone. And if you want more money, imagine something believable and satisfying that you would do with that money, like writing a check out to your favorite charity, buying your mom a house, or going on an exciting vacation. If you choose something that creates overt conflict for you, such as a sum of money that is so great you don't really believe you can get it, you run the risk of unconsciously sabotaging your efforts.

You don't have to choose an image initially. Dabbling in many images will help you decide on one that works.

Tinker with first- and third-person perspectives: Many brain-imaging studies have shown that the brain is powerfully stimulated by both first-person and third-person images—by imagining yourself actually doing something, and by watching yourself doing something. First-person images make you feel like you are in an actual situation, and they are often more vivid, but they can also make you anxious because they are so real. So if first-person images make you anxious, start with third-person images. (Recall how second-person self-talk reduces stress!) Better yet, tinker with both, to get different "camera angles" of the same situation.

Tinker with believability: When you believe something is difficult or impossible, your brain will strain to mount an image of it. For example, imagine rotating your left hand to ninety degrees; then imagine rotating it three hundred degrees. In the first case, your brain will quickly produce an image of that possibility, but in the second, it will take much longer to mount an image.

Based on this, we can safely assume that if you have a goal (e.g., to lose thirty pounds, to fall in love, or to make $100,000), you may have to adjust it until your brain "buys" it. Imagining losing five pounds, going on a successful date, or making $20,000 more than you do already may be easier. Adjust as necessary—using belief as a guide—until you get the right numbers.

Tinker specifically with your target: In 2011, Bärbel Knäuper, a psychology professor, took a group of college students who wanted to eat more fruit and divided them into three groups. One intended to eat more fruit, another intended to eat a specific fruit at a specific time, and another *imagined* eating a specific fruit at a specific time—they didn't just *intend* it.

This study found that the third group, those who *imagined* eating a specific fruit at a specific time, were much more likely to actually eat fruit. Imagining (not just intending) what you want *specifically* adds to the possibility of getting or doing it. You chisel away at the image until it comes into clear view. Focus and unfocus work together to create a clear specific image. So if you have a greatness goal, then be as specific as you can be with what you imagine. Imagining something specifically will make it more likely that you will actually do it.

THE POWER OF THE UNDERDOG
IN THE IMAGINATION

There are five types of imagery that you can use in your quest for greatness: winning, coming from behind, practicing a weakness, seeing a strategy on a board in front of you, or feeling excited about getting what you want.

In 2009, kinesiology professor Craig Hall and his colleagues examined 345 athletes to see which types of imagery improved their confidence at crunch time. They found that only two types actually improved confidence: working on specific weaknesses and imagining coming from behind. Dabbling in these two kinds of images will help you feel the confidence you need for your greatness pursuits.

Tinker with image quality: Once you imagine what you want in the first and third person, are specific about it, believe it, and feel confident about it, you have to take another look at the image to make some corrections.

When you imagine something, engage all your senses. Try to feel what you would feel in that situation, and imagine the taste or the smell if that pertains to the situation. Make it as real as you can. Imagining in these many ways will make you less anxious and more confident. Since stress can deactivate your imagining brain, this sensory approach is especially helpful. Mindfulness meditation (a great unfocus activity!) can also help you destress and prepare your mind for the image. Also, ensure that your image is clearly delineated and rewarding. What colors do you see? How does it make you feel? Is your image in 3-D? All this taken together will help clarify your image so your brain can use it as a blueprint to conjure up a plan to get you to your goal.

A HAWK'S-EYE VIEW

Ray Kurzweil, the director of engineering at Google, is one of the world's most famous futurists. A stunning 86 percent of his predictions about the future have been correct. In 1999, he predicted that personal computers would come in a variety of shapes and that they would be wearable in ten years. He also predicted that portable computers would be a trend by 2009. In 2000, he predicted very-high-bandwidth wireless communication to the Internet at all times by 2010. That year he also correctly predicted that in ten years, computers would tap into a worldwide mesh forming vast supercomputers and memory banks. He was right on all accounts. His accuracy in predicting the future is astounding.

Currently Kurzweil predicts that search engines will soon provide spontaneous feedback to us. If we look up a new restaurant opening, for instance, this imagined new search engine will remind us when it opens and might even send us a menu. It acts as an ancillary brain. Even bolder, Kurzweil predicts that nanobots made from our DNA will be scurrying through our bloodstreams. They will connect us to the cloud, and we will be able to send email and photos directly from our brains.

If you examine Kurzweil's thinking carefully, you will see that he has a very focused and intricate knowledge of people and machines. In addition, he is able to project into the future to imagine the tipping point at which exponential progress will occur. Unfocus, when it activates the DMN, sets up your slow-wave rhythms and helps you create possible versions of the future. But how does Kurzweil unfocus to come up with such radical ideas, and how can he be correct so often?

Freeman Dyson, a theoretical physicist and mathematician, suggests an explanation. He divides natural scientists into the hawks that fly above the confusing particularity of nature and the frogs that muck around in the messy details. Kurzweil is a hawk, content to unfocus from time to time to see the big picture. When he does, he is able to project possibilities far into the future.

Becoming the hawk and asking big-picture questions will bring you closer to your greatness. You don't have to be predicting flying drones and nanobots either. You can ask big questions about your own life, such as *If I look at the greatest exponential opportunity in my business in the next six months, what would that be?*

For Jeff Bezos, unfocus takes the form of what he calls the "regret minimization framework." Three components could apply to your life: project your life out to when you are eighty years old; ask your eighty-year-old self if he or she regrets that you didn't try out your big idea; then ask yourself if you'd regret leaving behind your job, your unpaid bonus, and your stability in order to pursue your passion. Taking this long-term perspective will awaken the hawk in your thinking.

Your brain can be a crystal ball because of the DMN, which unfocus will activate. It will get the connections within itself buzzing, and it will turn on the connections between the DMN and brain regions that put puzzle pieces together to predict the future. Rather than sticking with the completed puzzles of the past, you tinker with the puzzle pieces of the future, stare at each possible picture, and rearrange the pieces until they make sense.

"TO BE, OR NOT TO BE"

In normal waking consciousness, you think logically, plan, analyze, and follow up on your intentions with action. In so doing, you capitalize on only a small amount of your brain's resources. But a higher level of intelligence governs your decision-making, removes brain biases, and clears your mind of the usual obstructions that prevent your access to your own greatness. Called *transcendental awareness*, it circumvents the distracting and misleading effects of ongoing mental chatter and helps you to have better thought control and make better decisions.

Having transcendental awareness involves being, not doing. Many practices can help you reach this state. Perhaps the best studied is mindfulness, a practice in which you focus on your breath, gently ignore your mental chatter, and return to your breath every time your mind wanders into the chatter. This practice (twenty minutes twice a day is a standard recommendation) will teach you how to deepen your self-awareness, control your emotions, and then see and experience yourself as part of the greater whole of the universe. You can also practice mindfulness by using the technique known as *open monitoring,* in which you simply receive all thoughts, feelings, and sensations without judgment and monitor them.

Aside from mindfulness meditation, transcendental meditation (TM), which is a mantra-based meditation, Qi Gong meditation, and even several forms of prayer have also shown psychological benefit. Don't be discouraged if you can't sit still, because there are walking forms of meditation too. And if you really can't sit still for long, try an app called Headspace, which is an interactive form of meditation. Funnily enough, Ryan Seacrest is one of the investors in it.

People often think of meditation—whether mantra- or breath-focused—as a kind of hyperfocus. But the focus you give your mantra or your breath actually leads to a wonderful kind of unfocus, and in this unfocus is transcendence of the self. With TM, it appears on brain scans as deactivation of the parietal lobe—a region associated with developing a sense of self. Disrupting or deactivating the sense of self minimizes your sense of separateness from others.

Mindfulness, on the other hand, stimulates regions in your brain that are responsible for empathy and social understanding. Like the DMN, they enhance your connection with those around you, allowing you to have deeper insights about how you fit into a social context and how that context can inform your thinking. Even in children with ADHD, mindfulness meditation—focusing on your breath rather than your silent mental chatter—improves attention.

THE FOCUS TRIAD

Three stages, from focus to unfocus, can move you toward transcendence.

In everyday life, you focus on your work, your chores, your children, and your health. At best, this happens when you can stop all distractions and just look at what is in front of you. This is laser-sharp focus.

The second stage in the evolution of focus is a continuous flow of perception. In this state, you are not just removed from distractions but actually move much more deeply into concentration where you are not restless or troubled by your desires. Your attention is not just focused but sustained. You may, for example, be able to repeat a word in your head five times before your mind wanders off in another direction and you have to bring it back. But when you have mastered concentration, you continuously mention the word, and your mind will not wander anymore.

In the final state, the boundary between you and what you are concentrating on is completely lost. You are *in* the former object of concentration. You and your word become one. If I ask you now what *table* is, for instance, you may describe it as an object that has four legs and a surface. But this is only using several words for one. In this final transcended state, when you look at the table, you experience its essence. In that state, you would describe a table very differently—perhaps as a collection of wood atoms that vibrate ever so slightly, remain bonded, and provide the potential energy necessary to resist the pull of gravity, should you place anything atop the horizontal vibrating atom collection. It's in such mind states that many scientific insights probably occur.

When all three states of consciousness happen at the same time, three types of attention coexist in different brain circuits. I call this the *attention triad*. In one room in your brain, the spotlight is on. In another, the recess lights are on. And in the third, light is streaming through the window making inside and outside indistinguishable. Talk about unfocus!

The widespread health benefits of meditation will help to sustain your greatness. In addition to reducing stress, meditation may also increase the duration of your life. In 2009, molecular biologist Elizabeth Blackburn was awarded the Nobel Prize for discovering protective caps on chromosomes called telomeres. She has also discovered an enzyme (telomerase) that protects the caps from the detrimental effects of aging. In an initial study she conducted, a group of thirty volunteers went to the Shambhala Mountain Center in northern Colorado for a three-month meditation retreat. With them, she found a 30 percent increase in telomerase activity. Subsequently many more studies have replicated this finding. If you meditate, no more telomere snipping with age. You live longer!

Putting It All Together for Your Personal Greatness

All these greatness principles can be found in three basic identities that you already likely possess.

THE INNER EXPLORER

Some people will tell you that greatness is a mountain you have to climb. It may be—but it's not outside you. Rather, it's a place you have to find within yourself after clearing away the fog. You do this by reconstructing your personal narrative, reexamining your memories, allowing the many sides of yourself to surface, and building an image of your future after tinkering with it over and over again. It is all about chipping away at the sculpture of you. That's what will reveal your greatness.

Years of indoctrination by formal education, social values, and early life insults may dupe you into thinking that greatness is beyond your reach. No matter what your age is, I'm here to tell you unequivocally that this is wrong. Greatness is a universal truth. I have seen it emerge over and over again in the most unlikely people in my therapy and coaching practice.

Every person is responsible for his or her own greatness. There's nothing fancy to practice in this belief. Know that you're great. It's one of life's axioms. Just as certainly as the sun will shine and as the ocean waves will ebb and flow, you've got to believe that you are great. And move on. If you doubt it, question the doubt. If you're afraid of it, question the fear. If you're in disbelief about it, question the disbelief. But never, ever question the greatness.

Rather, unfocus. Take time off to go on a run. Spend time in relaxing activities that you enjoy. The more you learn to daydream and to connect your daydreams to your desires and spontaneous realizations, the closer you'll get to your overall goals. Greatness, in that sense, is a lifestyle!

THE SEARCH ENGINEER

Search engine optimization (SEO) is a way to organize the content of your website so that it shows up higher in page ranks—the better your SEO, the more people will visit your site because it will come up first (or close to the top) in searches of a related term.

(It's likely what helped Amazon become so successful!) But another kind of SEO is *self-esteem optimization,* which enhances your self-esteem. As opposed to simply protecting your self-esteem to maintain the status quo (*self-esteem maintenance,* SEM), SEO can take your life to the next level.

For example, when Jeff Bezos left his job on Wall Street, his self-esteem would have been subjected to uncertainty. Had he "protected" it, he might have backtracked for SEM. Instead, he chose to optimize it—to acknowledge and live out his desires. To manage your self-esteem best, you need to go from SEM to SEO.

In some situations, it may not be obvious that you're stuck in SEM. For example, downsizing and simplifying your life can take a huge burden off your shoulders, and you may think you're optimizing, but you could actually be lowering the bar to handle the stress of life more effectively. You're self-handicapping! That's why, for every downsizing and simplifying decision in life, ask yourself, *What if I took my life to the next level up?* That's the kind of question you ask for SEO. But be prepared for your brain to fight back.

In my therapy and coaching practice, I encourage people to up their game. It often backfires at first. They dig their heels in, not realizing that that's the SEM talking. SEM is often the superordinate goal—the goal above all other goals. It will race all other goals to the finish line unless you do something about it. When your brain says, *Why try?* it's a sign that your greatness is breaking down. You've got to build it up.

Rather than SEM, make SEO your superordinate goal. To do so, you literally use self-talk.

You acknowledge that there is a price to pay. Build an image of what you want, and realize that your future is built from your mind and not from your current circumstances. Try to dig into your paradoxes. Write out three stereotypes that confine you, and defy each one with a concrete behavior. For instance, if you think you are "not a creative person," doodle for fifteen minutes a day and examine your doodles at the end of the month. You'll likely see things that you like, and certain ineffable patterns will emerge.

When you examine SEM, you'll see how it keeps you in your unhealthy eating habits, away from the gym, stuck in a socioeconomic bracket, stagnant in your relationships, and away from fun. Engaging in SEO means you've decided to take your self-esteem apart, so that you can put it back together. Great people engage in SEO throughout their lives.

Consider this metaphor: when you work out, your muscles actually tear before they repair to make you bigger and stronger. Similarly, self-esteem that comes apart in the right way can be reconstituted so that you feel much stronger and more prepared for success. In a sense, you submit to it. That's what positive disintegration is about.

LIFE'S OLYMPIAN

An Olympic figure skater moving on the ice must be focused to execute on her technical prowess, but when she leaps into the air, she has to let go. Many elite athletes point to their ability to activate their unconscious mind in the most competitive and high-stress moments as the X factor that defines their places in history. They surrender!

This isn't as Zen as it may sound. Many athletes at the top of their profession talk about learning to stop thinking. They are talking about surrender, the process of releasing their minds from the stress of focusing on what they have learned. The brains of world-class gymnasts, for example, have particularly strong DMN connections compared to the general population. This makes sense, given that gymnasts often do things during which focus would be a liability. If you aren't sure if you're upside-down or right side up, or if you're falling or flying, maybe it's better not to ask. Better to trust, be mindful, and surrender, rather than be vigilant.

Whether you are a world-class athlete, a top-level strategist in a business, or simply an ordinary person trying to access your greatness, learning the mental competencies associated with a surrender mindset is critical. Greatness is something you surrender to when you get logic, memories, and confusion about your contradictions out of the way.

The singer who belts out a note so high that it gives you chills, the firefighter who rescues a baby, the soccer player who dribbles the ball successfully to score a goal, and the runner who breaks through the tape at the finish line first—all these people can be so grand only because they have learned to surrender to the moment that calls.

Keep in mind that it's often preferable to surf the waves than to control the ocean. Expertise isn't just about control—it's also about knowing when to give it up.

The problem with trying to be great is that every time you step onto your surfboard, the waves may knock you down. If this happens over and over again, you may even give up trying to surf. But anyone who has surfed will tell you that if you get back on that board, you'll make it eventually. Some days will be rougher than others. You may pack up the surfboard, but you'll always return. That's positive disintegration in action. Take time off to be with your mind—go for a stroll. Any top performer will tell you that downtime is as important as "on" time. So release your goals from time to time. Just be present.

Sometimes it's hard to talk about presence without sounding too abstract. But I'm talking about something simpler. Just practice letting go of your goals from time to time. Unfocus on them. Maybe you don't want to make all that money this year, or to get that promotion. Maybe you do. But if you bring things in and out of focus, you will feel more connected to them. Staying focused on goals means that unfocus can't work its magic for you.

In a sense, this whole book has been about your greatness. To resolve your horizontal conflicts, to shift vertically to your higher self, to escape the trappings of memory, and to build a future without resistance from reality, remember to incorporate the unfocused competencies in this table.

Focused Mindset	Unfocused Mindset Shift
You've got to be "together" to be great.	Positive disintegration allows you to reconfigure your life continuously.
Don't be hypocritical.	Relax into your paradoxes and own them.
Purpose requires a goal.	Purpose will lead you to your goal—activate it with crises and spontaneity.
Keep your eye on the ball at all times.	Practice surrendering to your spontaneity.
Be realistic.	Change your reality with your imagination.

THE TINKER MANIFESTO

A lot of people in our industry haven't had very diverse experiences. So they don't have enough dots to connect, and they end up with very linear solutions without a broad perspective on the problem. The broader one's understanding of the human experience, the better design we will have.

—Steve Jobs

I cdnuolt blveiee that I cluod aulaclty uesdnatnrd what I was rdanieg. Were you surprised that you were able to comprehend the garbled words in that sentence? According to psychologist Graham Rawlinson, all you need is the first and last letter in place, and your brain will automatically unscramble the rest to spell out the word correctly. Notwithstanding some caveats and exceptions, this illustrates one of the basic tenets of this book: that your brain doesn't have to logically focus on every component in sequence in order to understand what's happening. The context and connecting ideas can help it make sense of things.

So it is with the information, advice, and strategies I've laid out in the preceding chapters. You can and should absorb the material that interests or inspires you, and come back for the rest when you feel yourself stuck or stymied by too much focus in one or more arenas of your life. That said, most people find it helpful to have the foundational principles of the tinkering mindset laid out all in one place.

Whether you're an individual looking to improve your life, or a company leader looking to engage your employees to improve profits, use these overarching credos as a guide. If you get lost as you wander back and forth between focus and unfocus, they will remind you of why you committed to these changes in the first place and help you to reset your cognitive rhythm.

PRACTICE SELF-FORGIVENESS

Notice that the title of this book includes the admonition *Try*. You won't ever *try* anything in life if you can't forgive yourself when you fail. The fact that you're trying implies that you're willing to fail, and when you do, you simply dig yourself out of the hole and keep going.

When you tinker, you are a mental traveler, sampler, and dancer. As a traveler, you will find new ideas but sometimes get lost; as a sampler, you will have the privilege of abandoning distasteful experiences quickly, yet the variety of potential experiences may be overwhelming to you as well; and as a dancer, you may enjoy synchronizing with others but lose touch with yourself from time to time. In all those roles, mistakes help you readjust your thoughts and behaviors. Can you imagine what would happen if, every time you saw a wrong-way sign while driving, you gave up on your journey and sat there regretting it without ever moving again—or if you just kept cursing yourself while driving on? You probably wouldn't get very far without driving yourself batty!

In a sense, idleness suits us, at least unconsciously. Living in guilt, as psychoanalytic scholars of motivations have pointed out, gives us unconscious license to avoid living fully—to stagnate, in order to defy the march to our seemingly inevitable mortality. But this strategy doesn't work. Death will meet us anyway. So why not learn to course correct and move forward with greater vitality?

Self-forgiveness is part of the rejuvenation or refueling process. You can be wrong, make a mistake, and learn from that mistake by exploring it; you can, and sometimes should, even regret your actions. But to discover anything new, and to stop repeating prior traumas, you have to move on. Tinkering allows you to ponder your life as you move forward.

Self-forgiveness is not just brushing something aside. It is a deep realization and acceptance that you are not perfect—and apparently were not designed to be. Your life can still be excellent, beautiful, and great. To a tinkerer, errors are not stop signs—they are signals for a detour. Sometimes these detours pay off if you allocate your attention to what's possible rather than blame yourself. Possibility thinking will help you get there.

Consider two examples from the world of pharmacology. The drug Minoxidil was developed for the treatment of high blood pressure, but it also happened to cause hair growth, and once scientists realized that this side effect could actually be a desired effect for other conditions, they developed it as a topical application for male pattern baldness. The common blood thinner Warfarin was first used to kill rats by causing them to bleed before scientists realized that same reaction could be harnessed in a life-extending way. Hence its development into a blood-thinning drug that could help dissolve dangerous blood clots in humans.

Focus makes you think of side effects as just that, side effects. Unfocus makes you ask, *If I take my mind off the obvious for a moment, how might this side effect give me a better result?* Managed effectively, conflicts build brain capacity, and errors signify the need to change course. Einstein reminded us that a person who has never made any mistakes has never tried anything new.

After more than two decades of studying and researching the brain, I am convinced that we are "wired funny." As rich as the experience of being human is, it is also fraught with things that don't make sense. Why does loving come with so much pain? Why does hard work come with varied gain? Why are we not wired to connect with and help each other rather than look to our differences—even fight about them—to find ourselves?

These inevitable contradictions are dazzlingly confusing. That's why we can be humble about being human—and why it makes sense to recognize our frequently faulty brain wiring and turn to our many-sided selves when we're looking for answers. The mother who recognizes that her organizational skills can just as easily be applied to running a business, or the business owner who recognizes that her skills can just as easily be applied to running a house—these people lead themselves and others with purpose to the proverbial promised land where they can be curious, adaptable, and free. There they will find their greatness.

Once you are released from the clutches of focus, it will pay to stop obsessing about your mistakes and spend more time discovering and expressing your ingenuity.

BE LIGHT

If you've ever held a helium balloon, then delighted in setting it free while still tied to a string that you're holding, you'll likely also know the mild panic that ensues when it escapes unexpectedly and floats off. It's one thing to be flying high, another altogether to be drifting aimlessly.

The call to one's own freedom is strong, yet few heed it, and when they do, they often feel untethered. Armed with the tinker tools that you now have, you can be sure that as you build and rebuild your life with cognitive rhythm, the glowing octopus of a DMN will help you put the puzzle pieces for possible new life scenarios together.

Not only does life include heaviness, but we also seek out its heaviness so that we don't flit meaninglessly from one thing to another. Even though we say we want to be happy and free, we also want to feel grounded. Being grounded is fine if it means being sensible. But it's not if you're grounded like a ship in dry dock, or like a child who is forbidden to leave the house.

There's clearly an upside to having a schedule, family, friends and a stable job. But as much as these elements can bring profound meaning and comfort to you, you may be unconsciously using them to weigh you down. As the Danish philosopher Søren Kierkegaard argued, too much freedom and too many possibilities make us anxious. The "dizziness of freedom," as he called it, creates a rebound reaction in which you hunker down with focus and hold on to your possessions and circumstances even more. But tinkering is a much better alternative. You can tinker your way to another level of comfort—learn to see the lessons in a little lighthearted hair loosening, even if you are a more serious person at heart.

In the same way that you cannot swim until you surrender to the water and let it keep you afloat, you cannot have freedom unless you give in to the lightness that comes with it. Relieve yourself of too much heaviness before it becomes a burden. You have a choice.

There appear to be two arguments about whether we have freedom to choose. Some people believe we have no free will, but clearly the characters showcased in this book do not have that problem! Instead, they, like many others, believe that we can be agents of our own freedom—we have some ability to choose where we want to go and what we do. To all of them, the alternative seems absurd. But in truth, the freedom to choose exists on a spectrum depending on what we're choosing. You can't choose your parents, for example, but you can choose how you relate to them. Just the belief in having a choice will activate your brain to start your journey, to tinker, to update, and if it is somehow stretched by stress, you now know how to reactivate your brain's spring coils too.

Unfocus circuits play a major role in helping you escape the confines of the environment to access your own ingenuity for solutions. When you tinker, dabble, doodle, and try, you will update what you know gradually. Freedom will become less intimidating.

LET LIFE ADD UP

Of all the individuals I highlighted in this book, you could interpret that any one of them got to their goals by using possibility thinking and sheer determination. That would be true, but it would be only a partial or relative truth, because every one of them also had struggles, doubts, and failures along the way. Who's to say that these adversities did not motivate these people even more?

Most of what you think is true is true only to some extent. Rarely are things absolute. Loving someone unconditionally, being completely motivated, being the greatest that you can be— these are all usually relative. As jarring and infrequent as the phrase "partial truths" may sound, they are more the norm than the exception. As you tinker on, it's important to accept partial truths because, being far more reliable and representative guides, they can lead you to the greatness you're looking for.

Even computers are now programmed for partial truths! Rather than using binary computer logic based on yes-or-no answers to develop artificial intelligence, programmers now increasingly use "fuzzy logic," which more closely approximates how the brain works because it is based on degrees of truth. With fuzzy logic, a computer, much like a brain, aggregates information that is more or less true, then uses these approximations to get to a more accurate answer. You don't need to focus on each fact, like the jumbled letters I showed you earlier. Instead, you think what you think and move on. That's the spirit of a tinkerer.

Dr. Kary Mullis stands out as an example of fuzzy thinking paying off. On the way to discovering PCR, according to his colleagues, he did not conduct well-controlled experiments. Instead, the findings leading up to this discovery were highly questionable and somewhat incomplete. In fact, one of his colleagues described him as "a tinkerer, a bricoleur," and as someone who "loves to play with things . . . loves to try things out . . . ignores people who say you can't do it." When you accumulate enough partial truths, fueled by a sense of possibility thinking, each new one may send you in a completely different direction that leads you to a realization.

Dr. Mullis did not use clearly defined and stepwise findings in successive experiments, yet he got the Nobel Prize in chemistry. This is true of most important discoveries—tinkering leading to an accumulation of partial truths that eventually cross a threshold. In retrospect, they may appear to be clear and logical because our brains airbrush things by connecting the dots backward—the way false memories are formed.

When you're a tinkerer, fuzzy logic and partial truths should not deter you. By tinkering with relative truths, you increase the chances that your brain will keep trying to fill the gaps within and between them to help you make sense of your life.

EMBRACE COMPLEXITY

Simple intentions are easy to understand. Do you need to go for a walk? Put on a pair of sneakers and go walking. Hungry? Make some food and eat dinner. For simple actions, you need what we call *simple cognition*. It's easy to be clear with your intentions and act. But for more complex things like wanting to be happy or rich or great, simple intentions are not enough. Those goals or the path toward them are often obscure. And even when you think you're clear, you're frequently not.

First and foremost, an increasing number of studies have demonstrated that unlike the action centers in the brain, there is no one primary intention center or circuit. Depending on your action—whether it is to speak, subtract, or move your hand—intentions activate different brain circuits.

Rather than being a single function, "intention" is the resulting force that promotes action depending on the alignment of memories, ideas, emotions, and thoughts. If, in the balance of things, you still think that something is impossible or that you are dumb, success will continue to be out of reach despite your hard efforts. First you have to align these various elements to build an intention. Unfocus will help you do that.

Also, your brain can stimulate an action long before you even have a conscious intention to act. By the time you have an intention, your brain has already caused you to have that intention, and when you act, it's not necessarily because you decided to act. Instead, sufficient unconscious data has accumulated to lead to that action—and it is independent of your conscious intention. Understanding this complexity will encourage you to be patient—to slowly recall different parts of yourself, one by one, until enough of "you" is represented in your brain. When a sufficient number of "self" elements are called up, you will have the presence to be motivated. You have to work on the coalescence of a sufficient number of self-attributes, not just on an intensification of your desire. In other words, you can't win at the game of life if *you* don't show up for it. On a day-to-day basis, most people leave their most important attributes behind in their waking lives.

One of the most interesting aspects of complex cognition is that your "consciousness" may be a result of more than actual brain circuits interacting with each other. Largely invisible magnetic forces may be at play as well.

There are many reasons to assume that consciousness is electromagnetic. In 2016, biophysicist Abraham R. Liboff pointed out that brain cells are able to generate electricity across their membranes and magnetic fields around them. Also, hemoglobin is magnetic, and when it runs through brain circuits, it could contribute to this electromagnetic effect.

These forces cannot be seen, yet they impact your brain profoundly. To understand it, think of how you cannot see a magnetic field, yet if you brought a magnet to a metal fridge, you would instantly see it in action. Your brain's electromagnetic field can be altered by unfocus techniques such as mindfulness, which start with focus, then lead to unfocused states.

DARE TO LEAP

The famous Double Slit Experiment is how we confirmed the way electrons—the tiny "particles" in your brain—behave. To understand this experiment, imagine being in front of a plate in which there are two big holes large enough for tennis balls to pass through. Now imagine a screen behind this plate, so that when you throw the tennis balls through the holes that match their size exactly, they will hit the screen. If you were throwing tennis balls straight through the holes, they would most likely hit the screen in line with the holes, right? But in the Double Slit Experiment, when you use electrons rather than tennis balls, something different happens.

Instead of seeing the electrons hit the screen in line with the slits, you will see electron "hits" in the form of bands all across the screen. The range of places that they hit is far broader than the tennis-ball-sized and positioned holes.

After thinking long and hard about this, scientists have deduced that when electrons go through the slits, they become waves and travel together toward the screen. These waves are like the concentric circles you might see if you simultaneously dropped two rocks close to each other, one with each hand, into a pond. In the same way that the rocks will create outwardly moving circles in a pond, the electron beams that go through the double slits create concentric circles moving toward the screen. These two concentric circle formations get bigger and bigger as they move toward the screen, and at some point, the lines of both crisscross each other. Eventually more and more wave lines intersect on the way to the screen.

The bands on the screen correspond to where the waves intersect. There are lots of points of intersection, so there are many bands on the screen. But here's where the story gets even stranger.

If you were to place a measuring device that observes the electrons as they pass through the slit (a metaphor for focus), the electrons stop behaving like waves and instead act like particles—like the tennis balls. You see them on the screen only directly in front of the slits on the screen. If you turn the device off (a metaphor for unfocus), they start behaving like waves again, and you see bands. Also, if you place the device in between the entrance and the screen, they behave in the same way when they cross the line of placement: particles if the observing device is on, waves if it is off.

It's as if the electrons "know" whether you are watching them. Even stranger is that scientists later demonstrated that you could hide the device so far away and present it for so little time that there would not be enough time for the electrons to "sense" it. Yet 93 percent of the time, they behave like particles when they are observed. How this occurs is still a mystery. But it's fair to say that electrons will be in more possible places when they are not being observed.

Now, we know that this phenomenon represents much of what quantum physics is about. And we know too that you can't apply principles that govern the behavior of small particles like electrons to larger objects like humans willy-nilly. Yet when you appreciate that electrons are what you're made up of, and that the very particles that make up your brain can change when unobserved, it gives you reason to pause and a deep respect for unfocus and the unknown.

Suppressing or repressing self-doubt is far inferior to replacing it with acceptance of mystery, possibility thinking, intuition, spontaneity, and operating from your psychological COG. When you do, you unfocus from the existing evidence (or lack of evidence) for success, and you use your brain to visualize and simulate templates of the future that you can explore. By accepting and accelerating on a more mysterious path, you don't allow focus to limit your possibilities or draw you down.

A focused frame of mind is one that is invested in conscious, linear, goal-directed, purposeful, productive, and sensible thinking. You can't do without it. Yet on its own, it is woefully inadequate for exponential gains. Rather, it is only when unfocus is added to the mix that you can take advantage of the speed of unconscious processing outside the realm of focus, reenergize your brain fatigued from focus, and dislodge hidden memories inaccessible to a focused mind. When you do, you put yourself in the position to make a quantum leap—an improvement in your life that is sudden, large, and often unexpected.

A tinkering mind is always on the lookout for the right moment to make this leap—to leave the hallowed ground of a focused mind and live a life that is partly planned and partly simulated and imagined. If it's not front and center, it's at least at the back of your mind. Each small tinkering step, each small dabbling experiment, brings you closer to the giant leap that fear would otherwise keep you from.

SEE BEADS ON A CHAIN, NOT ISOLATED BUOYS AT SEA

It is a biological reality that our brains are all connected. There are holes in your skull (eyes, ears, nose, mouth, skin) and a brain within it—your brain is open to the world! Our heads are more like multiple beads, joined by an invisible thread, than single buoys floating out at sea. There's plenty of evidence to suggest that in addition to having separate brains joined by this thread, our brains may be part of one bigger chain called universal consciousness.

Just because you can't "see" this universal consciousness doesn't mean it doesn't exist. For example, we believe that we can reliably see the world around us with our eyes, yet every human being has a literal blind spot in the eye, so that it is possible to completely miss something. Similarly, any sound that has a frequency of 17,400 Hz can be heard only by teenagers. If you are over eighteen, you're unlikely to hear it. And similar limitations apply to taste, touch, and smell. The world is filled with more information than your senses will process. Mirror neurons are proof of our instant connection. These brain circuits in *your* head are turned on when they "reflect" (like a mirror) *my* movement, intention, and emotions when you are near me.

Your brain can form a picture of what is going on in my brain without any effort at all on your part. Somehow, something between you and me "transmits" this information. Call it air, radio waves, or whatever you want—a line of communication is open between you and me, and the effect is instant. Watch a figure skater leap into the air, and you feel magnificent because your brain is mounting a response as if you were doing the same—but it's below the threshold for movement or is suppressed, which is why you're not leaping off the couch. Talk to someone who has malicious intent, and your brain mirrors this intent. The same goes for a person whose smile is contagious—your mirror neurons are reflecting the intention and emotion in your own brain, automatically.

Amazingly, you don't even have to be close to me for our brains to communicate—the Internet can connect thoughts as well. In 2014, psychiatrist Carles Grau and his colleagues conducted an experiment in which they proved that a person thinking of the word *hola* or *ciao* in India could communicate this to people in France without saying it out loud, being seen, or typing it. The takeaway? Thought is electricity. And when you use the Internet, this electricity can be communicated across large distances.

We can synchronize our brains with one another automatically. In 2015, psychologist Yulia Golland and her colleagues showed that when people watch a movie together, their brain waves become synchronized. The more synchronized their brain waves are, the more closely tied to each other their emotional states are. Even when people are not deliberately connected with one another, just being in the same physical space synchronizes their physiology.

All these ideas suggest that a "communication line" exists between us—an "Internet" connecting our brains.

When you look at the world, do you see it as a *collection* or *connection* of many things? (Remember lumpers and splitters?) Your perceptions would have you believe that the world is a collection of many things, but when you suspend your perceptions, you see the world as a connection of things, as one giant coordinated universe. Great minds are able to move from focus to unfocus by seeing the world as a collection and then as a connection. They move back and forth between the two with ease.

Our tendency to see things as a collection of separate items can be traced back to infancy, when our brains develop the ability to differentiate ourselves from others. When an infant first learns how to grasp things, like a person's thumb, it heralds their first experience of a "self" as separate from "other." Neurons in the parietal cortex are largely responsible for this experience when they are adequately developed. And as you grow, you continue to see the world as objects outside yourself, and you think this is a fact of life set in stone. It's not. Remember how meditation can change this?

Focus cannot help you see the connections in this "Internet of things." No matter how hard you look for a tangible sign of it, you won't see it. That's why we need to rely on ways of "seeing" that are beyond perception. We need to settle into unfocus for this connection to become more apparent.

Seeing the world as connected has many other upsides too, especially when it defines a new mindset. The airplane, the telephone, and the Internet could not have been invented if the inventors did not at least partially believe that people could be connected across large distances. And we may be more likely to solve social problems such as prejudice by seeing the world as a connection. Seeing men and women as different has led to flawed arguments and injustice time and time again, against both parties. Seeing men and women as people makes us understand that we have more in common than we might think and that due to this connection we are responsible for one another.

REPLACE EVOLUTION

A long time ago evolutionary biologists recognized that the human body evolved over time. When certain things become unnecessary, the body does away with them. And when new competencies are needed, the body scrambles to develop them. I believe that unfocus is a relatively new brain habit that has evolved to reclaim the glories of the Renaissance and to meet the demands of an ever-changing world—a new and modern Renaissance.

The brain does not, however, simply pull a new and clear function out of a hat. It develops its advances through tinkering. As evolution tinkers with our brains to endow us with the capacity to unfocus, we need to learn how to leverage this capacity to make the best of it.

But in many respects we are faster than evolution. And in any case, we can't wait for evolution to catch up with the changing world that we are creating. Instead, tinkerers have to work *with* evolution. They realize that their survival brains are simply fueling fear and taking them away from opportunity. They challenge the survival brain with possibility thinking and a brain that is more willing to understand the vast possibilities of the world by being in cognitive rhythm.

These mindset shifts can only occur when tinkerers take over from evolution—with the full power, productivity, and passion that this manifesto represents about the new, raw human potential.

THE TINKER MANIFESTO

I value self-forgiveness

I work with lightness—not against it

I am happy to be productive in a fuzzy world

I embrace complexity

I embrace the unknown

I am part of the Internet of Things

I can work faster than evolution in this life

ACKNOWLEDGMENTS

I am deeply indebted and grateful to the team that has allowed this book to become a reality.

The concept and book would probably have remained in my imagination were it not for the brilliant, incisive, and "nail on the head" mentality of my agent, Celeste Fine. Celeste saw my pressing need to encourage all people to find greatness within their own complexity—at a time when the term *complexity* bordered on profanity. With her nurturing sense of belief and promise and her deep-lying sensitivities and intellectual faculties, she helped me bring this book to life.

Before *Tinker* was born, Celeste asked me to engage in a monologue for an hour, in order to see what I was doing and why I loved my life and work so much. After hearing my seemingly endless ramblings, she looked at me and said, "Unfocus—you have to write about why unfocus is such a good idea, and how people can make it work for themselves in their lives. You've done it. Why not share it?" Celeste is not simply a representative. She knows deeply who her writers are. She advocated *for* me, and also read, thought, wondered, and pondered with me throughout this process. With never a wasted word, she is a master of communication, incorrigibly her own, and as inspiring of "self-ownership" as one could possibly be. Her entire team, including John Maas and Sarah Passick, helped me stay with this book, even when, at times, the concept seemed to have run away into obscurity.

In fact, it might have, were it not for the mind-blowing experience of working with my editor, Marnie Cochran. I'm not sure where to start—with her brilliant sensibility that makes every word want to blossom into the fullness that it can be, or slip into a space that was just waiting for it? Or with her lighthearted depth, so clearly obvious in her relentless dedication to the clarity of the writing? Or with my very large luck and good fortune that she did not give in to her probably quite frequent temptations to wash her hands of what at times was a book that seemed to want to become ether, or a mirror of all-too-intense aspects of humanity that would have obscured its core message? Marnie, thank you for your amazing talent and your supreme understanding and professionalism in working *with* me so adaptively and collaboratively, even when my words were untamed, far too irreverent, or simply caught up in the excitement of themselves. Thank you for bothering to talk, listen, understand, change, or stay your course when you believed in it, and for working with me in articulating the immense power of unfocus. And so much thanks, too, to Liz Stein and Janet Biehl, who worked with us to help polish the words on the page.

Then there are all the people in my life who have tolerated my obsession with this book and my social media outreach to the world, despite their intense need for privacy. I acknowledge them in these brief mentions: To Uma—you are magic beyond compare, a stalwart presence of love, understanding, and critical feedback, and a bastion of support and faith in ethereal and transcendent ways. To Rajiv—your iconoclastic presence and gifts of insight have been so enlightening, and your tireless ability to accompany me and let me accompany you in neurotic entanglements personify unfocus. To Rajan—thank you for covering for me like a "mindguard," allaying my anxieties about our family, my choices, myself, and showing me the belief that has inspired this book to its completion. To my parents, Raz and Sava, I owe so much gratitude. They are in every intention and word in this book, and inextricably linked with my psyche—my mom, still my greatest fan, and a veritable miracle to behold; my dad, passed, yet ever present in my work ethic and reminders to reset to "no-nonsense." To Paula, whose patience, inspiration, intelligence, work ethic, and dedication I have benefited from. And to Vicky and Irina, for helping me manage my life.

And how can I forget the unsung heroes of this process in my extended family and among my friends—Uncle Bobby, Mano, Shan, Jaya, Babes, Shunna, Jean, Bob, Pragasen, Brandon, Mahadev, Dennis, Stephen, Daphne, Phillip, JT, Daron, Zach, Brenda, and Gideon, people whose love, dedication, presence, support, and "beingness" have touched and supported this book in intangible yet essential and fundamental ways.

I grew up in a family of characters, with cousins who evolve out of that same matrix too: Boonch, Thumbiemama, Boyamama, Perima, Dayamama, Surya, Sagrie, Prakash, Monty, Pinglan, Naveen, Loges, Bashni, Georgie, Devan, Doris, Anna, Aggie—a potpourri of names and diversity of characters, but a foundational experience in my understanding of nondual consciousness. For that I am immensely grateful.

No book gets written without its teachers in mind either. I must thank and acknowledge Dr. P. D. Naidoo, one of my first inspirations to study the brain; Dr. Margaret Nair, for inspiring me to pursue an education in psychiatry; Dr. Shervert Frazier, for guiding me out of many dark holes, often in reverie, before his untimely recent passing; Dr. Bruce Cohen, for setting me on the path that was to become my academic life; Dr. Ross Baldessarini, for encouraging me to always question; Drs. Debbye Yurgelun-Todd and Perry Renshaw, for including me in the world's most innovative brain-imaging center of its time at Harvard; Dr. Bill Carter, for seeing in me something that I am, often before I do, and often surprisingly too; Dr. Les Havens, for bothering to manifest as a human on earth, when you clearly had other things to do; and, of course, Dr. Jonathan Cole, for believing in me and the tinker process, and for opening the doors to my home and my identity's place of rest and reinvention, in America. Also, I would be remiss if I were not to mention my colleagues from downtown—Dr. Maurizio Fava, for helping me do my initial research, and Drs. John Herman and Jerry Rosenbaum, for being there soon after I graduated, and for offering to be there if ever I needed them.

Finally, none of this would be possible if it were for not for my patients, coaching clients, and online community, who teach me and remind me endlessly that life hides in secret places; that "self" as we see it is an illusion; that we owe it to *ourselves* to find ourselves in ways that logic alone could never reveal. I bow to you, feeling now a place of reverence that I call God—a force that I humbly submit to, whatever it is—in deep and profound gratitude.

Tinker Dabble Doodle Try is not just meant to be a book; it is meant to herald a new and invigorated movement. In reading this book, I hope that you will be inspired to own and manifest your identity as an adventurer, and if you already do, to take it to another level.

We are wired to be self-aware, but also to wander into ourselves, so that we may taste the magic of being alive and rise to the occasion of this opportunity to truly live—tinkeringly!

NOTES

INTRODUCTION: LEAVING THE CULT OF FOCUS

xi **One Friday night in 1983** K. Mullis, "Polymerase Chain Reaction," *Dr. Kary Banks Mullis,* n.d.: http://www.karymullis.com/pcr.shtml.

xi **"My little silver Honda's"** K. Mullis, *Dancing Naked in the Minefield* (New York: Vintage Books, 1998), pp. 3–4.

xii **Dr. Kary Banks Mullis** "Biography," *Dr. Kary Banks Mullis,* n.d.: http://www.karymullis.com/biography.shtml.

xiv *inattentional blindness,* **wherein** C. Kreitz, P. Furley, et al., "The Influence of Attention Set, Working Memory Capacity, and Expectations on Inattentional Blindness," *Perception* 45, no. 4 (2016): 386–99.

xiv **police officer in Boston** C. F. Chabris, A. Weinberger, et al., "You Do Not Talk About Fight Club If You Do Not Notice Fight Club: Inattentional Blindness for a Simulated Real-World Assault," *Iperception* 2, no. 2 (2011): 150–53.

xv **invisible gorilla experiment** D. J. Simons and C. F. Chabris, "Gorillas in Our Midst: Sustained Inattentional Blindness for Dynamic Events," *Perception* 28, no. 9 (1999): 1059–74.

xv **too much focus or hyperfocus** B. Hahn, A. N. Harvey, et al., "Hyperdeactivation of the Default Mode Network in People with Schizophrenia When Focusing Attention in Space," *Schizophrenia Bulletin* (February 28, 2016).

xvi *long-term discounting* C. Chen and G. He, "The Contrast Effect in Temporal and Probabilistic Discounting," *Frontiers in Psychology* 7 (2016): 304.

xvi *loss of caring* C. N. Dewall, R. F. Baumeister, et al., "Depletion Makes the Heart Grow Less Helpful: Helping as a Function of Self-

Regulatory Energy and Genetic Relatedness," *Personality and Social Psychology Bulletin* 34, no. 12 (December 2008): 1653–62.

xvi **Rosabeth Moss Kanter** R. M. Kanter, "Innovation: The Classic Traps," *Harvard Business Review* 84, no. 11 (2006): 154.

xvii **After obtaining his Ph.D.** E. Yoffe, "Is Kary Mullis God?" *Esquire* 122, no. 1 (1994): 68.

xix **Unfocusing reduces amygdala activation** K. McRae, B. Hughes, et al., "The Neural Bases of Distraction and Reappraisal," *Journal of Cognitive Neuroscience* 22, no. 2 (2010): 248–62.

xix **the *frontopolar cortex*** A. E. Green, M. S. Cohen, et al., "Frontopolar Activity and Connectivity Support Dynamic Conscious Augmentation of Creative State," *Human Brain Mapping* (2014), conference abstract.

xix ***anterior insula* activity** H. C. Lou, H. Nowak, and T. W. Kjaer, "The Mental Self," *Progress in Brain Research* 150 (2005): 197–204.

xx ***prefrontal cortex* activity** A. Golkar, E. Johansson, et al., "The Influence of Work-Related Chronic Stress on the Regulation of Emotion and on Functional Connectivity in the Brain," *PLoS One* 9, no. 9 (2014): e104550.

xx **improves long-term memory** T. Amer, K. W. Ngo, and L. Hasher, "Cultural Differences in Visual Attention: Implications for Distraction Processing," *British Journal of Psychology* (2016), epub. ahead of print.

xx ***default mode network*** A. Kucyi, M. J. Hove, et al., "Dynamic Brain Network Correlates of Spontaneous Fluctuations in Attention," *Cerebral Cortex* (2016), epub. ahead of print.

xx **in diseases like Alzheimer's** L. L. Beason-Held, T. J. Hohman, et al., "Brain Network Changes and Memory Decline in Aging," *Brain Imaging and Behavior* (2016), epub. ahead of print.

xx **DMN that is not synchronized** K. Mevel, G. Chételat, et al., "The Default Mode Network in Healthy Aging and Alzheimer's Disease," *International Journal of Alzheimer's Disease* 2011 (2011): http://dx.doi.org/10.4061/2011/535816.

xx **Reduced connectivity in the unfocus** S. Sandrone and M. Catani, "Journal Club: Default-Mode Network Connectivity in Cognitively Unimpaired Patients with Parkinson Disease," *Neurology* 81, no. 23 (2013): e172–75.

xx **build cognitive reserve** R. S. Wilson, C. F. Mendes de Leon, et al., "Participation in Cognitively Stimulating Activities and Risk of Incident Alzheimer Disease," *Journal of the American Medical Association* 287 (2002): 742–48.

xx **protect your thinking brain** C. Fabrigoule, L. Letenneur, et al., "Social and Leisure Activities and Risk of Dementia: A Prospective Longitudinal Study," *Journal of the American Geriatrics Society* 43 (1995): 485–90; C. Helmer, D. Damon, et al., "Marital Status and Risk of Alzheimer's Disease: A French Population-Based Cohort Study," *Neurology* 53 (1999): 1953–58; J. Verghese, R. B. Lipton, et al., "Leisure Activities and the Risk of Dementia in the Elderly," *New England Journal of Medicine* 348, no. 25 (2003): 2508–16; X. Zhang, C. Li, and M. Zhang, "Psychosocial Risk Factors of Alzheimer's Disease," *Zhonghua Yi Xue Za Zhi* 79 (1999): 335–38.

CHAPTER 1: THE BEAT OF YOUR BRAIN

5 **brains manage focus and unfocus** D. Gui, S. Xu, et al., "Resting Spontaneous Activity in the Default Mode Network Predicts Performance Decline During Prolonged Attention Workload," *NeuroImage* 120 (October 15, 2015): 323–30.

6 **Your brain will shut down** M. Tanaka, A. Ishii, and Y. Watanabe, "Neural Effects of Mental Fatigue Caused by Continuous Attention Load: A Magnetoencephalography Study," *Brain Research* 1561 (May 2, 2014): 60–66.

6 **in mini-mental journeys** M. A. Killingsworth and D. T. Gilbert, "A Wandering Mind Is an Unhappy Mind," *Science* 330, no. 6006 (November 12, 2010): 932.

6 **a brain cell's resting voltage** J. E. Dowling, *Creating Minds: How the Brain Works* (New York: W. W. Norton, 1999), p. 22; M. A. Persinger, "Brain Electromagnetic Activity and Lightning: Potentially Congruent Scale-Invariant Quantitative Properties," *Frontiers in Integrative Neuroscience* 6 (2012): 19.

6 **100 billion brain cells** S. Herculano-Houzel, "The Human Brain in Numbers: A Linearly Scaled-up Primate Brain," *Frontiers in Human Neuroscience* 3 (2009): 31.

7 **your brain's attention fluctuates** A. Kucyi, M. J. Hove, et al., "Dynamic Brain Network Correlates of Spontaneous Fluctuations in Attention," *Cerebral Cortex* (February 13, 2016).

7 **continuum from more to less** N. H. Liu, C. Y. Chiang, and H. C. Chu, "Recognizing the Degree of Human Attention Using EEG Signals from Mobile Sensors," *Sensors* (Basel) 13, no. 8 (2013): 10273–86.

7 **Gamma waves are the odd** X. Jia and A. Kohn, "Gamma Rhythms in the Brain," *PLoS Biology* 9, no. 4 (April 2011): e1001045.

7 **Faster than beta waves** J. W. Kim, B. N. Kim, et al., "Desynchronization of Theta-Phase Gamma-Amplitude Coupling During a Mental Arithmetic Task in Children with Attention Deficit/Hyperactivity Disorder," *PLoS One* 11, no. 3 (2016): e0145288.

7 **Being a peak performer at** M. Graczyk, M. Pachalska, et al., "Neuro-feedback Training for Peak Performance," *Annals of Agricultural and Environmental Medicine* 21, no. 4 (2014): 871–75; S. di Fronso, C. Robazza, et al., "Neural Markers of Performance States in an Olympic Athlete: An EEG Case Study in Air-Pistol Shooting," *Journal of Sports Science and Medicine* 15, no. 2 (June 2016): 214–22; T. Hulsdunker, A. Mierau, and H. K. Struder, "Higher Balance Task Demands Are Associated with an Increase in Individual Alpha Peak Frequency," *Frontiers in Human Neuroscience* 9 (2015): 695.

7 **Georg Philipp Telemann** S. Zohn, *Music for a Mixed Taste: Style, Genre and Meaning in Telemann's Instrumental Works* (New York: Oxford University Press, 2008), p. 20.

7 **Benjamin Franklin invented** L. Gensel, "The Medical World of Benjamin Franklin," *Journal of the Royal Society of Medicine* 98, no. 12 (December 2005): 534–38; M. W. Jernegan, "Benjamin Franklin's 'Electrical Kite' and Lightning Rod," *New England Quarterly* 1, no. 2 (1928): 180–96.

7 **the frontoparietal cortex** S. Vossel, J. J. Geng, and G. R. Fink, "Dorsal and Ventral Attention Systems: Distinct Neural Circuits but Collaborative Roles," *Neuroscientist* 20, no. 2 (April 2014): 150–59.

8 *central executive network* L. E. Sherman, J. D. Rudie, et al., "Development of the Default Mode and Central Executive Networks across Early Adolescence: A Longitudinal Study," *Developmental Cognitive Neuroscience* 10 (October 2014): 148–59.

8 **The brain circuit that allows** D. Tomasi, N. D. Volkow, et al., "Dopamine Transporters in Striatum Correlate with Deactivation in the Default Mode Network During Visuospatial Attention," *PLoS One* 4, no. 6 (2009): e6102.

8 **"Do Mostly Nothing"** A. Mohan, A. J. Roberto, et al., "The Significance of the Default Mode Network (DMN) in Neurological and Neuropsychiatric Disorders: A Review," *Yale Journal of Biology and Medicine* 89, no. 1 (2016): 49–57.

8 **one of the greatest consumers** I. Neuner, J. Arrubla, et al., "The Default Mode Network and EEG Regional Spectral Power: A Simultaneous fMRI-EEG Study," *PLoS One* 9, no. 2 (2014): e88214.

8 **connected with the focus circuits** A. Karten, S. P. Pantazatos, et al., "Dynamic Coupling between the Lateral Occipital-Cortex, Default-Mode, and Frontoparietal Networks During Bistable Perception," *Brain Connectivity* 3, no. 3 (2013): 286–93; T. Piccoli, G. Valente, et al., "The Default Mode Network and the Working Memory Network Are Not Anti-Correlated During All Phases of a Working Memory Task," *PLoS One* 10, no. 4 (2015): e0123354.

9 **a mix of brainwaves** F. Lopes de Silva, "Neural Mechanisms Underlying Brain Waves: From Neural Membranes to Networks," *Electroencephalography and Clinical Neurophysiology* 79, no. 2 (1991): 81–93; Neuner, Arrubla, et al., "Default Mode Network"; W. Gao, J. H. Gilmore, et al., "The Dynamic Reorganization of the Default-Mode Network During a Visual Classification Task," *Frontiers in Systems Neuroscience* 7 (2013): 34; X. Di and B. B. Biswal, "Dynamic Brain Functional Connectivity Modulated by Resting-State Networks," *Brain Structure and Function* 220, no. 1 (January 2015): 37–46; R. N. Spreng, W. D. Stevens, et al., "Default Network Activity, Coupled with the Frontoparietal Control Network, Supports Goal-Directed Cognition," *NeuroImage* 53, no. 1 (October 15, 2010): 303–17.

9 **It's we who stop this** G. Bush, "Attention-Deficit/Hyperactivity Disorder and Attention Networks," *Neuropsychopharmacology* 35, no. 1 (January 2010): 278–300; M. Schecklmann, A. C. Ehlis, et al., "Diminished Prefrontal Oxygenation with Normal and Above-Average Verbal Fluency Performance in Adult ADHD," *Journal of Psychiatric Research* 43, no. 2 (December 2008): 98–106.

9 **Unfocus circuits bring on** M. Drolet, R. I. Schubotz, and J. Fischer, "Authenticity Affects the Recognition of Emotions in Speech: Behavioral and fMRI Evidence," *Cognitive, Affective and Behavioral Neuroscience* 12, no. 1 (March 2012): 140–50; C. G. Davey, J. Pujol, and B. J. Harrison, "Mapping the Self in the Brain's Default Mode Network," *NeuroImage* 132 (May 15, 2016): 390–97.

9 **And they can be trained** K. L. Hyde, J. Lerch, et al., "Musical Training Shapes Structural Brain Development," *Journal of Neuroscience* 29, no. 10 (March 11, 2009): 3019–25; L. Jancke, "Music Drives Brain Plasticity," *F1000 Biology Reports* 1 (2009): 78.

9 **Fritz Reiner, a twentieth-century** P. Hart, *Fritz Reiner: A Biography* (Evanston, IL: Northwestern University Press, 1994); H. Edgar, "CSO Unveils Fritz Reiner Bust at Symphony Center," *Chicago Maroon* (June 15, 2016): http://chicagomaroon.com/2016/06/15/cso-unveils-fritz-reiner-bust-at-symphony-center/; "The Forgotten Great Conductors," *Gramophone* (October 12, 2013): http://www.gramophone.co.uk/features/focus/the-forgotten-great-conductors.

9 **"You're not men"** G. Stein, "Fritz Reiner: A Marriage of Talent and Terror," *Dr. Gerald Stein: Blogging About Psychotherapy from Chicago* (October 12, 2013): https://drgeraldstein.wordpress.com/tag/our-strengths-are-our-weaknesses/.

10 **The Many Notes of Your** A. Anticevic, M. W. Cole, et al., "The Role of Default Network Deactivation in Cognition and Disease," *Trends in Cognitive Sciences* 16, no. 12 (December 2012): 584–92.

10 *a distraction filter* M. Ziaei, N. Peira, and J. Persson, "Brain Systems Underlying Attentional Control and Emotional Distraction During Working Memory Encoding," *NeuroImage* 87 (February 15, 2014): 276–86; T. Piccoli, G. Valente, et al., "The Default Mode Network and the Working Memory Network Are Not Anti-Correlated During All Phases of a Working Memory Task," *PLoS One* 10, no. 4 (2015): e0123354.

10 *builds mental flexibility* D. Vatansever, A. E. Manktelow, et al., "Cognitive Flexibility: A Default Network and Basal Ganglia Connectivity Perspective," *Brain Connectivity* 6, no. 3 (April 2016): 201–7; A. W. Sali, S. M. Courtney, and S. Yantis, "Spontaneous Fluctuations in the Flexible Control of Covert Attention," *Journal of Neuroscience* 36, no. 2 (January 13, 2016): 445–54.

11 *connects you more deeply* C. G. Davey, J. Pujol, and B. J. Harrison, "Mapping the Self in the Brain's Default Mode Network," *NeuroImage* 132 (May 15, 2016): 390–97; P. Qin, S. Grimm, et al., "Spontaneous Activity in Default-Mode Network Predicts Ascription of Self-Relatedness to Stimuli," *Social Cognitive and Affective Neuroscience* 11, no. 4 (April 2016): 693–702.

11 *activates "social connection" circuits* W. Li, X. Mai, and C. Liu, "The Default Mode Network and Social Understanding of Others: What Do Brain Connectivity Studies Tell Us," *Frontiers in Human Neuroscience* 8 (2014): 74; R. B. Mars, F. X. Neubert, et al., "On the Relationship between the 'Default Mode Network' and the 'Social Brain,' " *Frontiers in Human Neuroscience* 6 (2012): 189.

11 *integrates the past, present* M. Konishi, D. G. McLaren, et al., "Shaped by the Past: The Default Mode Network Supports Cognition That Is Independent of Immediate Perceptual Input," *PLoS One* 10, no. 6 (2015): e0132209; Y. Ostby, K. B. Walhovd, et al., "Mental Time Travel and Default-Mode Network Functional Connectivity in the Developing Brain," *Proceedings of the National Academy of Sciences* 109, no. 42 (October 16, 2012): 16800–4.

11 *express your creativity* R. E. Beaty, M. Benedek, et al., "Creativity and the Default Network: A Functional Connectivity Analysis of the Creative Brain at Rest," *Neuropsychologia* 64C (September 20, 2014): 92–98; N. C. Andreasen, "A Journey into Chaos: Creativity and the Unconscious," *Mens Sana Monographs* 9, no. 1 (January 2011): 42–53.

11 *dredge up intangible memories* J. Yang, X. Weng, et al., "Sustained Activity within the Default Mode Network During an Implicit Memory Task," *Cortex* 46, no. 3 (March 2010): 354–66; T. Ino, R. Nakai, et al., "Brain Activation During Autobiographical Memory Retrieval

with Special Reference to Default Mode Network," *Open Neuroimaging Journal* 5 (2011): 14–23.

12 **maintain the status quo** S. M. Fleming, C. L. Thomas, and R. J. Dolan, "Overcoming Status Quo Bias in the Human Brain," *Proceedings of the National Academy of Sciences* 107, no. 13 (March 30, 2010): 6005–9.

12 *cognitive dissonance,* **which is** K. Izuma, M. Matsumoto, et al., "Neural Correlates of Cognitive Dissonance and Choice-Induced Preference Change," *Proceedings of the National Academy of Sciences* 107, no. 51 (December 21, 2010): 22014–19.

13 **Switch cost comes in the** S. Yin, T. Wang, et al., "Task-Switching Cost and Intrinsic Functional Connectivity in the Human Brain: Toward Understanding Individual Differences in Cognitive Flexibility," *PLoS One* 10, no. 12 (2015): e0145826; P. S. Cooper, P. M. Garrett, et al., "Task Uncertainty Can Account for Mixing and Switch Costs in Task-Switching," *PLoS One* 10, no. 6 (2015): e0131556.

13 **called** *spreading of alternatives* E. Harmon-Jones, C. Harmon-Jones, et al., "Left Frontal Cortical Activation and Spreading of Alternatives: Tests of the Action-Based Model of Dissonance," *Journal of Personality and Social Psychology* 94, no. 1 (January 2008): 1–15.

13 **professor Issidoros Sarinopoulos** I. Sarinopoulos, D. W. Grupe, et al., "Uncertainty During Anticipation Modulates Neural Responses to Aversion in Human Insula and Amygdala," *Cerebral Cortex* 20, no. 4 (April 2010): 929–40.

14 **focus casts a magic spell** B. R. Payne, J. J. Jackson, et al., "In the Zone: Flow State and Cognition in Older Adults," *Psychology and Aging* 26, no. 3 (September 2011): 738–43.

14 **more psychologically comfortable** S. B. Ostlund and B. W. Balleine, "On Habits and Addiction: An Associative Analysis of Compulsive Drug Seeking," *Drug Discovery Today: Disease Models* 5, no. 4 (Winter 2008): 235–45.

15 **feeling more drained** M. A. Boksem, T. F. Meijman, and M. M. Lorist, "Effects of Mental Fatigue on Attention: An ERP Study," *Brain Research: Cognitive Brain Research* 25, no. 1 (September 2005): 107–16.

15 **they either choke or just** R. Yu, "Choking Under Pressure: The Neuropsychological Mechanisms of Incentive-Induced Performance Decrements," *Frontiers of Behavioral Neuroscience* 9 (2015): 19.

16 **fatigued by focus** D. van der Linden, M. Frese, and T. F. Meijman, "Mental Fatigue and the Control of Cognitive Processes: Effects on Perseveration and Planning," *Acta Psychologica* 113, no. 1 (May 2003): 45–65.

16 **making the same mistake** M. C. Stevens, K. A. Kiehl, et al., "Brain Network Dynamics During Error Commission," *Human Brain Mapping* 30, no. 1 (January 2009): 24–37.

16 **quickly or repeatedly overwhelmed** A. F. Arnsten, "Stress Signalling Pathways That Impair Prefrontal Cortex Structure and Function," *Nature Reviews Neuroscience* 10, no. 6 (June 2009): 410–22.

16 **settling is a sign** T. Thompson and A. Richardson, "Self-Handicapping Status, Claimed Self-Handicaps and Reduced Practice Effort Following Success and Failure Feedback," *British Journal of Educational Psychology* 71, pt. 1 (March 2001): 151–70.

16 **disenchanted with where you are** R. N. Spreng, E. DuPre, et al., "Goal-Congruent Default Network Activity Facilitates Cognitive Control," *Journal of Neuroscience* 34, no. 42 (October 15, 2014): 14108–14.

18 **Reverie is a form** T. H. Ogden, "Reverie and Interpretation," *Psychoanalytic Quarterly* 66, no. 4 (October 1997): 567–95.

18 **letting your mind wander** J. Smallwood and J. Andrews-Hanna, "Not All Minds That Wander Are Lost: The Importance of a Balanced Perspective on the Mind-Wandering State," *Frontiers in Psychology* 4 (2013): 441.

18 **Unlike mindfulness** C. M. Zedelius and J. W. Schooler, "Mind Wandering 'Ahas' Versus Mindful Reasoning: Alternative Routes to Creative Solutions," *Frontiers in Psychology* 6 (2015): 834.

19 **projecting into the future** R. N. Spreng, R. A. Mar, and A. S. Kim, "The Common Neural Basis of Autobiographical Memory, Prospection, Navigation, Theory of Mind, and the Default Mode: A Quantitative Meta-Analysis," *Journal of Cognitive Neuroscience* 21, no. 3 (March 2009): 489–510.

19 **it must not be stressful** R. L. McMillan, S. B. Kaufman, and J. L. Singer, "Ode to Positive Constructive Daydreaming," *Frontiers in Psychology* 4 (2013): 626.

19 **usefulness of self-talk** E. Kross, E. Bruehlman-Senecal, et al., "Self-Talk as a Regulatory Mechanism: How You Do It Matters," *Journal of Personality and Social Psychology* 106, no. 2 (February 2014): 304–24.

20 **value of reframing your thoughts** D. Cutuli, "Cognitive Reappraisal and Expressive Suppression Strategies Role in the Emotion Regulation: An Overview on Their Modulatory Effects and Neural Correlates," *Frontiers in Systems Neuroscience* 8 (2014): 175.

20 **Psychologist Daniel Wegner** D. M. Wegner, "Ironic Processes of Mental Control," *Psychological Review* 101, no. 1 (1994): 34–52; D. M. Wegner, "How to Think, Say, or Do Precisely the Worst Thing for Any Occasion," *Science* 325, no. 5936 (2009): 48–50.

20 **a "do not" instruction** D. M. Wegner, R. Erber, and S. Zanakos, "Ironic Processes in the Mental Control of Mood and Mood-Related Thought," *Journal of Personality and Social Psychology* 65, no. 6 (December 1993): 1093–104.

20 **use your body to activate** M. Oppezzo and D. L. Schwartz, "Give Your Ideas Some Legs: The Positive Effect of Walking on Creative Thinking," *Journal of Experimental Psychology, Learning, Memory, and Cognition* 40, no. 4 (July 2014): 1142–52.

20 **One person may want to** R. A. Atchley, D. L. Strayer, and P. Atchley, "Creativity in the Wild: Improving Creative Reasoning through Immersion in Natural Settings," *PLoS One* 7, no. 12 (2012): e51474.

21 **Regardless of the technique** J. Xu, A. Vik, et al., "Nondirective Meditation Activates Default Mode Network and Areas Associated with Memory Retrieval and Emotional Processing," *Frontiers in Human Neuroscience* 8 (2014): 86.

24 **Ana Luisa Pinho** A. L. Pinho, O. de Manzano, et al., "Connecting to Create: Expertise in Musical Improvisation Is Associated with Increased Functional Connectivity between Premotor and Prefrontal Areas," *Journal of Neuroscience* 34, no. 18 (April 30, 2014): 6156–63.

25 **psychologist Anika Maraz** A. Maraz, O. Kiraly, et al., "Why Do You Dance? Development of the Dance Motivation Inventory (DMI)," *PLoS One* 10, no. 3 (2015): e0122866.

26 **John Elfreth Watkins** E. Watkins, "What May Happen in the Next Hundred Years?" *Ladies' Home Journal* (1900): 8.

26 **may not always be correct** S. Sandrone, "The Brain as a Crystal Ball: The Predictive Potential of Default Mode Network," *Frontiers in Human Neuroscience* 6 (2012): 261.

27 **neuroscientist Julia Mossbridge** J. Mossbridge, P. Tressoldi, and J. Utts, "Predictive Physiological Anticipation Preceding Seemingly Unpredictable Stimuli: A Meta-Analysis," *Frontiers in Psychology* 3 (2012): 390.

27 **an active role in this prediction** C. S. Soon, A. H. He, et al., "Predicting Free Choices for Abstract Intentions," *Proceedings of the National Academy of Sciences* 110, no. 15 (April 9, 2013): 6217–22.

27 **Some kind of unconscious mirroring** M. Iacoboni, I. Molnar-Szakacs, et al., "Grasping the Intentions of Others with One's Own Mirror Neuron System," *PLoS Biology* 3, no. 3 (March 2005): e79.

27 **theories based on quantum physics** S. Hameroff, "How Quantum Brain Biology Can Rescue Conscious Free Will," *Frontiers in Integrative Neuroscience* 6 (2012): 93.

27 **Children who learn to play** E. A. Miendlarzewska and W. J. Trost, "How Musical Training Affects Cognitive Development: Rhythm,

Reward and Other Modulating Variables," *Frontiers in Neuroscience* 7 (2013): 279.

CHAPTER 2: CONJURING CREATIVITY

30 **Brazilian artist Vik Muniz** V. Muniz, "Art with Wire, Sugar, Chocolate and String," *TED* (April 2007): https://www.ted.com/talks/vik _muniz_makes_art_with_wire_sugar/transcript?language=en.

30 **peanut butter and jelly** M. Schwendener, "Smile and Say 'Peanut Butter,' Mona Lisa," *New York Times* (March 2, 2007): http://www .nytimes.com/2007/03/02/arts/design/02muni.html?_r=0.

30 **brings to life potential conflicts** Erkan, "10 Most Creative Artworks Made from Unexpected Materials By Vik Muniz," *Most 10* (February 19, 2013): http://www.themost10.com/creative-artworks -unexpected-materials/.

31 **researcher Melissa Ellamil** M. Ellamil, C. Dobson, et al., "Evaluative and Generative Modes of Thought During the Creative Process," *NeuroImage* 59, no. 2 (January 16, 2012): 1783–94.

32 **hired Edelman Berland** Edelman Berland (for Adobe), "Seeking Creative Candidates: Hiring for the Future" *Adobe* (September 2014): http://www.images.adobe.com/content/dam/Adobe/en/education /pdfs/creative-candidates-study-0914.pdf?scid=social33220386.

32 **situations of uncertainty** J. S. Mueller, S. Melwani, and J. A. Goncalo, "The Bias Against Creativity: Why People Desire but Reject Creative Ideas," *Psychological Science* 23, no. 1 (January 1, 2012): 13–17.

33 **when you focus exclusively** M. Gilead, N. Liberman, and A. Maril, "From Mind to Matter: Neural Correlates of Abstract and Concrete Mindsets," *Social Cognitive and Affective Neuroscience* 9, no. 5 (May 2014): 638–45.

34 **fast and unconscious reorganization** S. M. Ritter and A. Dijksterhuis, "Creativity—The Unconscious Foundations of the Incubation Period," *Frontiers in Human Neuroscience* 8 (2014): 215.

34 **ability to surrender to chaos** D. Safan-Gerard, "Chaos and Control in the Creative Process," *Journal of the American Academy of Psychoanalysis* 13, no. 1 (January 1985): 129–38.

34 **a state of tension** M. Faust and Y. N. Kenett, "Rigidity, Chaos and Integration: Hemispheric Interaction and Individual Differences in Metaphor Comprehension," *Frontiers in Human Neuroscience* 8 (2014): 511; N. C. Andreasen, "A Journey into Chaos: Creativity and the Unconscious," *Mens Sana Monographs* 9, no. 1 (January 2011): 42–53.

34 **"Philosophy of science"** Attributed to R. Feynman, quoted by S.

Weinberg, in D. Overbye, "Laws of Nature, Source Unknown," *New York Times* (December 2007).

34 **Kevin Dunbar's research** K. Dunbar, "How Scientists Really Reason: Scientific Reasoning in Real World Laboratories," in R. Sternberg and J. Davidson, eds., *The Nature of Insight* (Cambridge, MA: MIT Press, 1995), pp. 365–96.

35 **Charles Limb is a doctor** C. J. Limb and A. R. Braun, "Neural Substrates of Spontaneous Musical Performance: An fMRI Study of Jazz Improvisation," *PLoS One* 3, no. 2 (2008): e1679.

36 **behavior expert Kenneth Resnicow** K. Resnicow and S. E. Page, "Embracing Chaos and Complexity: A Quantum Change for Public Health," *American Journal of Public Health* 98, no. 8 (August 2008): 1382–89.

37 **Arno Penzias and Robert Wilson** "Penzias and Wilson Discover Cosmic Microwave Radiation," PBS, 1965: http://www.pbs.org/wgbh/aso/databank/entries/dp65co.html; R. Schoenstein, "The Big Bang's Echo," *All Things Considered*, NPR, May 17, 2005: http://www.npr.org/templates/story/story.php?storyId=4655517; "June 1963: Discovery of the Cosmic Microwave Background," *APS News*, July 2002: https://www.aps.org/publications/apsnews/200207/history.cfm.

39 **like a mind pop** L. Zhang, W. Li, et al., "The Association between the Brain and Mind Pops: A Voxel-Based Morphometry Study in 256 Chinese College Students," *Brain Imaging and Behavior* 10, no. 2 (June 2016): 332–41.

39 **Yet inspiration actually has** V. C. Oleynick, T. M. Thrash, et al., "The Scientific Study of Inspiration in the Creative Process: Challenges and Opportunities," *Frontiers in Human Neuroscience* 8 (2014): 436.

40 **A natural way to prompt** G. M. Morriss-Kay, "The Evolution of Human Artistic Creativity," *Journal of Anatomy* 216, no. 2 (February 2010): 158–76.

41 *simplified semantic structures* D. Landy, C. Allen, and C. Zednik, "A Perceptual Account of Symbolic Reasoning," *Frontiers in Psychology* 5 (2014): 275.

41 **Metaphors are implicit comparisons** O. Vartanian, "Dissociable Neural Systems for Analogy and Metaphor: Implications for the Neuroscience of Creativity," *British Journal of Psychology* 103, no. 3 (August 2012): 302–16.

41 **The higher the quality** M. Benedek, R. Beaty, et al., "Creating Metaphors: The Neural Basis of Figurative Language Production," *NeuroImage* 90 (April 15, 2014): 99–106.

42 **"split thinking" or in "lumping"** E. Jauk, M. Benedek, and A. C. Neu-

bauer, "Tackling Creativity at Its Roots: Evidence for Different Patterns of EEG Alpha Activity Related to Convergent and Divergent Modes of Task Processing," *International Journal of Psychophysiology* 84, no. 2 (May 2012): 219–25.

43 **signals from gut bacteria** L. Galland, "The Gut Microbiome and the Brain," *Journal of Medicinal Food* 17, no. 12 (December 2014): 1261–72.

43 **Parkinson's disease—previously** E. Svensson, E. Horvath-Puho, et al., "Vagotomy and Subsequent Risk of Parkinson's Disease," *Annals of Neurology* 78, no. 4 (October 2015): 522–29.

43 **psychologist Tony McCaffrey** T. McCaffrey, "Innovation Relies on the Obscure: A Key to Overcoming the Classic Problem of Functional Fixedness," *Psychological Science* 23, no. 3 (March 2012): 215–18.

43 **"Openness to experience"** W. Li, X. Li, et al., "Brain Structure Links Trait Creativity to Openness to Experience," *Social Cognitive and Affective Neuroscience* (April 7, 2014): 191–98; B. Shi, D. Y. Dai, and Y. Lu, "Openness to Experience as a Moderator of the Relationship between Intelligence and Creative Thinking: A Study of Chinese Children in Urban and Rural Areas," *Frontiers in Psychology* 7 (2016): 641; S. B. Kaufman, L. C. Quilty, et al., "Openness to Experience and Intellect Differentially Predict Creative Achievement in the Arts and Sciences," *Journal of Personality* (December 8, 2014): 248–58.

43 **"normal" people are** D. Wood, S. D. Gosling, and J. Potter, "Normality Evaluations and Their Relation to Personality Traits and Well-Being," *Journal of Personality and Social Psychology* 93, no. 5 (November 2007): 861–79.

44 **people who have openness** R. E. Beaty, S. B. Kaufman, et al., "Personality and Complex Brain Networks: The Role of Openness to Experience in Default Network Efficiency," *Human Brain Mapping* 37, no. 2 (February 2016): 773–79.

44 **A freak accident** C. Kino, "Where Art Meets Trash and Transforms Life," *New York Times* (October 21, 2010): http://www.nytimes.com/2010/10/24/arts/design/24muniz.html?_r=0.

44 **Intuition is the brain's ability** E. Nahmias, J. Shepard, and S. Reuter, "It's OK If 'My Brain Made Me Do It': People's Intuitions About Free Will and Neuroscientific Prediction," *Cognition* 133, no. 2 (November 2014): 502–16.

44 **form an intuition network** T. Zander, N. K. Horr, et al., "Intuitive Decision Making as a Gradual Process: Investigating Semantic Intuition-Based and Priming-Based Decisions with fMRI," *Brain and Behavior* 6, no. 1 (January 2016): e00420; K. G. Volz, R. Rubsamen,

and D. Y. von Cramon, "Cortical Regions Activated by the Subjective Sense of Perceptual Coherence of Environmental Sounds: A Proposal for a Neuroscience of Intuition," *Cognitive Affective and Behavioral Neuroscience* 8, no. 3 (September 2008): 318–28.

45 **serial hypothesis testing** R. C. Wilson and Y. Niv, "Inferring Relevance in a Changing World," *Frontiers in Human Neuroscience* 5 (2011): 189.

45 **is *predictive inference*** A. K. Seth, K. Suzuki, and H. D. Critchley, "An Interoceptive Predictive Coding Model of Conscious Presence," *Frontiers in Psychology* 2 (2011): 395.

46 **a mind pop activates** L. Zhang, W. Li, et al., "The Association Between the Brain and Mind Pops: A Voxel-Based Morphometry Study in 256 Chinese College Students," *Brain Imaging and Behavior* 10, no. 2 (June 2016): 332–41.

47 **Vik Muniz is a living example** C. Kino, "Where Art Meets Trash and Transforms Life," *The New York Times* (October 21, 2010): http://www.nytimes.com/2010/10/24/arts/design/24muniz.html?_r=0.

47 **famous Stanford commencement speech** S. Jobs, "You've Got to Find What You Love," Commencement Address at Stanford University, June 12, 2005: http://news.stanford.edu/2005/06/14/jobs -061505/.

47 **scientists' and artists' brains** N. C. Andreasen and K. Ramchandran, "Creativity in Art and Science: Are There Two Cultures?" *Dialogues in Clinical Neuroscience* 14, no. 1 (March 2012): 49–54.

48 **Henri Poincaré, a mathematician** A. Miller, *Einstein, Picasso: Space, Time, and the Beauty That Causes Havoc* (New York: Basic Books, 2002), pp. 1–5.

49 **organizational psychologist Kevin Eschelman** K. J. Eschleman, J. Madsen, et al., "Benefiting from Creative Activity: The Positive Relationships Between Creative Activity, Recovery Experiences, and Performance-Related Outcomes," *Journal of Occupational and Organizational Psychology* 87, no. 3 (September 2014): 579–98.

50 **professor Robert Root-Bernstein** R. S. Root-Bernstein, M. Bernstein, and H. Garnier, "Correlations Between Avocations, Scientific Style, Work Habits, and Professional Impact of Scientists," *Creativity Research Journal* 8, no. 2 (April 1995): 115–37.

50 **example of Kirin Sinha** J. Chu, "Getting a Move On in Math," *MIT News* (December 23, 2013): http://news.mit.edu/2013/getting-a -move-on-in-math-1223.

51 **The ancient Greeks considered** W. Eamon, "The Invention of Discovery," *William Eamon* (January 16, 2014): http://williameamon .com/?p=972.

51 **psychologists Matthew Killingsworth** M. A. Killingsworth and D. T. Gilbert, "A Wandering Mind Is an Unhappy Mind," *Science* 330, no. 6006 (November 12, 2010): 932.

52 **"what is a novel but"** O. Pamuk, *Other Colors* (New York: Vintage, 2008), p. 7.

52 **Called *volitional daydreaming*** R. L. McMillan, S. B. Kaufman, and J. L. Singer, "Ode to Positive Constructive Daydreaming," *Frontiers in Psychology* 4 (2013): 626.

53 **psychologist Benjamin Baird** B. Baird, J. Smallwood, et al., "Inspired by Distraction: Mind Wandering Facilitates Creative Incubation," *Psychological Science* 23, no. 10 (October 1, 2012): 1117–22.

54 **writer Rebecca McMillan** McMillan, Kaufman, and Singer, "Ode to Positive Constructive Daydreaming."

54 **"art of pausing."** M. Popova, "The Psychology of How Mind Wandering and 'Positive Constructive Daydreaming' Boost Our Creativity and Social Skills," *Brain Pickings*, n.d.: https://www.brainpickings.org/2013/10/09/mind-wandering-and-creativity/.

55 **Writer's block is connected** A. W. Flaherty, "Frontotemporal and Dopaminergic Control of Idea Generation and Creative Drive," *Journal of Comparative Neurology* 493, no. 1 (December 5, 2005): 147–53.

55 **To overcome writer's block** P. Huston, "Resolving Writer's Block," *Canadian Family Physician* 44 (January 1998): 92–97.

55 **professor Angela K. Leung** A. K. Leung, S. Kim, et al., "Embodied Metaphors and Creative 'Acts,' " *Psychological Science* 23, no. 5 (May 1, 2012): 502–9.

56 **fluid arm movements** M. L. Slepian and N. Ambady, "Fluid Movement and Creativity," *Journal of Experimental Psychology: General* 141, no. 4 (November 2012): 625–29.

57 **sleep comes in two phases** P. McNamara, P. Johnson, et al., "REM and NREM Sleep Mentation," *International Review of Neurobiology* 92 (2010): 69–86.

57 **works its magic** S. M. Ritter, M. Strick, et al., "Good Morning Creativity: Task Reactivation During Sleep Enhances Beneficial Effect of Sleep on Creative Performance," *Journal of Sleep Research* 21, no. 6 (December 2012): 643–47.

57 **Dreaming—the ultimate tinkering** D. Kahn, "Brain Basis of Self: Self-Organization and Lessons from Dreaming," *Frontiers in Psychology* 4 (2013): 408.

57 **Carl Jung argued** S. Khodarahimi, "Dreams in Jungian Psychology: The Use of Dreams as an Instrument for Research, Diagnosis and Treatment of Social Phobia," *Malaysian Journal of Medical Science* 16, no. 4 (October 2009): 42–49.

57 **Paul McCartney reportedly** S. Turner, *A Hard Day's Write: The Sto-ries Behind Every Beatles Song,* 3rd ed. (New York: Harper, 2005).

57 **Albert Einstein famously dreamed** T. McIsaac, "5 Scientific Discoveries Made in Dreams," *Epoch Times* (June 4, 2015): http://www .theepochtimes.com/n3/1380669-5-scientific-discoveries-made-in -dreams/.

57 **sleep expert Matthew Walker** M. P. Walker and R. Stickgold, "Overnight Alchemy: Sleep-Dependent Memory Evolution," *Nature Reviews Neuroscience* 11, no. 3 (March 2010): 218; author reply on 18.

58 **Napping is a great way** S. C. Mednick, D. J. Cai, et al., "Comparing the Benefits of Caffeine, Naps and Placebo on Verbal, Motor and Perceptual Memory," *Behavioural Brain Research* 193, no. 1 (November 3, 2008): 79–86.

58 **researcher Felipe Beijamini** F. Beijamini, S. I. Pereira, et al., "After Being Challenged by a Video Game Problem, Sleep Increases the Chance to Solve It," *PLoS One* 9, no. 1 (2014): e84342.

59 **psychiatrist Sara Mednick** D. J. Cai, S. A. Mednick, et al., "REM, Not Incubation, Improves Creativity by Priming Associative Networks," *Proceedings of the National Academy of Sciences* 106, no. 25 (June 23, 2009): 10130–34.

59 **created four conditions** A. J. Tietzel and L. C. Lack, "The Recuperative Value of Brief and Ultra-Brief Naps on Alertness and Cognitive Performance," *Journal of Sleep Research* 11, no. 3 (September 2002): 213–18.

59 **Haruki Murakami sleeps** M. Currey, *Daily Rituals: How Artists Work* (New York: Knopf, 2013).

61 **Creativity is perspiration as much** V. C. Oleynick, T. M. Thrash, et al., "The Scientific Study of Inspiration in the Creative Process: Challenges and Opportunities," *Frontiers in Human Neuroscience* 8 (2014): 436.

62 **immerse yourself in a different identity** D. Dumas and K. N. Dunbar, "The Creative Stereotype Effect," *PLoS One* 11, no. 2 (2016): e0142567.

62 **Rosa Aurora Chavez** R. A. Chavez, "Imagery as a Core Process in the Creativity of Successful and Awarded Artists and Scientists and Its Neurobiological Correlates," *Frontiers in Psychology* 7 (2016): 351.

CHAPTER 3: DYNAMIC LEARNING IN A BRAVE NEW WORLD

64 **"Fuckup Nights" is a phenomenon** "What Is Fuckup Nights?" *Fuckup Nights,* n.d.: http://fuckupnights.com; C. D. Von Kaenel, "Failure Has Never Been More Successful," *Fast Company* (November 14, 2014): http://www.fastcompany.com/3038446/innovation-agents /failure-has-never-been-more-successful.

64 **Yet it's common** D. Gage, "The Venture Capital Secret: 3 Out of 4 Start-Ups Fail," *Wall Street Journal* (September 20, 2012): http://www.wsj.com/articles/SB10000872396390443720204578004980476 429190; C. Nobel, "Why Companies Fail—and How Their Founders Can Bounce Back," *Harvard Business School: Working Knowledge* (March 7, 2011): http://hbswk.hbs.edu/item/why-companies -failand-how-their-founders-can-bounce-back.

65 **sad or frustrated** J. Goldman and J. McCarthy, "Job Market Optimism Up Sharply in Northern America, Europe," *Gallup* (May 21, 2015): http://www.gallup.com/poll/183380/job-market-optimism -sharply-northern-america-europe.aspx.

65 **failure, rather than** A. C. Edmondson, "Strategies of Learning from Failure," *Harvard Business Review* 89, no. 4 (April 2011): 48–55, 137; M. Lindstrom, "The Truth About Being 'Done' Versus Being 'Perfect,' " *Fast Company* (April 25, 2012): http://www.fastcompany .com/3001533/truth-about-being-done-versus-being-perfect; R. Asghar, "Why Silicon Valley's 'Fail Fast' Mantra Is Just Hype," *Forbes* (July 14, 2014): http://www.forbes.com/sites/robasghar/2014/07 /14/why-silicon-valleys-fail-fast-mantra-is-just-hype/#46b8da722236.

66 **Brightworks School, and its** "Brightworks: An Extraordinary School," *Brightworks,* n.d.: http://www.sfbrightworks.org.

67 **physics Peter Galison** E. Keto, "Visual Research: Galison Brings Together Art and Science in Scholarship, Filmmaking," *Harvard Crimson* (April 26, 2016): http://www.thecrimson.com/article/2016/4 /26/galison-profile/.

68 **MIT has a "Hobby Shop"** T. Moroney, "MIT Hobby Shop Spawns Offbeat Creations Like 'Hairball,' " *Bloomberg* (May 21, 2014): http://www.bloomberg.com/news/articles/2014-05-21/mit-hobby -shop-spawns-offbeat-creations-like-hairball-.

68 **Google's hiring practice** A. Bryant, "In Head-Hunting, Big Data May Not Be Such a Big Deal," *New York Times,* June 19, 2013: http://www .nytimes.com/2013/06/20/business/in-head-hunting-big-data-may -not-be-such-a-big-deal.html?partner=socialflow&smid=tw-nytimes business&_r=0.

69 **No wonder the DMN** M. E. Raichle, "The Restless Brain: How Intrinsic Activity Organizes Brain Function," *Philosophical Transactions of the Royal Society of London. Series B: Biological Sciences* 370, no. 1668 (May 19, 2015).

69 **psychologist Jackie Andrade** J. Andrade, "What Does Doodling Do?" *Applied Cognitive Psychology* 24, no. 1 (2008): 100–106.

72 **One Laptop per Child** D. Talbot, "Given Tablets but No Teachers, Ethiopian Children Teach Themselves," *MIT Technology Review*

(October 29, 2012): https://www.technologyreview.com/s/506466
/given-tablets-but-no-teachers-ethiopian-children-teach-themselves/.

72 **restaurateur Jonathan Waxman** K. Tannenbaum, "Interview with
Jonathan Waxman," *Institute of Culinary Education* (January 2013):
http://www.ice.edu/press/the-ice-interviews/interview-with-jon
athan-waxman.

72 **Waxman grew up** C. Bell, "Jonathan Waxman," *Prezi* (September
17, 2014): https://prezi.com/2cfsgdsdj0nz/jonathan-waxman/.

72 **An accomplished trombone player** "Jonathan Waxman," *Music City
Food + Wine* (September 17 and 18, 2016): http://www.musiccity
foodandwinefestival.com/2015-talent/jonathan-waxman/.

73 **casino pit bands** M. Rogers, "Barbuto's Jonathan Waxman Talks
Music City Eats, Maintaining Momentum," *Nashville Eater* (September 16, 2013): http://nashville.eater.com/2013/9/16/6371261
/barbutos-jonathan-waxman-talks-music-city-eats-maintaining-mo
mentum.

73 **long blond hair** C. Lucas-Zenk, "Celebrity Chefs Gather to Cook,
Raise Money," *West Hawaii Today* (January 17, 2013): http://west
hawaiitoday.com/sections/news/local-news/celebrity-chefs-gather
-cook-raise-money.html.

73 **he sold Ferraris** L. McLaughlin, "Decades Later, Jonathan Waxman's Barbuto Is Still Ingredients Crazy," *Edible Manhattan* (September 2, 2010): http://www.ediblemanhattan.com/z/topics/back
-of-the-house/jonathan-waxmans-barbuto/; "Jonathan Waxman,"
Austin Food and Wine Festival (April 22–24, 2016): http://www.aus
tinfoodandwinefestival.com/2016-talent/jonathan-waxman/.

73 **"There is a strong"** Rogers, "Barbuto's Jonathan Waxman."

73 **"How many times did"** O. Stren, "Rock Star Chef Minus the Ego
Brings Success in the Kitchen," *Globe and Mail* (October 14, 2012):
http://www.theglobeandmail.com/life/food-and-wine/food-trends
/rock-star-chef-minus-the-ego-brings-success-in-the-kitchen/article
21089862/.

73 **Two years later Waxman returned** "Jonathan Waxman," *Music City
Food + Wine.*

74 **delicious and revolutionary** D. C. Hamilton, "Episode 17: Jonathan
Waxman," *Chef's Story* (September 5, 2012): http://heritageradionet
work.org/podcast/chef-039-s-story-episode-17-jonathan-waxman/.

74 **The pièce de résistance** R. Sietsema, "Jonathan Waxman Rides
Again at Jams and Barbuto," *New York Eater* (October 20, 2015):
http://ny.eater.com/2015/10/20/9544087/jams-midtown-review.

74 **food was so tasty** B. Landman, "Why This NYC Chef Turned Down
Being Painted by Andy Warhol," *New York Post* (September 19,

2015): http://nypost.com/2015/09/19/why-this-nyc-chef-turned
-down-being-painted-by-andy-warhol/

74 **Waxman recalls entering** McLaughlin, "Decades Later, Waxman's
Barbuto."

74 **transferred his creative skills** "Jonathan Waxman," *Music City Food
+ Wine.*

74 **market crashed in 1987** McLaughlin, "Decades Later, Waxman's
Barbuto."

75 **"a bit of French"** A. Friedman, "Jonathan Waxman Looks Back on
10 Years of Barbuto," *New York Eater* (February 11, 2014): http://
ny.eater.com/2014/2/11/6281721/jonathan-waxman-looks-back
-on-10-years-of-barbuto; F. Bruni, "The Secret of the Humble Chick-
ens," *New York Times* (January 9, 2008): http://www.nytimes.com
/2008/01/09/dining/reviews/09rest.html.

75 **Adele's in Nashville** C. Chamberlain, "Jonathan Waxman Opens Up
Adele's in Music City," *Nashville Lifestyles,* n.d.: http://www.nash
villelifestyles.com/restaurants/jonathan-waxman-opens-adeles-in
-music-city.

76 **a psychological COG** M. Benedek, E. Jauk, et al., "Brain Mechanisms Associated with Internally Directed Attention and Self-
Generated Thought," *Scientific Reports* 6 (2016): 22959.

76 **grows from this place** M. Benedek, E. Jauk, et al., "To Create or to
Recall? Neural Mechanisms Underlying the Generation of Creative
New Ideas," *NeuroImage* 88 (March 2014): 125–33; R. Puente-Diaz,
"Creative Self-Efficacy: An Exploration of Its Antecedents, Conse-
quences, and Applied Implications," *Journal of Psychology* 150, no. 2
(2016): 175–95.

76 **tap into this inner compass** A. Peine, K. Kabino, and C. Spreckelsen,
"Self-Directed Learning Can Outperform Direct Instruction in the
Course of a Modern German Medical Curriculum—Results of a
Mixed Methods Trial," *BMC Medical Education* 16 (2016): 158; R.
Kaplan, C. F. Doeller, et al., "Movement-Related Theta Rhythm in
Humans: Coordinating Self-Directed Hippocampal Learning,"
PLoS Biology 10, no. 2 (2012): e1001267; D. Markant, S. DuBrow, et
al., "Deconstructing the Effect of Self-Directed Study on Episodic
Memory," *Memory and Cognition* 42, no. 8 (November 2014): 1211–
24; Benedek, Jauk, et al., "Brain Mechanisms Associated."

77 **Waxman seems to have** J. Bolois, "Jonathan Waxman on the Perils
of NYC Dining Culture and Surrendering Ego," *First We Feast* (April
21, 2016): http://firstwefeast.com/eat/2016/04/jonathan-waxman
-soapbox-interivew.

77 **Before farm-to-table food** A. Betker, "Jonathan Waxman's Jams

Opens in New York," *WWD* (August 17, 2015): http://wwd.com/eye/food/jonathan-waxmans-jams-10203118/.

77 **the fresh quality** McLaughlin, "Decades Later, Waxman's Barbuto."

77 **restaurant in Napa** Ibid.

77 **stick with investing** P. Lynch, *One Up on Wall Street: How to Use What You Already Know to Make Money in the Market* (New York: Simon & Schuster, 1989).

78 **The best way to tap** C. G. Davey, J. Pujol, and B. J. Harrison, "Mapping the Self in the Brain's Default Mode Network," *NeuroImage* 132 (May 15 2016): 390–97; P. Qin, S. Grimm, et al., "Spontaneous Activity in Default-Mode Network Predicts Ascription of Self-Relatedness to Stimuli," *Social Cognitive and Affective Neuroscience* 11, no. 4 (April 2016): 693–702.

78 **Meditating, listening to music** J. Xu, A. Vik, et al., "Nondirective Meditation Activates Default Mode Network and Areas Associated with Memory Retrieval and Emotional Processing," *Frontiers in Human Neuroscience* 8 (2014): 86; V. A. Taylor, V. Daneault, et al., "Impact of Meditation Training on the Default Mode Network During a Restful State," *Social Cognitive and Affective Neuroscience* 8, no. 1 (January 2013): 4–14; E. A. Vessel, G. G. Starr, and N. Rubin, "Art Reaches Within: Aesthetic Experience, the Self and the Default Mode Network," *Frontiers in Neuroscience* 7 (2013): 258; E. A. Vessel, G. G. Starr, and N. Rubin, "The Brain on Art: Intense Aesthetic Experience Activates the Default Mode Network," *Frontiers in Human Neuroscience* 6 (2012): 66; L. K. Miles, K. Karpinska, et al., "The Meandering Mind: Vection and Mental Time Travel," *PLoS One* 5, no. 5 (2010): e10825.

78 **Exercise is both a great** C. E. Krafft, J. E. Pierce, et al., "An Eight Month Randomized Controlled Exercise Intervention Alters Resting State Synchrony in Overweight Children," *Neuroscience* 256 (January 3, 2014): 445–55; M. W. Voss, R. S. Prakash, et al., "Plasticity of Brain Networks in a Randomized Intervention Trial of Exercise Training in Older Adults," *Frontiers in Aging Neuroscience* 2 (2010).

79 **brain researcher Christopher Davey** Davey, Pujol, and Harrison, "Mapping the Self."

80 **Psychologist Martin Seligman** M. E. Seligman, "Learned Helplessness," *Annual Review of Medicine* 23 (1972): 407–12.

80 **psychologist Carol Dweck** C. S. Dweck and E. L. Leggett, "A Social-Cognitive Approach to Motivation and Personality," *Psychological Review* 95, no. 2 (1988): 256.

80 **David Franklin and Daniel Wolpert** D. W. Franklin and D. M. Wolpert, "Computational Mechanisms of Sensorimotor Control," *Neuron* 72, no. 3 (November 3, 2011): 425–42.

82 **Columbia psychologist Jennifer Mangels** J. A. Mangels, B. Butterfield, et al., "Why Do Beliefs About Intelligence Influence Learning Success? A Social Cognitive Neuroscience Model," *Frontiers in Aging Neuroscience* 1, no. 2 (September 2006): 75–86.

85 ***Systematic forecasting*, as** J. M. Stogner, "Predictions Instead of Panics: The Framework and Utility of Systematic Forecasting of Novel Psychoactive Drug Trends," *American Journal of Drug and Alcohol Abuse* 41, no. 6 (2015): 519–26.

85 **neuroscientist Moshe Bar** M. Bar, "The Proactive Brain: Memory for Predictions," *Philosophical Transactions of the Royal Society B* 364, no. 1521 (May 12, 2009): 1235–43.

88 **limitation as an opportunity** D. Maurer, "Waxman Fails to Wax Competition on *Top Chef: Masters*," *Grubstreet* (July 23, 2009): http://www.grubstreet.com/2009/07/waxman_fails_to_wax _competitio.html.

88 **the traditional BLT** J. M. Hirsh, "Tips for Building a Better BLT: More Fat, More Contrasting Flavors," *StarNews Online* (January 30, 2008): http://www.starnewsonline.com/lifestyle/20080130/tips-for -building-a-better-blt-more-fat-more-contrasting-flavors.

88 **reactionary and revolutionary** McLaughlin, "Decades Later, Waxman's Barbuto."

88 **When Hunter Lewis** R. Martin, "12 Things You Can and Should Learn from Jonathan Waxman," *Food Republic* (September 3, 2014): http://www.foodrepublic.com/2014/09/03/12-things-you-can-and -should-learn-from-jonathan-waxman/.

90 **mental simulation, or imagining** R. E. Beaty, S. B. Kaufman, et al., "Personality and Complex Brain Networks: The Role of Openness to Experience in Default Network Efficiency," *Human Brain Mapping* 37, no. 2 (February 2016): 773–79.

91 **neuroscientist Matthias Gruber** M. J. Gruber, B. D. Gelman, and C. Ranganath, "States of Curiosity Modulate Hippocampus-Dependent Learning via the Dopaminergic Circuit," *Neuron* 84, no. 2 (October 22, 2014): 486–96.

92 **Columbia psychologist Dean Mobbs** D. Mobbs, C. C. Hagan, et al., "Reflected Glory and Failure: The Role of the Medial Prefrontal Cortex and Ventral Striatum in Self vs Other Relevance During Advice-Giving Outcomes," *Social Cognitive and Affective Neuroscience* 10, no. 10 (October 2015): 1323–28.

93 **neuroeconomist Jan Engelmann** J. B. Engelmann, C. M. Capra, et al., "Expert Financial Advice Neurobiologically 'Offloads' Financial Decision-Making Under Risk," *PLoS One* 4, no. 3 (2009): e4957.

93 **Vinod Khosla, co-founder** V. Khosla, " '20-Percent Doctor Included' & Doctor Algorithm: Speculations and Musings of a Technology

Optimist," *Khosla Ventures* (August 1, 2015): http://www.khosla ventures.com/20-percent-doctor-included-speculations-and-musings -of-a-technology-optimist.

94 **researcher Matthew Winter** M. Winter, J. Kam, et al., "The Use of Portable Video Media (Pvm) Versus Standard Verbal Communication (Svc) in the Urological Consent Process: A Multicentre, Randomised Controlled, Crossover Trial," *BJU International* (July 21, 2016), epub ahead of print.

94 **Oxford University researchers** C. B. Frey and M. A. Osborne, "The Future of Employment: How Susceptible Are Jobs to Computerisation?" *Oxford Martin* (Oxford, U.K.: Oxford Martin Programme on Technology and Employment, 2013): http://www.oxfordmartin.ox .ac.uk/downloads/academic/future-of-employment.pdf.

94 **World Economic Forum** "The Future of Jobs: Employment, Skills and Workforce Strategy for the Fourth Industrial Revolution," World Economic Forum (2016): 13–15: http://www3.weforum.org /docs/Media/WEF_Future_of_Jobs_embargoed.pdf.

94 **Tech-No-Logic has made** "The Robotic Private Chef that Frees Your Cooking Time," *One Cook,* n.d.: http://onecook4.me.

94 **Momentum Machines has made** M. McNeal, "Rise of the Machines: The Future Has Lots of Robots, Few Jobs for Humans" *Wired* (April 2015): http://www.wired.com/brandlab/2015/04/rise-machines -future-lots-robots-jobs-humans/.

95 **entrepreneur Kevin Ashton** A. Wood, "The Internet of Things Is Revolutionising Our Lives, but Standards Are a Must," *Guardian* (March 31, 2015): https://www.theguardian.com/media-network /2015/mar/31/the-internet-of-things-is-revolutionising-our-lives -but-standards-are-a-must.

95 **"We want Google to be"** N. Saint, "Google Launches Google Instant, Search Results That Stream Instantly As You Type," *Business Insider* (September 8, 2010): http://www.businessinsider.com /google-search-event-live-2010-9.

CHAPTER 4: MASTERING MULTITASKING

97 *wobbly brain syndrome* W. C. Clapp, M. T. Rubens, et al., "Deficit in Switching Between Functional Brain Networks Underlies the Impact of Multitasking on Working Memory in Older Adults," *Proceedings of the National Academy of Sciences* 108, no. 17 (April 26, 2011): 7212–17.

98 **Kep Kee Loh** K. K. Loh and R. Kanai, "Higher Media Multi-Tasking Activity Is Associated with Smaller Gray-Matter Density in the Anterior Cingulate Cortex," *PLoS One* 9, no. 9 (2014): e106698.

99 **Psychologists Jason Watson** J. M. Watson and D. L. Strayer, "Super-

taskers: Profiles in Extraordinary Multitasking Ability," *Psychonomic Bulletin and Review* 17, no. 4 (August 2010): 479–85.

100 **As busy as popcorn** L. McKenzie, "Ryan Seacrest to Launch Clothing, Hollywood Reporter," *Randa* (August 12, 2014): http://www.randa.net/news/press-article/ryan-seacrest-to-launch-clothing-hollywood-reporter.

100 **On most days** L. Melton, "Ryan Seacrest: Portrait of a Multi-Tasking Media Master," *Axs* (August 23, 2014): http://www.axs.com/ryan-seacrest-portrait-of-a-multi-tasking-media-master-17462; J. Patterson, "The King of Multitasking the Entertainment Industry," *Taipei Times* (June 28, 2007): http://www.taipeitimes.com/News/feat/archives/2007/06/28/2003367248.

100 **what is working right** J. Duncan and D. J. Mitchell, "Training Refines Brain Representations for Multitasking," *Proceedings of the National Academy of Sciences* 112, no. 46 (November 17, 2015): 14127–28; M. K. Rothbart and M. I. Posner, "The Developing Brain in a Multitasking World," *Developmental Review* 35 (March 1, 2015): 42–63; A. Verghese, K. G. Garner, et al., "Prefrontal Cortex Structure Predicts Training-Induced Improvements in Multitasking Performance," *Journal of Neuroscience* 36, no. 9 (March 2, 2016): 2638–45.

101 **Cognitive rhythm** H. Koshino, T. Minamoto, et al., "Anterior Medial Prefrontal Cortex Exhibits Activation During Task Preparation but Deactivation During Task Execution," *PLoS One* 6, no. 8 (2011): e22909; M. Moayedi, T. V. Salomons, et al., "Connectivity-Based Parcellation of the Human Frontal Polar Cortex," *Brain Structure and Function* 220, no. 5 (September 2015): 2603–16.

101 **A little stress—called *eustress*** M. Kumar, S. Sharma, et al., "Effect of Stress on Academic Performance in Medical Students: A Cross Sectional Study," *Indian Journal of Physiology and Pharmacology* 58, no. 1 (January–March 2014): 81–86.

101 **A recent study compared** J. M. Soares, A. Sampaio, et al., "Stress Impact on Resting State Brain Networks," *PLoS One* 8, no. 6 (2013): e66500.

101 **numerous things to reduce** J. E. van der Zwan, W. de Vente, et al., "Physical Activity, Mindfulness Meditation, or Heart Rate Variability Biofeedback for Stress Reduction: A Randomized Controlled Trial," *Applied Psychophysiology and Biofeedback* 40, no. 4 (December 2015): 257–68.

101 **normalize DMN function** J. Xu, A. Vik, et al., "Nondirective Meditation Activates Default Mode Network and Areas Associated with Memory Retrieval and Emotional Processing," *Frontiers in Human*

Neuroscience 8 (2014): 86; C. J. Boraxbekk, A. Salami, et al., "Physical Activity over a Decade Modifies Age-Related Decline in Perfusion, Gray Matter Volume, and Functional Connectivity of the Posterior Default-Mode Network: A Multimodal Approach," *NeuroImage* 131 (May 1, 2016): 133–41.

101 **use self-talk to reframe** Y. Kivity and J. D. Huppert, "Does Cognitive Reappraisal Reduce Anxiety? A Daily Diary Study of a Micro-Intervention with Individuals with High Social Anxiety," *Journal of Consulting and Clinical Psychology* 84, no. 3 (March 2016): 269–83; T. Shore, K. C. Kadosh, et al., "Investigating the Effectiveness of Brief Cognitive Reappraisal Training to Reduce Fear in Adolescents," *Cognition and Emotion* (June 13, 2016): 1–10.

102 **deactivate your amygdala** A. Zilverstand, M. A. Parvaz, and R. Z. Goldstein, "Neuroimaging Cognitive Reappraisal in Clinical Populations to Define Neural Targets for Enhancing Emotion Regulation. A Systematic Review," *NeuroImage* (June 8, 2016); X. Xie, S. Mulej Bratec, et al., "How Do You Make Me Feel Better? Social Cognitive Emotion Regulation and the Default Mode Network," *NeuroImage* 134 (July 1, 2016): 270–80; J. Ferri, J. Schmidt, et al., "Emotion Regulation and Amygdala-Precuneus Connectivity: Focusing on Attentional Deployment," *Cognitive, Affective and Behavioral Neuroscience* (July 21, 2016); M. Quirin, M. Kent, et al., "Integration of Negative Experiences: A Neuropsychological Framework for Human Resilience," *Behavioral and Brain Sciences* 38 (2015): e116.

102 **give yourself over to it** G. L. Poerio, P. Totterdell, et al., "Social Daydreaming and Adjustment: An Experience-Sampling Study of Socio-Emotional Adaptation During a Life Transition," *Frontiers in Psychology* 7 (2016): 13; J. B. Banks and A. Boals, "Understanding the Role of Mind Wandering in Stress-Related Working Memory Impairments," *Cognition and Emotion* (May 4, 2016): 1–8; W. C. Taylor, K. E. King, et al., "Booster Breaks in the Workplace: Participants' Perspectives on Health-Promoting Work Breaks," *Health Education Research* 28, no. 3 (June 2013): 414–25; B. W. Mooneyham and J. W. Schooler, "Mind Wandering Minimizes Mind Numbing: Reducing Semantic-Satiation Effects through Absorptive Lapses of Attention," *Psychonomic Bulltin and Review* 23, no. 4 (August 2016): 1273–79.

102 **companies like Google** J. B. Stewart, "Looking for a Lesson in Google's Perks," *The New York Times* (March 15, 2013): http://www .nytimes.com/2013/03/16/business/at-google-a-place-to-work-and -play.html.

102 **cognitive neuroscientist E. L. Maclin** E. L. Maclin, K. E. Mathewson, et al., "Learning to Multitask: Effects of Video Game Practice on

Electrophysiological Indices of Attention and Resource Allocation," *Psychophysiology* 48, no. 9 (September 2011): 1173–83.

103 **kinesiologist Joaquin Anguera** J. A. Anguera, J. Boccanfuso, et al., "Video Game Training Enhances Cognitive Control in Older Adults," *Nature* 501, no. 7465 (September 5, 2013): 97–101.

103 **This alliance of the conscious** H. Pashler and J. C. Johnston, "Attentional Limitations in Dual Task Performance," in H. Pashler, ed., *Attention (Studies in Cognition)* (New York: Psychology Press, 1998), p. 155.

103 **Like George Hyde-Lees** R. Ellman, *Yeats: The Man and The Masks* (New York: W. W. Norton, 1948), p. 224.

104 **Sir Arthur Conan Doyle** A. Conan Doyle, *The New Revelation* (Auckland, New Zealand: Floating Press, 2010).

104 **psychologist Wilma Koutstaal** W. Koutstaal, "Skirting the Abyss: A History of Experimental Explorations of Automatic Writing in Psychology," *Journal of the History of the Behavioral Sciences* 28 (1992): 5–27.

104 **voluntarily switching your state** Z. Lin and S. He, "Seeing the Invisible: The Scope and Limits of Unconscious Processing in Binocular Rivalry," *Progress in Neurobiology* 87, no. 4 (April 2009): 195–211; J. Lisman and E. J. Sternberg, "Habit and Nonhabit Systems for Unconscious and Conscious Behavior: Implications for Multitasking," *Journal of Cognitive Neuroscience* 25, no. 2 (February 2013): 273–83.

104 **seeing and guiding** V. van Polanen and M. Davare, "Interactions Between Dorsal and Ventral Streams for Controlling Skilled Grasp," *Neuropsychologia* 79, pt. B (December 2015): 186–91.

105 **a mixed bag** J. A. Bargh and E. Morsella, "The Unconscious Mind," *Perspectives on Psychological Science* 3, no. 1 (January 2008): 73–79; W. Meredith-Owen, "Jung's Shadow: Negation and Narcissism of the Self," *Journal of Analytical Psychology* 56, no. 5 (November 2011): 674–91.

105 **stir the unconscious** J. Schimel, T. Psyszczynski, et al., "Running from the Shadow: Psychological Distancing from Others to Deny Characteristics People Fear in Themselves," *Journal of Personality and Social Psychology* 78, no. 3 (March 2000): 446–62.

105 **One way to activate** J. Sayers, "Marion Milner, Mysticism and Psychoanalysis," *International Journal of Psycho-Analysis* 83, pt. 1 (February 2002): 105–20.

105 **Marion Milner finds** M. Milner, *On Not Being Able to Paint* (New York: Routledge, 2010).

105 **Psychologist Robert Burns** S. Juan, "Why Do We Doodle?" *Register* (October 13, 2006): http://www.theregister.co.uk/2006/10/13/the_odd_body_doodling/.

106 **hesitate to doodle** C. Magazine and D. Greenberg, *Presidential Doodles: Two Centuries of Scribbles, Scratches, Squiggles, and Scrawls from the Oval Office* (New York: Basic Books, 2006).

106 **Albrecht Dürer, also doodled** G. D. Schott, "Doodling and the Default Network of the Brain," *Lancet* 378, no. 9797 (September 24, 2011): 1133–34.

106 **"Try to pose for yourself"** T. Dostoyevsky and D. Patterson, *Winter Notes on Summer Impressions* (Evanston, IL: Northwestern University Press, 1997), p. 49.

106 **Daniel Wegner's research** D. M. Wegner, "Ironic Processes of Mental Control," *Psychological Review* 101, no. 1 (January 1994): 34–52.

106 **four months of musical training** S. Seinfeld, H. Figueroa, et al., "Effects of Music Learning and Piano Practice on Cognitive Function, Mood and Quality of Life in Older Adults," *Frontiers in Psychology* 4 (2013): 810.

106 **increase your overall IQ** E. A. Miendlarzewska and W. J. Trost, "How Musical Training Affects Cognitive Development: Rhythm, Reward and Other Modulating Variables," *Frontiers in Neuroscience* 7 (2013): 279; K. Hille, K. Gust, et al., "Associations between Music Education, Intelligence, and Spelling Ability in Elementary School," *Advances in Cognitive Psychology* 7 (2011): 1–6.

106 **musical training lights up** C. Y. Wan and G. Schlaug, "Music Making as a Tool for Promoting Brain Plasticity Across the Life Span," *Neuroscientist* 16, no. 5 (October 2010): 566–77; L. Jancke, "Music Drives Brain Plasticity," *F1000 Biology Reports* 1 (2009): 78.

107 **or *serial processing*** R. Fischer and F. Plessow, "Efficient Multitasking: Parallel Versus Serial Processing of Multiple Tasks," *Frontiers in Psychology* 6 (2015): 1366.

107 **neuroscientist Omar Al-Hashimi** O. Al-Hashimi, T. P. Zanto, and A. Gazzaley, "Neural Sources of Performance Decline During Continuous Multitasking," *Cortex* 71 (2015): 49–57.

110 **researcher Hansjörg Neth** H. Neth, S. S. Khemlani, and W. D. Gray, "Feedback Design for the Control of a Dynamic Multitasking System: Dissociating Outcome Feedback from Control Feedback," *Human Factors* 50, no. 4 (2008): 643–51.

115 **Todd Kelley and Steven Yantis** T. A. Kelley and S. Yantis, "Neural Correlates of Learning to Attend," *Frontiers in Human Neuroscience* 4 (2010): 216.

116 **neuroscientist Wesley Clapp** W. C. Clapp, M. T. Rubens, and A. Gazzaley, "Mechanisms of Working Memory Disruption by External Interference," *Cerebral Cortex* 20, no. 4 (2010): 859–72.

118 **neuroscientist Jaak Panksepp** J. Panksepp, "Can PLAY Diminish ADHD and Facilitate the Construction of the Social Brain?" *Journal*

of the Canadian Academy of Child and Adolescent Psychiatry 16, no. 2 (2007): 57–66.

120 **psychologist Arie Kruglanski** A. W. Kruglanski and G. Gigerenzer, "Intuitive and Deliberate Judgments Are Based on Common Principles," *Psychological Review* 118, no. 1 (2011): 97–109.

CHAPTER 5: GETTING UNSTUCK

125 **pops into your head** L. Kvavilashvili and G. Mandler, "Out of One's Mind: A Study of Involuntary Semantic Memories," *Cognitive Psychology* 48, no. 1 (January 2004): 47–94.

125 **get more emotionally neutral** J. H. Mace, "Involuntary Autobiographical Memory Chains: Implications for Autobiographical Memory Organization," *Frontiers in Psychiatry* 5 (2014): 183; J. H. Mace, *Involuntary Memory* (Malden, MA: Wiley-Blackwell, 2007).

126 **reduce your brain opioids** J. K. Zubieta, J. A. Bueller, et al., "Placebo Effects Mediated by Endogenous Opioid Activity on Mu-Opioid Receptors," *Journal of Neuroscience* 25, no. 34 (August 24, 2005): 7754–62; A. Piedimonte, F. Benedetti, and E. Carlino, "Placebo-Induced Decrease in Fatigue: Evidence for a Central Action on the Preparatory Phase of Movement," *European Journal of Neuroscience* 41, no. 4 (February 2015): 492–97; F. Benedetti, E. Carlino, and A. Pollo, "How Placebos Change the Patient's Brain," *Neuropsychopharmacology* 36, no. 1 (January 2011): 339–54; A. Pollo, E. Carlino, et al., "Preventing Motor Training Through Nocebo Suggestions," *European Journal of Applied Physiology and Occupational Physiology* 112, no. 11 (November 2012): 3893–903.

126 **Such *attention shifting*** D. R. Johnson, "Emotional Attention Set-Shifting and Its Relationship to Anxiety and Emotion Regulation," *Emotion* 9, no. 5 (October 2009): 681–90; D. Di Nocera, A. Finzi, et al., "The Role of Intrinsic Motivations in Attention Allocation and Shifting," *Frontiers in Psychology* 5 (2014): 273.

127 **"Buying" into this idea** J. Groopman, "The Anatomy of Hope," *Permanente Journal* 8, no. 2 (Spring 2004): 43–47.

127 **try *affect labeling*** E. Constantinou, M. Van Den Houte, et al., "Can Words Heal? Using Affect Labeling to Reduce the Effects of Unpleasant Cues on Symptom Reporting," *Frontiers in Psychology* 5 (2014): 807; S. H. Hemenover, A. A. Augustine, et al., "Individual Differences in Negative Affect Repair," *Emotion* 8, no. 4 (August 2008): 468–78.

127 **putting up a barrier** M. D. Lieberman, N. I. Eisenberger, et al., "Putting Feelings into Words: Affect Labeling Disrupts Amygdala Activity in Response to Affective Stimuli," *Psychological Science* 18, no. 5

(May 2007): 421–28; S. J. Torrisi, M. D. Lieberman, et al., "Advancing Understanding of Affect Labeling with Dynamic Causal Modeling," *NeuroImage* 82 (November 15, 2013): 481–88.

128 **reframing emotions calms** J. M. Cisler, B. A. Sigel, et al., "Changes in Functional Connectivity of the Amygdala During Cognitive Reappraisal Predict Symptom Reduction During Trauma-Focused Cognitive-Behavioral Therapy Among Adolescent Girls with Post-Traumatic Stress Disorder," *Psychological Medicine* (August 15, 2016): 1–11; J. Ferri, J. Schmidt, et al., "Emotion Regulation and Amygdala-Precuneus Connectivity: Focusing on Attentional Deployment," *Cognitive, Affective and Behavioral Neuroscience* (July 21, 2016); C. E. Waugh, P. Zarolia, et al., "Emotion Regulation Changes the Duration of the Bold Response to Emotional Stimuli," *Social, Cognitive and Affective Neuroscience* (May 19, 2016).

128 **using focused techniques** Y. Zhai and Y. Zhu, "Study of Effect on Solution-Focused Approach in Improving the Negative Emotion of Surgical Patients in Department of Vascular Surgery," *Pakistan Journal of Pharmaceutical Sciences* 29, 2 Suppl. (March 2016): 719–22; M. J. Rohrbaugh and V. Shoham, "Brief Therapy Based on Interrupting Ironic Processes: The Palo Alto Model," *Clinical Psychology* (New York) 8, no. 1 (2001): 66–81.

129 **Doubt will add to** C. Schuster, S. E. Martiny, and T. Schmader, "Distracted by the Unthought: Suppression and Reappraisal of Mind Wandering under Stereotype Threat," *PLoS One* 10, no. 3 (2015): e0122207; K. C. Oleson, K. M. Poehlmann, et al., "Subjective Overachievement: Individual Differences in Self-Doubt and Concern with Performance," *Journal of Personality* 68, no. 3 (June 2000): 491–524.

129 **panacea to an exhausted brain** U. Bingel, V. Wanigasekera, et al., "The Effect of Treatment Expectation on Drug Efficacy: Imaging the Analgesic Benefit of the Opioid Remifentanil," *Science Translational Medicine* 3, no. 70 (February 16, 2011): 70ra14.

130 **These proclamations reflect cases** "Fisher Sees Stocks Permanently High," *New York Times* (October 16, 1929): http://query.nytimes .com/gst/abstract.html?res=9806E6DF1639E03ABC4E52DFB66783 82639EDE&legacy=true; V. Navasky, "Tomorrow Never Knows," *New York Times Magazine* (September 29, 1996): http://www.nytimes .com/1996/09/29/magazine/tomorrow-never-knows.html; J. Sanburn, "Top 10 Failed Predictions: Four-Piece Groups with Guitars Are Finished," *Time* (October 21, 2011): http://content.time.com/time /specials/packages/article/0,28804,2097462_2097456_2097466,00 .html; H. Davies, *The Beatles: The Authorized Biography* (New York:

McGraw-Hill, 1968); U. Saiidi, "Here's Why the Majority of Brexit Polls Were Wrong," *CNBC* (July 4, 2016): http://www.cnbc.com /2016/07/04/why-the-majority-of-brexit-polls-were-wrong.html; J. Edwards, "Pollsters Now Know Why They Were Wrong About Brexit," *Business Insider* (July 24, 2016): http://www.businessinsider .com/pollsters-know-why-they-were-wrong-about-brexit-2016-7; S. Lohr and N. Singer, "How Data Failed Us in Calling an Election," *New York Times* (November 10, 2016): https://www.nytimes .com/2016/11/10/technology/the-data-said-clinton-would-win -why-you-shouldnt-have-believed-it.html.

131 **Smallpox, an infectious disease** E. A. Voigt, R. B. Kennedy, and G. A. Poland, "Defending Against Smallpox: A Focus on Vaccines," *Expert Review of Vaccines* (April 28, 2016): 1–15; D. A. Koplow, *Smallpox: The Fight to Eradicate a Global Scourge* (Berkeley: University of California Press, 2003).

131 **In the Elephant War** A. M. Behbehani, "The Smallpox Story: Life and Death of an Old Disease," *Microbiological Reviews* 47, no. 4 (December 1983): 455–509.

131 **it obliterated Hottentots** "Smallpox Epidemic Strikes at the Cape," *South African History Online,* 2014: http://www.sahistory.org.za /dated-event/smallpox-epidemic-strikes-cape.

131 **half the Cherokee Indian** "Smallpox Blankets," *Cherokee Heritage Documentation Center,* n.d.: http://cherokeeregistry.com/index .php?option=com_content&view=article&id=407&Itemid=617.

131 **the Continental Army** M. Becker, "Smallpox in Washington's Army: Strategic Implications of the Disease During the American Revolutionary War," *Journal of Military History* 68, no. 2 (April 2004): 381–430.

131 **discovery of a vaccine** S. Riedel, "Edward Jenner and the History of Smallpox and Vaccination," *Proceedings (Baylor University Medical Center)* 18, no. 1 (January 2005): 21–25; E. A. Belongia and A. L. Naleway, "Smallpox Vaccine: The Good, the Bad, and the Ugly," *Clinical Medicine and Research* 1, no. 2 (April 2003): 87–92.

131 **psychologist Tor D. Wager** T. D. Wager, D. J. Scott, and J. K. Zubieta, "Placebo Effects on Human Mu-Opioid Activity During Pain," *Proceedings of the National Academy of Sciences* 104, no. 26 (June 26, 2007): 11056–61.

132 **researcher Sonya Freeman** S. Freeman, R. Yu, et al., "Distinct Neural Representations of Placebo and Nocebo Effects," *NeuroImage* 112 (May 15, 2015): 197–207.

133 **psychologist Charles S. Carver** C. S. Carver and S. L. Johnson, "Authentic and Hubristic Pride: Differential Relations to Aspects of

Goal Regulation, Affect, and Self-Control," *Journal of Research in Personality* 44, no. 6 (December 2010): 698–703.

133 **your brain's compass** J. Boedecker, T. Lampe, and M. Riedmiller, "Modeling Effects of Intrinsic and Extrinsic Rewards on the Competition between Striatal Learning Systems," *Frontiers in Psychology* 4 (2013): 739.

133 **extrinsic rewards play a role** J. S. Carton, "The Differential Effects of Tangible Rewards and Praise on Intrinsic Motivation: A Comparison of Cognitive Evaluation Theory and Operant Theory," *Behavior Analysis* 19, no. 2 (Fall 1996): 237–55.

134 **moment things become** K. Murayama, M. Matsumoto, et al., "Neural Basis of the Undermining Effect of Monetary Reward on Intrinsic Motivation," *Proceedings of the National Academy of Sciences* 107, no. 49 (December 7, 2010): 20911–16.

134 **orient and motivate you** S. Reiss, "Extrinsic and Intrinsic Motivation at 30: Unresolved Scientific Issues," *Behavior Analysis* 28, no. 1 (2005): 1–14.

135 **Releasing focus makes it glow** Y. Ostby, K. B. Walhovd, et al., "Mental Time Travel and Default-Mode Network Functional Connectivity in the Developing Brain," *Proceedings of the National Academy of Sciences* 109, no. 42 (October 16, 2012): 16800–4.

135 **called *autonoetic consciousness*** J. R. Andrews-Hanna, "The Brain's Default Network and Its Adaptive Role in Internal Mentation," *Neuroscientist* 18, no. 3 (June 2012): 251–70.

135 **spontaneous thoughts are** A. Berkovich-Ohana and J. Glicksohn, "The Consciousness State Space (Css): A Unifying Model for Consciousness and Self," *Frontiers in Psychology* 5 (2014): 341.

136 **a sign that you** B. J. Baars, "Spontaneous Repetitive Thoughts Can Be Adaptive: Postscript on 'Mind Wandering,'" *Psychological Bulletin* 136, no. 2 (March 2010): 208–10.

136 **that's a good thing** C. E. Giblin, C. K. Morewedge, and M. I. Norton, "Unexpected Benefits of Deciding by Mind Wandering," *Frontiers in Psychology* 4 (2013): 598.

136 **Your conscious brain processes** T. Nørretranders, *The User Illusion: Cutting Consciousness Down to Size* (New York: Viking, 1998); T. D. Wilson, *Strangers to Ourselves: Discovering the Adaptive Unconscious* (Cambridge, MA: Harvard University Press, 2002); A. Dijksterhuis, "Think Different: The Merits of Unconscious Thought in Preference Development and Decision Making," *Journal of Personality and Social Psychology* 87, no. 5 (November 2004): 586–98.

136 **can be less accurate** L. M. Augusto, "Unconscious Knowledge: A Survey," *Advances in Cognitive Psychology* 6 (2010): 116–41; P. C.

Trimmer, A. I. Houston, et al., "Mammalian Choices: Combining Fast-but-Inaccurate and Slow-but-Accurate Decision-Making Systems," *Proceedings of the Royal Society B Biological Sciences* 275, no. 1649 (October 22, 2008): 2353–61.

137 **"Contrary to popular opinion"** A. Foege, "Guest Column: America's 'Tinkering' Spirit: Alive and Well, and Making Our Nation Great," *Northwest Georgia News* (June 12, 2013): http://www.northwestgeor gianews.com/rome/guest-column-america-s-tinkering-spirit-alive -and-well-and/article_b62f2334-8c18-53b6-863d-e140ab7dbb96 .html.

138 **Nassim Taleb, professor** N. N. Taleb, *Antifragile* (New York: Random House, 2012).

139 **brain researcher Luigi F. Agnati** L. F. Agnati, D. Guidolin, et al., "The Neurobiology of Imagination: Possible Role of Interaction-Dominant Dynamics and Default Mode Network," *Frontiers in Psychology* 4 (2013): 296.

139 **cognitive psychologist Marieke Jepma** M. Jepma, R. G. Verdonschot, et al., "Neural Mechanisms Underlying the Induction and Relief of Perceptual Curiosity," *Frontiers in Behavioral Neuroscience* 6 (2012): 5.

140 **"decided to drop out"** S. Jobs, " 'You've Got to Find What You Love,' Jobs Says," *News Stanford* (June 14, 2005): http://news.stanford .edu/2005/06/14/jobs-061505/.

140 **at an ashram** A. Gowen, "Inside the Indian Temple That Draws America's Tech Titans," *Washington Post* (October 31, 2015): https:// www.washingtonpost.com/world/asia_pacific/inside-the-indian -temple-that-draws-americas-tech-titans/2015/10/30/03b646d8 -7cb9-11e5-bfb6-65300a5ff562_story.html.

140 **he founded Apple** N. Rawlinson, "History of Apple, 1976–2016: The Story of Steve Jobs and the Company He Founded," *Macworld* (April 1, 2016): http://www.macworld.co.uk/feature/apple/his tory-of-apple-steve-jobs-what-happened-mac-computer-3606104/.

140 **founder Mark Zuckerberg** Gowen, "Inside the Indian Temple."

140 **Bill Gates still takes** R. A. Guth, "In Secret Hideaway, Bill Gates Ponders Microsoft's Future," *Wall Street Journal* (March 28, 2005): http://www.wsj.com/articles/SB111196625830690477.

141 **Bryce Huebner and Robert D. Rupert** B. Huebner and R. D. Rupert, "Massively Representational Minds Are Not Always Driven by Goals, Conscious or Otherwise," *Behavioral and Brain Sciences* 37, no. 2 (April 2014): 145–46.

143 **allows your predictive brain** M. Bar, "The Proactive Brain: Memory for Predictions," *Philosophical Transactions of the Royal Society of London. Series B: Biological Sciences* 364, no. 1521 (May 12, 2009):

1235–43; S. L. Mullally and E. A. Maguire, "Memory, Imagination, and Predicting the Future: A Common Brain Mechanism?" *Neuroscientist* 20, no. 3 (June 2014): 220–34.

143 **complete and whole** C. G. Davey, J. Pujol, and B. J. Harrison, "Mapping the Self in the Brain's Default Mode Network," *NeuroImage* 132 (May 15, 2016): 390–97.

143 **fuels your path** J. F. Cornwell, B. Franks, and E. T. Higgins, "Truth, Control, and Value Motivations: The 'What,' 'How,' and 'Why' of Approach and Avoidance," *Frontiers in Systems Neuroscience* 8 (2014): 194.

144 **"When I let go"** L. Tze, *Tao Te Ching* (New York: Dover, 1997).

145 **biologist Alexander Fleming** "Discovery and Development of Penicillin," American Chemical Society, n.d.: http://www.acs.org/content/acs/en/education/whatischemistry/landmarks/flemingpenicillin.html; B. L. Ligon, "Penicillin: Its Discovery and Early Development," *Seminars in Pediatric Infectious Disease* 15, no. 1 (January 2004): 52–57.

145 **drug company Pfizer** T. A. Ban, "The Role of Serendipity in Drug Discovery," *Dialogues in Clinical Neuroscience* 8, no. 3 (2006): 335–44.

146 **Henk van Steenbergen** H. van Steenbergen, G. P. Band, et al., "Hedonic Hotspots Regulate Cingulate-Driven Adaptation to Cognitive Demands," *Cerebral Cortex* 25, no. 7 (July 2015): 1746–56.

148 **psychologist Jack Brehm** J. W. Brehm, "Postdecision Changes in the Desirability of Alternatives," *Journal of Abnormal Psychology* 52, no. 3 (May 1956): 384–89.

149 **psychologist Robert E. Knox** R. E. Knox and J. A. Inkster, "Postdecision Dissonance at Post Time," *Journal of Personality and Social Psychology* 8, no. 4 (April 1968): 319–23.

149 **self-talk in the second person** E. Kross, E. Bruehlman-Senecal, et al., "Self-Talk as a Regulatory Mechanism: How You Do It Matters," *Journal of Personality and Social Psychology* 106, no. 2 (February 2014): 304–24.

150 **dopamine D4 receptor gene** R. P. Ebstein and R. H. Belmaker, "Saga of an Adventure Gene: Novelty Seeking, Substance Abuse and the Dopamine D4 Receptor (D4DR) Exon III Repeat Polymorphism," *Molecular Psychiatry* 2, no. 5 (September 1997): 381–84; J. Benjamin, L. Li, et al., "Population and Familial Association Between the D4 Dopamine Receptor Gene and Measures of Novelty Seeking," *Nature Genetics* 12, no. 1 (January 1996): 81–84.

150 **keeps you stuck** L. Schwabe and O. T. Wolf, "Stress Prompts Habit Behavior in Humans," *Journal of Neuroscience* 29, no. 22 (June 3, 2009): 7191–98.

150 **internist Colin P. West** C. P. West, L. N. Dyrbye, et al., "Intervention

to Promote Physician Well-Being, Job Satisfaction, and Professionalism: A Randomized Clinical Trial," *JAMA Internal Medicine* 174, no. 4 (April 2014): 527–33.

151 **psychologist Nicholas Spanos** N. P. Spanos, R. J. Stenstrom, and J. C. Johnston, "Hypnosis, Placebo, and Suggestion in the Treatment of Warts," *Psychosomatic Medicine* 50, no. 3 (May–June 1988): 245–60.

152 **"biochemical battle strategies."** T. S. Sathyanarayana Rao, M. R. Asha, et al., "The Biochemistry of Belief," *Indian Journal of Psychiatry* 51, no. 4 (October–December 2009): 239–41.

152 **limits as horizons** S. Yoshimura, Y. Okamoto, et al., "Neural Basis of Anticipatory Anxiety Reappraisals," *PLoS One* 9, no. 7 (2014): e102836.

153 **Yale psychologist Jerome Singer** R. L. McMillan, S. B. Kaufman, and J. L. Singer, "Ode to Positive Constructive Daydreaming," *Frontiers in Psychology* 4 (2013): 626.

154 **half of our waking time** M. A. Killingsworth and D. T. Gilbert, "A Wandering Mind Is an Unhappy Mind," *Science* 330, no. 6006 (November 12, 2010): 932.

154 **brain's emotional centers** P. Feng, Y. Zheng, and T. Feng, "Resting-State Functional Connectivity between Amygdala and the Ventromedial Prefrontal Cortex Following Fear Reminder Predicts Fear Extinction," *Social Cognitive and Affective Neuroscience* 11, no. 6 (June 2016): 991–1001; C. J. Reppucci and G. D. Petrovich, "Organization of Connections between the Amygdala, Medial Prefrontal Cortex, and Lateral Hypothalamus: A Single and Double Retrograde Tracing Study in Rats," *Brain Structure and Function* 221, no. 6 (July 2016): 2937–62.

154 **neurologist Antonio Damasio** A. Damasio, *Descartes' Error: Emotion, Reason, and the Human Brain* (New York: Penguin, 1995).

155 **John Cassavetes, the Greek-American** J. Loewen, "John Cassavetes from *A Personal Journey with Martin Scorsese Through American Movies*," YouTube: https://www.youtube.com/watch?v=UR3jKqsMI_c.

CHAPTER 6: FROM DISENCHANTMENT TO GREATNESS

157 **a son was born** "Jeff Bezos Biography," *Biography*, n.d.: http://www.biography.com/people/jeff-bezos-9542209.

157 **married a Cuban** "Jeff Bezos Biography," *Famous People*, n.d.: http://www.thefamouspeople.com/profiles/jeff-bezos-4868.php.

157 **boy never saw** J. Yarow, "The Astonishing Story of Jeff Bezos' Biological Father Who Didn't Even Know Bezos Existed Until the End of Last Year," *Business Insider* (October 10, 2013): http://www.businessinsider.com/jeff-bezos-biological-father-2013-10.

157 **took it apart** K. Russell, "The 9 Most Interesting Facts About Jeff Bezos from the Big New Amazon Book," *Business Insider* (November 18, 2013): http://www.businessinsider.in/The-9-Most-Interesting-Facts-About-Jeff-Bezos-From-The-Big-New-Amazon-Book/articleshow/25996451.cms?format=slideshow.

157 **rigged an electric alarm** "Jeff Bezos Fun Facts," *Celebrity Fun Facts* (August 20, 2016): http://www.celebrityfunfacts.com/jeff-bezos/f67m89/.

157 **an automatic gate closer** J. Ostdick, "e-vangelist," *Success* (June 30, 2011): http://www.success.com/article/e-vangelist.

157 **a book on "bright minds,"** N. Carlson, "Jeff Bezos: Here's Why He Won," *Business Insider* (May 16, 2011): http://www.businessinsider.com/jeff-bezos-visionary-2011-4.

158 **the Dream Institute** "Bezos Biography," *Biography*.

158 **person of the year** "Bezos Biography," *Famous People*.

158 **America's best leaders** D. LaGasse, "America's Best Leaders: Jeff Bezos, Amazon.com CEO," *U.S. News & World Report* (November 19, 2008): http://www.usnews.com/news/best-leaders/articles/2008/11/19/americas-best-leaders-jeff-bezos-amazoncom-ceo.

158 **businessperson of the year** "2012 Business Person of the Year," *Fortune* (November 16, 2012): http://fortune.com/2012/11/16/2012-businessperson-of-the-year/.

158 **fourth-wealthiest person** "The Richest People in America," *Forbes* (August 20, 2016): http://www.forbes.com/forbes-400/gallery/jeff-bezos.

158 **second-best CEO** "The Best Performing CEOs," *Harvard Business Review* (November 2015): 49–59.

158 **consistency of thought** A. W. Kosner, "Jeff Bezos on How to Change Your Mind," *Forbes* (October 19, 2012): http://www.forbes.com/sites/anthonykosner/2012/10/19/jeff-bezos-on-people-who-are-right-a-lot-vs-wrong-a-lot-has-he-got-it-right/#92c790762ed3.

159 **brain can change** C. M. van Heugten, R. W. Ponds, and R. P. Kessels, "Brain Training: Hype or Hope?" *Neuropsychological Rehabilitation* 26, nos. 5–6 (October 2016): 639–44.

159 **origin of this focus** Ibid.; A. P. Jha, J. Krompinger, and M. J. Baime, "Mindfulness Training Modifies Subsystems of Attention," *Cognitive, Affective and Behavioral Neuroscience* 7, no. 2 (June 2007): 109–19.

160 **more generous CEOs** P. Dey, "9 Most Generous CEOs of Our Time," *Best Mankind*, n.d.: http://www.bestmankind.com/most-generous-ceos-of-our-time/; J. Kantor and D. Streitfeld, "Inside Amazon: Wrestling Big Ideas in a Bruising Workplace," *New York Times* (August 16, 2015): http://www.nytimes.com/2015/08/16/technology/inside-amazon-wrestling-big-ideas-in-a-bruising-workplace.html.

160 **also quite playful** A. Deutschman, "Inside the Mind of Jeff Bezos," *Fast Company* (August, 1, 2004): http://www.fastcompany.com /50106/inside-mind-jeff-bezos.

161 **be stubborn and flexible** Ibid.

161 **sometimes sell something** Ibid.

161 **release of "pleasure" chemicals** A. S. Sprouse-Blum, G. Smith, et al., "Understanding Endorphins and Their Importance in Pain Management," *Hawaii Medical Journal* 69, no. 3 (March 2010): 70–71.

161 **direct your attention** B. Salehi, M. I. Cordero, and C. Sandi, "Learning Under Stress: The Inverted-U-Shape Function Revisited," *Learning and Memory* 17, no. 10 (October 2010): 522–30.

161 **love and hatred** E. Meaux and P. Vuilleumier, "Facing Mixed Emotions: Analytic and Holistic Perception of Facial Emotion Expressions Engages Separate Brain Networks," *NeuroImage* 141 (July 5, 2016): 154–73; H. E. Heshfield, S. Scheibe, et al., "When Feeling Bad Can Be Good: Mixed Emotions Benefit Physical Health across Adulthood," *Social Psychological and Personality Science* 4, no. 1 (January 2013): 54–61; S. Zeki and J. P. Romaya, "Neural Correlates of Hate," *PLoS One* 3, no. 10 (2008): e3556.

161 **also connects you** I. Molnar-Szakacs and L. Q. Uddin, "Self-Processing and the Default Mode Network: Interactions with the Mirror Neuron System," *Frontiers in Human Neuroscience* 7 (2013): 571.

162 **reward center is activated** A. S. Heller, C. M. van Reekum, et al., "Sustained Striatal Activity Predicts Eudaimonic Well-Being and Cortisol Output," *Psychological Science* 24, no. 11 (November 1, 2013): 2191–200.

163 **hundred most influential** "The 100 Most Influential People," *Time* (April 21, 2016): http://time.com/collection/2016-time-100/.

164 **Called *self-handicapping*** M. Zuckerman and F. F. Tsai, "Costs of Self-Handicapping," *Journal of Personality* 73, no. 2 (April 2005): 411–42.

164 **Make self-handicapping a habit** H. Takeuchi, Y. Taki, et al., "Anatomical Correlates of Self-Handicapping Tendency," *Cortex* 49, no. 4 (April 2013): 1148–54.

164 **Kazimierz Dabrowski, a Polish** K. Dabrowski, "[On Positive Disintegration. An Outline of the Theory Concerning the Psychological Development of Man through Unbalanced States, Nervous States, Neuroses and Psychoses]," *Annales Medico-Psychologiques* 117, no. 2 (November 1959): 643–68; K. Dabrowski, "[Remarks on Typology Based on the Theory of Positive Disintegration]," *Annales Medico-Psychologiques* 118, no. 2 (October 1960): 401–6.

164 **Billie Jean King** B. J. King, *Pressure Is a Privilege: Lessons I've Learned from Life and the Battle of the Sexes* (New York: LifeTime Media, 2008).

165 **depends on three factors** W. Tillier, "The Basic Concepts of Dabrowski's Theory of Positive Disintegration," in W. Tillier, ed., *Perspectives on the Self: Proceedings of the Second Biennial Conference on Dabrowski's Theory of Positive Disintegration* (unpublished, 1996): 5–14.

165 **Gifted students often** S. Mendaglio, "Dabrowski's Theory of Positive Disintegration: Some Implications for Teachers of Gifted Students," *AGATE* 15, no. 2 (Fall 2002): 14–22.

165 **referred to as "dynamisms"** Ibid.

166 **achieve positive disintegration** W. Tillier, "Dabrowski 101: The Theory of Positive Disintegration," *Positive Disintegration* (December 6, 2014): http://positivedisintegration.com/Dabrowski101.pdf.

167 **psychologist Andrea Berger** A. Berger, G. Tzur, and M. I. Posner, "Infant Brains Detect Arithmetic Errors," *Proceedings of the National Academy of Sciences* 103, no. 33 (August 15, 2006): 12649–53.

168 **brain's control regions relax** C. J. Limb and A. R. Braun, "Neural Substrates of Spontaneous Musical Performance: An fMRI Study of Jazz Improvisation," *PLoS One* 3, no. 2 (2008): e1679; M. C. Anderson, K. N. Ochsner, et al., "Neural Systems Underlying the Suppression of Unwanted Memories," *Science* 303, no. 5655 (January 9, 2004): 232–35.

168 **the improvisation circuit** A. Engel and P. E. Keller, "The Perception of Musical Spontaneity in Improvised and Imitated Jazz Performances," *Frontiers in Psychology* 2 (2011): 83.

168 **Jazz musicians, for example** R. E. Beaty, "The Neuroscience of Musical Improvisation," *Neuroscience and Biobehavioral Reviews* 51 (April 2015): 108–17.

168 **switches into "purring"** U. Debarnot, M. Sperduti, et al., "Experts Bodies, Experts Minds: How Physical and Mental Training Shape the Brain," *Frontiers in Human Neuroscience* 8 (2014): 280.

168 **race car drivers** G. Bernardi, L. Cecchetti, et al., "It's Not All in Your Car: Functional and Structural Correlates of Exceptional Driving Skills in Professional Racers," *Frontiers in Human Neuroscience* 8 (2014): 888; G. Bernardi, E. Ricciardi, et al., "How Skill Expertise Shapes the Brain Functional Architecture: An fMRI Study of Visuo-Spatial and Motor Processing in Professional Racing-Car and Naive Drivers," *PLoS One* 8, no. 10 (2013): e77764.

169 **archers' brain activation** J. Seo, Y. T. Kim, et al., "Stronger Activation and Deactivation in Archery Experts for Differential Cognitive

Strategy in Visuospatial Working Memory Processing," *Behavioural Brain Research* 229, no. 1 (April 1, 2012): 185–93.

169 **elite Ping-Pong players** S. Wolf, E. Brolz, et al., "Winning the Game: Brain Processes in Expert, Young Elite and Amateur Table Tennis Players," *Frontiers in Behavioral Neuroscience* 8 (2014): 370.

170 **consultant Andrew Campbell** A. Campbell, J. Whitehead, and S. Finkelstein, "Why Good Leaders Make Bad Decisions," *Harvard Business Review* 87, no. 2 (February 2009): 60–66, 109.

170 **psychologists Chad Dodson** C. S. Dodson and L. E. Krueger, "I Misremember It Well: Why Older Adults Are Unreliable Eyewitnesses," *Psychonomic Bulletin Review* 13, no. 5 (October 2006): 770–75.

171 **lists of related words** D. R. Cann, K. McRae, and A. N. Katz, "False Recall in the Deese-Roediger-McDermott Paradigm: The Roles of Gist and Associative Strength," *Quarterly Journal of Experimental Psychology* (Hove) 64, no. 8 (August 2011): 1515–42.

171 **able to remember** J. Storbeck and G. L. Clore, "With Sadness Comes Accuracy; with Happiness, False Memory: Mood and the False Memory Effect," *Psychological Science* 16, no. 10 (October 2005): 785–91.

171 **psychologists Youssef Ezzyat** Y. Ezzyat and L. Davachi, "Similarity Breeds Proximity: Pattern Similarity Within and Across Contexts Is Related to Later Mnemonic Judgments of Temporal Proximity," *Neuron* 81, no. 5 (March 5, 2014): 1179–89.

172 **gastroenterologist Jin-Yong Kang** J. Y. Kang, K. G. Yeoh, et al., "Chili—Protective Factor Against Peptic Ulcer?" *Digestive Diseases and Sciences* 40, no. 3 (March 1995): 576–79.

172 **the active ingredient** M. N. Satyanarayana, "Capsaicin and Gastric Ulcers," *Critical Reviews in Food Science and Nutrition* 46, no. 4 (2006): 275–328.

172 **researcher Martijn Mulder** M. J. Mulder, E. J. Wagenmakers, et al., "Bias in the Brain: A Diffusion Model Analysis of Prior Probability and Potential Payoff," *Journal of Neuroscience* 32, no. 7 (February 15, 2012): 2335–43.

173 **researcher Mariela Jaskelioff** M. Jaskelioff, F. L. Muller, et al., "Telomerase Reactivation Reverses Tissue Degeneration in Aged Telomerase-Deficient Mice," *Nature* 469, no. 7328 (January 6, 2011): 102–6.

173 **David Sinclair and** A. P. Gomes, N. L. Price, et al., "Declining Nad(+) Induces a Pseudohypoxic State Disrupting Nuclear-Mitochondrial Communication During Aging," *Cell* 155, no. 7 (December 19, 2013): 1624–38.

174 **geneticist George Church** G. Church, "Where Do We Go from Here?" *Future of Genetic Medicine* IX (March 3, 2016): https://www

.scripps.org/sparkle-assets/documents/brochure_future_of
_genomic_medicine_ix.pdf.

174 **doctoral student Daniela Aisenberg** D. Aisenberg, N. Cohen, et al.,
"Social Priming Improves Cognitive Control in Elderly Adults—
Evidence from the Simon Task," *PLoS One* 10, no. 1 (2015):
e0117151.

174 **doctoral student Deirdre Robertson** D. A. Robertson, G. M. Savva, et
al., "Negative Perceptions of Aging and Decline in Walking Speed:
A Self-Fulfilling Prophecy," *PLoS One* 10, no. 4 (2015): e0123260.

174 **psychologist Malgorzata Gocłowska** M. Gocłowska, "Can Counter-
Stereotypes Boost Flexible Thinking?" *Group Processes and Inter-
group Relations* 16, no. 2 (2013): 217–31.

175 **researchers Daniel Webster** D. M. Webster and A. W. Kruglanski,
"Individual Differences in Need for Cognitive Closure," *Journal
of Personality and Social Psychology* 67, no. 6 (December 1994):
1049–62.

176 **High levels of NCC** Y. Tanaka, J. Fujino, et al., "Are Ambiguity Aversion and Ambiguity Intolerance Identical? A Neuroeconomics In-
vestigation," *Frontiers in Psychology* 5 (2014): 1550.

176 **neurologist Marc Jeannerod** M. Jeannerod and J. Decety, "Mental
Motor Imagery: A Window into the Representational Stages of Action," *Current Opinion in Neurobiology* 5, no. 6 (December 1995):
727–32; M. Jeannerod, "Mental Imagery in the Motor Context,"
Neuropsychologia 33, no. 11 (November 1995): 1419–32.

177 **brain researcher Chang-Hyun Park** C. H. Park, W. H. Chang, et al.,
"Which Motor Cortical Region Best Predicts Imagined Movement?"
NeuroImage 113 (June 2015): 101–10.

177 **neurophysiologist Floriana Pichiorri** F. Pichiorri, G. Morone, et al.,
"Brain-Computer Interface Boosts Motor Imagery Practice During
Stroke Recovery," *Annals of Neurology* 77, no. 5 (May 2015): 851–65.

178 **brain is powerfully stimulated** K. Iseki, T. Hanakawa, et al., "Neural
Mechanisms Involved in Mental Imagery and Observation of Gait,"
NeuroImage 41, no. 3 (July 1, 2008): 1021–31.

178 **First-person images make you** H. J. Rice and D. C. Rubin, "I Can
See It Both Ways: First- and Third-Person Visual Perspectives at Retrieval," *Consciousness and Cognition* 18, no. 4 (December 2009):
877–90; A. R. Sutin and R. W. Robins, "Correlates and Phenomenol-
ogy of First and Third Person Memories," *Memory* 18, no. 6 (August
2010): 625–37.

179 **produce an image** A. P. Lameira, L. G. Gawryszewski, et al., "Hand
Posture Effects on Handedness Recognition as Revealed by the
Simon Effect," *Frontiers in Human Neuroscience* 3 (2009): 59.

179 **Bärbel Knäuper, a psychology** B. Knäuper, A. McCollam, et al., "Fruitful Plans: Adding Targeted Mental Imagery to Implementation Intentions Increases Fruit Consumption," *Psychological Health* 26, no. 5 (May 2011): 601–17.

179 **professor Craig Hall** C. R. Hall, K. J. Munroe-Chandler, et al., "Imagery and Observational Learning Use and Their Relationship to Sport Confidence," *Journal of Sports Sciences* 27, no. 4 (2009): 327–37.

180 **take another look** L. F. Agnati, D. Guidolin, et al.,"The Neurobiology of Imagination: Possible Role of Interaction-Dominant Dynamics and Default Mode Network," *Frontiers in Psychology* 4 (2013): 296.

180 **engage all your senses** J. Andrade, M. Khalil, et al., "Functional Imagery Training to Reduce Snacking: Testing a Novel Motivational Intervention Based on Elaborated Intrusion Theory," *Appetite* 100 (May 1, 2016): 256–62; C. McNorgan, "A Meta-Analytic Review of Multisensory Imagery Identifies the Neural Correlates of Modality-Specific and Modality-General Imagery," *Frontiers in Human Neuroscience* 6 (2012): 285.

180 **prepare your mind** B. Khoury, M. Sharma, et al., "Mindfulness-Based Stress Reduction for Healthy Individuals: A Meta-Analysis," *Journal of Psychosomatic Research* 78, no. 6 (June 2015): 519–28.

180 **stunning 86 percent** A. Knapp, "Ray Kurzweil Defends His 2009 Predictions," *Forbes* (March 21, 2012): http://www.forbes.com/sites/alexknapp/2012/03/21/ray-kurzweil-defends-his-2009-predictions/.

180 **he predicted that personal** D. Baer, "5 Amazing Predictions by Futurist Ray Kurzweil That Came True—And 4 That Haven't," *Tech Insider* (October 20, 2015): http://til.ink/2cY5gia.

181 **provide spontaneous feedback** S. Rosenbush, "Google's Ray Kurzweil Envisions New Era of Search," *Wall Street Journal* blogs (February 4, 2014): http://blogs.wsj.com/cio/2014/02/04/googles-ray-kurzweil-envisions-new-era-of-search/.

181 **nanobots made from** K. Miles, "Ray Kurzweil: In the 2030s, Nanobots in Our Brains Will Make Us 'Godlike,'" *Huffington Post* (October 1, 2015): http://www.huffingtonpost.com/entry/ray-kurzweil-nanobots-brain-godlike_us_560555a0e4b0af3706dbe1e2.

181 **slow-wave rhythms** F. M. Carvalho, K. T. Chaim, et al., "Time-Perception Network and Default Mode Network Are Associated with Temporal Prediction in a Periodic Motion Task," *Frontiers in Human Neuroscience* 10 (2016): 268; S. Sandrone, "The Brain as a Crystal Ball: The Predictive Potential of Default Mode Network," *Frontiers in Human Neuroscience* 6 (2012): 261.

181 **Freeman Dyson, a theoretical** J. Kagan, "Review: The Future of the Mind: The Scientific Quest to Understand, Enhance, and Empower the Mind," *Cerebrum* 2014 (May–June 2014): 7.

182 **"regret minimization framework"** M. Thompson, "Jeff Bezos— Regret Minimization Framework," YouTube (December 20, 2008): https://www.youtube.com/watch?v=jwG_qR6XmDQ.

182 **a crystal ball** Sandrone, "Brain as a Crystal Ball."

182 **Called *transcendental awareness*** D. R. Vago and D. A. Silbersweig, "Self-Awareness, Self-Regulation, and Self-Transcendence (S-Art): A Framework for Understanding the Neurobiological Mechanisms of Mindfulness," *Frontiers in Human Neuroscience* 6 (2012): 296.

182 **mindfulness, a practice** C. Noone, B. Bunting, and M. J. Hogan, "Does Mindfulness Enhance Critical Thinking? Evidence for the Mediating Effects of Executive Functioning in the Relationship Between Mindfulness and Critical Thinking," *Frontiers in Psychology* 6 (2015): 2043.

183 **known as *open monitoring*** D. P. Lippelt, B. Hommel, and L. S. Colzato, "Focused Attention, Open Monitoring and Loving Kindness Meditation: Effects on Attention, Conflict Monitoring, and Creativity—a Review," *Frontiers in Psychology* 5 (2014): 1083; H. Uusberg, A. Uusberg, et al., "Mechanisms of Mindfulness: The Dynamics of Affective Adaptation During Open Monitoring," *Biological Psychology* 118 (July 2016): 94–106.

183 **transcendental meditation (TM)** K. W. Chen, C. C. Berger, et al., "Meditative Therapies for Reducing Anxiety: A Systematic Review and Meta-Analysis of Randomized Controlled Trials," *Depression and Anxiety* 29, no. 7 (July 2012): 545–62.

183 **app called Headspace** A. Puddicome, "10 Minutes Could Change Your Whole Day," *Headspace*, n.d.: https://www.headspace.com/headspace-meditation-app.

183 **Ryan Seacrest is** T. Geller, "Jared Leto, Ryan Seacrest, Jessica Alba Invest in Headspace with the Chernin Group," *Wrap* (September 16, 2015): http://www.thewrap.com/jared-leto-ryan-seacrest-jessica-alba-invest-in-headspace-with-the-chernin-group/.

183 **deactivation of the parietal** Vago and Silbersweig, "Self-Awareness, Self-Regulation"; E. Mohandas, "Neurobiology of Spirituality," *Mens Sana Monographs* 6, no. 1 (January 2008): 63–80; F. Travis, D. A. Haaga, et al., "A Self-Referential Default Brain State: Patterns of Coherence, Power, and Eloreta Sources During Eyes-Closed Rest and Transcendental Meditation Practice," *Cognitive Processing* 11, no. 1 (February 2010): 21–30.

183 **empathy and social understanding** N. A. Farb, A. K. Anderson, and

Z. V. Segal, "The Mindful Brain and Emotion Regulation in Mood Disorders," *Canadian Journal of Psychiatry/Revue Canadienne de Psychiatrie* 57, no. 2 (February 2012): 70–77; R. Simon and M. Engstrom, "The Default Mode Network as a Biomarker for Monitoring the Therapeutic Effects of Meditation," *Frontiers in Psychology* 6 (2015): 776.

183 **children with ADHD** J. T. Mitchell, L. Zylowska, and S. H. Kollins, "Mindfulness Meditation Training for Attention-Deficit/Hyperactivity Disorder in Adulthood: Current Empirical Support, Treatment Overview, and Future Directions," *Cognitive and Behavioral Practice* 22, no. 2 (May 2015): 172–91; L. Zylowska, D. L. Ackerman, et al., "Mindfulness Meditation Training in Adults and Adolescents with ADHD: A Feasibility Study," *Journal of Attention Disorders* 11, no. 6 (May 2008): 737–46.

184 **Three stages, from focus** S. Satchidananda, *The Yoga Sutras of Patanjali* (Buckingham, VA: Integral Yoga Publications, 1990): 171–75.

185 **widespread health benefits** P. H. Canter, "The Therapeutic Effects of Meditation," *British Medical Journal* 326, no. 7398 (May 17, 2003): 1049–50; H. Sharma, "Meditation: Process and Effects," *Ayu* 36, no. 3 (July–September 2015): 233–37.

185 **biologist Elizabeth Blackburn** K. Harmon, "Work on Telomeres Wins Nobel Prize in Physiology or Medicine for 3 U.S. Genetic Researchers [Update]," *Scientific American* (October 5, 2009): http://www.scientificamerican.com/article/nobel-prize-medicine-2009-genetics/.

185 **Shambhala Mountain Center** Q. Conklin, B. King, et al., "Telomere Lengthening After Three Weeks of an Intensive Insight Meditation Retreat," *Psychoneuroendocrinology* 61 (November 2015): 26–27.

187 **protecting your self-esteem** R. A. Josephs, J. K. Bosson, and C. G. Jacobs, "Self-Esteem Maintenance Processes: Why Low Self-Esteem May Be Resistant to Change," *Personality and Social Psychology Bulletin* 29, no. 7 (July 2003): 920–33; A. D. Hermann, G. Leonardelli, and R. M. Arkin, "Self-Doubt and Self-Esteem: A Threat from Within," *Personality and Social Psychology Bulletin* 28 (2002): 395–408.

188 **brains of world-class gymnasts** R. Huang, M. Lu, et al., "Long-Term Intensive Training Induced Brain Structural Changes in World Class Gymnasts," *Brain Structure and Function* 220, no. 2 (March 2015): 625–44; B. Wang, Y. Fan, et al., "Brain Anatomical Networks in World Class Gymnasts: A DTI Tractography Study," *NeuroImage* 65 (January 15, 2013): 476–87; J. Wang, M. Lu, et al., "Exploring Brain Functional Plasticity in World Class Gymnasts: A Network Analysis," *Brain Structure and Function* (September 29, 2015).

CONCLUSION: THE TINKER MANIFESTO

191 **psychologist Graham Rawlinson** G. E. Rawlinson, "The Significance of Letter Position in Word Recognition," unpublished Ph.D. thesis, University of Nottingham, U.K., 1976.

192 **license to avoid living fully** R. H. Lehto and K. F. Stein, "Death Anxiety: An Analysis of an Evolving Concept," *Research and Theory for Nursing Practice* 23, no. 1 (2009): 23–41; L. Razinsky, *Freud, Psychoanalysis and Death* (Cambridge, U.K.: Cambridge University Press, 2014).

193 **Self-forgiveness is part** D. E. Davis, M. Y. Ho, et al., "Forgiving the Self and Physical and Mental Health Correlates: A Meta-Analytic Review," *Journal of Counseling Psychology* 62, no. 2 (April 2015): 329–35.

193 **The drug Minoxidil** A. G. Messenger and J. Rundegren, "Minoxidil: Mechanisms of Action on Hair Growth," *British Journal of Dermatology* 150, no. 2 (February 2004): 186–94.

193 **blood thinner Warfarin** D. Wardrop and D. Keeling, "The Story of the Discovery of Heparin and Warfarin," *British Journal of Haematology* 141, no. 6 (June 2008): 757–63.

193 **conflicts build brain capacity** M. C. Stevens, K. A. Kiehl, et al., "Brain Network Dynamics During Error Commission," *Human Brain Mapping* 30, no. 1 (January 2009): 24–37.

195 **philosopher Søren Kierkegaard** S. Kierkegaard, *The Concept of Anxiety* (Princeton, NJ: Princeton University Press, 1981).

195 **belief in having** E. Filevich, P. Vanneste, et al., "Brain Correlates of Subjective Freedom of Choice," *Consciousness and Cognition* 22, no. 4 (December 2013): 1271–84.

196 **Unfocus circuits play** I. Molnar-Szakacs and L. Q. Uddin, "Self-Processing and the Default Mode Network: Interactions with the Mirror Neuron System," *Frontiers in Human Neuroscience* 7 (2013): 571; S. Sandrone, "Self Through the Mirror (Neurons) and Default Mode Network: What Neuroscientists Found and What Can Still Be Found There," *Frontiers in Human Neuroscience* 7 (2013): 383; F. Travis, D. A. Haaga, et al., "A Self-Referential Default Brain State: Patterns of Coherence, Power, and Eloreta Sources During Eyes-Closed Rest and Transcendental Meditation Practice," *Cognitive Processing* 11, no. 1 (February 2010): 21–30.

196 **"fuzzy logic," which** S. S. Godil, M. S. Shamim, et al., "Fuzzy Logic: A 'Simple' Solution for Complexities in Neurosciences?" *Surgical Neurology International* 2 (2011): 24.

197 **were highly questionable** N. Wade, "Scientist at Work/Kary Mullis; After the 'Eureka,' a Nobelist Drops Out," *New York Times* (Septem-

ber 15, 1998): http://www.nytimes.com/1998/09/15/science/sci
entist-at-work-kary-mullis-after-the-eureka-a-nobelist-drops-out.html
?pagewanted=all&_r=0.

197 **"a tinkerer, a bricoleur"** Ibid.

198 **for more complex things** P. Dayan, "Simple Substrates for Complex
Cognition," *Frontiers in Neuroscience* 2, no. 2 (December 2008):
255–63.

198 **no one primary intention center** S. Uithol, D. C. Burnston, and P.
Haselager, "Why We May Not Find Intentions in the Brain," *Neuropsychologia* 56 (April 2014): 129–39.

198 **success will continue** J. A. Mangels, B. Butterfield, et al., "Why Do
Beliefs About Intelligence Influence Learning Success? A Social
Cognitive Neuroscience Model," *Social Cognitive and Affective Neu-
roscience* 1, no. 2 (September 2006): 75–86.

198 **brain can stimulate** B. Libet, "The Neural Time Factor in Conscious
and Unconscious Events," *Ciba Foundation Symposium* 174 (1993):
123–37, discussion 37–46; B. Libet, C. A. Gleason, et al., "Time of
Conscious Intention to Act in Relation to Onset of Cerebral Activity
(Readiness-Potential): The Unconscious Initiation of a Freely Vol-
untary Act," *Brain* 106, pt. 3 (September 1983): 623–42.

198 **will encourage you** B. Huebner and R. D. Rupert, "Massively Representational Minds Are Not Always Driven by Goals, Conscious or
Otherwise," *Behavioral and Brain Sciences* 37, no. 2 (April 2014):
145–46.

199 **biophysicist Abraham R. Liboff** A. R. Liboff, "Magnetic Correlates
in Electromagnetic Consciousness," *Electromagnetic Biology and
Medicine* 35, no. 3 (2016): 228–36.

199 **The famous Double Slit Experiment** I. Orion and M. Laitman, "The
Double-Slit Experiment and Particle-Wave Duality: Toward a Novel
Quantum Interpretation," *Journal of Modern Physics* 1, no. 1 (2010):
90–92; E. Strambini, K. S. Makarenko, et al., "Geometric Reduction
of Dynamical Nonlocality in Nanoscale Quantum Circuits," *Scientific Reports* 6 (2016): 18827.

200 **hide the device** "This Will Mindfuck You: The Double-Slit Experiment," *High Existence,* n.d.: http://highexistence.com/this-will
-mindfuck-you-the-double-slit-experiment/.

202 **our brains are all** R. S. Bobrow, "Evidence for a Communal Consciousness," *Explore* (New York) 7, no. 4 (July–August 2011): 246–
48; W. Hirstein, "Mindmelding: Connected Brains and the Problem
of Consciousness," *Mens Sana Monographs* 6, no. 1 (January 2008):
110–30.

202 **reliably see the world** P. A. Miller, G. Wallis, et al., "Reducing the

Size of the Human Physiological Blind Spot through Training," *Current Biology* 25, no. 17 (August 31, 2015): R747–48.

202 **any sound that has** G. A. Gates and J. H. Mills, "Presbycusis," *Lancet* 366, no. 9491 (September 24–30, 2005): 1111–20; L. Kenney, "Try It: Can You Hear These Sounds Only Young People Hear?" *Yahoo* (March 3, 2015): https://www.yahoo.com/beauty/try-it-can-you-hear-these-sounds-only-young-112627654778.html.

202 **form a picture** V. Gallese, L. Fadiga, et al., "Action Recognition in the Premotor Cortex," *Brain* 119, pt. 2 (April 1996): 593–609; V. Gallese, C. Keysers, and G. Rizzolatti, "A Unifying View of the Basis of Social Cognition," *Trends in Cognitive Sciences* 8, no. 9 (September 2004): 396–403; V. Gallese and C. Sinigaglia, "Understanding Action with the Motor System," *Behavioral and Brain Sciences* 37, no. 2 (April 2014): 199–200; M. Iacoboni, I. Molnar-Szakacs, et al., "Grasping the Intentions of Others with One's Own Mirror Neuron System," *PLoS Biology* 3, no. 3 (March 2005): e79.

203 **psychiatrist Carles Grau** C. Grau, R. Ginhoux, et al., "Conscious Brain-to-Brain Communication in Humans Using Non-Invasive Technologies," *PLoS One* 9, no. 8 (2014): e105225.

203 **psychologist Yulia Golland** Y. Golland, Y. Arzouan, and N. Levit-Binnun, "The Mere Co-Presence: Synchronization of Autonomic Signals and Emotional Responses Across Co-Present Individuals Not Engaged in Direct Interaction," *PLoS One* 10, no. 5 (2015): e0125804.

203 **Neurons in the parietal** S. Kaplan, "Grasping at Ontological Straws: Overcoming Reductionism in the Advaita Vedanta—Neuroscience Dialogue," *Journal of the American Academy of Religion* 77, no. 2 (2009): 238–74.

204 **human body evolved** F. Jacob, "Evolution and Tinkering," *Science* 196, no. 4295 (June 10, 1977): 1161–66.

INDEX

ABOUT THE AUTHOR

SRINI PILLAY, M.D., is a Harvard-trained practicing psychiatrist, a brain-imaging researcher, and a brain-based technology innovator. Currently a part-time assistant professor at Harvard Medical School, he is also an invited faculty member in the executive education programs at Harvard Business School and Duke Corporate Education. He is the founder and CEO of NeuroBusiness Group, an executive coaching, consulting, and technology business, which was named one of the top 20 leadership training Movers and Shakers in the world by Training Industry. His previous book, *Life Unlocked: 7 Revolutionary Lessons to Overcome Fear,* won a Books for a Better Life Award. Born in Durban, South Africa, he lives in Newton, Massachusetts.

drsrinipillay.com
Facebook.com/SriniPillayMD
@srinipillay

ABOUT THE TYPE

This book was set in Baskerville, a typeface designed by John Baskerville (1706–75), an amateur printer and typefounder, and cut for him by John Handy in 1750. The type became popular again when the Lanston Monotype Corporation of London revived the classic roman face in 1923. The Mergenthaler Linotype Company in England and the United States cut a version of Baskerville in 1931, making it one of the most widely used typefaces today.